OPERATION
NEPTUNE

OPERATION NEPTUNE

THE PRELUDE TO

D-DAY

DAVID WRAGG

First published 2014
by Spellmount, an imprint of The History Press
The Mill, Brimscombe Port
Stroud, Gloucestershire, GL5 2QG
www.thehistorypress.co.uk

British Library Cataloguing in Publication Data.
A catalogue record for this book is available from the British Library.

ISBN 978 0 7524 8922 3

Typesetting and origination by The History Press
Printed in Great Britain

CONTENTS

PREFACE

This is the BBC Home Service – and here is a special bulletin read by John Snagge. D-Day has come. Early this morning the Allies began the assault on the north-western face of Hitler's European fortress.

The very term 'D-Day' has a ring to it, even seventy years and more after the Allied invasion of France. Sometimes referred to as either the 'Normandy landings' or 'Operation Overlord', it is still known popularly as 'D-Day', even though there have been many D-days elsewhere, designating the launch of many operations.

It is impossible, however, to overstate the importance of the Allied invasion of France on 6 June 1944. It was not the end of the Second World War, not even of the Second World War in Europe, and those who thought that Germany would be forced to surrender by Christmas were soon proved wrong. There was much hard fighting ahead, but the balance of power had changed completely and could not be reversed. Germany, which had seemed unstoppable in 1940 with the Allied defeat in the Battle of France, the humiliation of the withdrawal from Dunkirk, all following on from the fall of Denmark, Norway, the Netherlands and Belgium, was now facing a combined British, American and Canadian assault aimed directly at the heart of its strength.

OPERATION NEPTUNE: THE PRELUDE TO D-DAY

One of the big developments of the Second World War was that assault was no longer over the ground, and even when landings were involved, they were not entirely from the sea. Airborne assault had already proved itself in the invasion of the Netherlands in May 1940. At Crete, where the Germans landed 17,530 men despite heavy losses amongst paratroops and air-landed troops, it was the airborne assault that saved them as the Royal Navy retained control of the seas, despite the losses suffered to Axis air power. Yet Crete was a close-run thing for the Germans, facing British, Commonwealth and Greek forces evacuated from the mainland totalling 35,000 men. What swung the balance in favour of the Germans was that the British and Greek forces had left behind their artillery and anti-aircraft weapons back in Greece, as well as their vehicles and their radios, so they lacked communications, transport and anything other than light weapons.

Operation Overlord was not simply going to be the biggest amphibious assault ever; it was also going to be the biggest airborne assault ever. It was going to have the largest fleet ever providing covering fire and mine clearance, as well as protection on its flanks from attacks by U-boats and E-boats. The latter had already enjoyed their first blood when by chance they happened on an American amphibious exercise and attacked and sank many landing craft.

Leaving nothing to chance in training the troops, a major exercise, 'Operation Tiger', was scheduled to run from 22 April to 30 April 1944, with 30,000 troops, who would be exposed to the use of live munitions so that they got used not simply to landing on a beach, but to the sounds and smells of warfare. The exercise was not without incident, with a case of friendly fire on 27 April, but the following day nine German E-boats evaded British patrols and found a convoy of eight landing ships, LSTs, in Lyme Bay. The ships were sailing in a straight line, which made attack easier, and had just one corvette as an escort. In the ensuing battle, two of the LSTs were sunk and one was badly damaged before the attackers withdrew unscathed, leaving 946 men dead and another 200 wounded.

To allow room for such a massive invasion force, the landings had been divided into five landing zones or beaches, each with its own code-name, with US forces taking Omaha and Utah beaches to the west of the British and Canadian forces landing on Gold, Juno and Sword beaches. To many, choosing Normandy for the invasion rather than the Pas-de-Calais, much closer to the English coast, might seem perverse, but short as the channel crossing might have been, it would have been too short of space and congested, with the ships providing easy targets, while the beaches of Normandy offered easier landing grounds.

Originally planned for 5 June 1944, Operation Overlord was delayed by a full twenty-four hours because of the weather. A severe storm had blown up, fortunately detected in time by the meteorologists advising the operation's commanders, who took the decision to order the delay. It is doubtful if their thoughtfulness was appreciated by those taking part in the landings as, while the storm may have blown over, the sea took much longer to calm down. For those who feel the first touches of *mal de mer* as soon as their feet touch the deck of a ship, the poor seaworthiness of flat-bottomed landing craft was something from beyond their worst nightmares. These creatures rolled and pitched, water slopped over the sides and onto the decks, and the helmets of those unfortunates aboard saw more use as receptacles for vomit than as protection from shrapnel and bullets.

True, the Germans had already lost North Africa, then Sicily, and were hard-pressed to stop the Allies advancing through Italy, Rome having fallen just two days earlier, on 4 June. Yet, there was the barrier of the Alps and much of northern Italy from just south of Florence in which to hold the Allies. Advancing through Austria meant facing many natural obstacles, and a population that included many supporters of the Nazis. Between France and Germany, the natural obstacles were much less severe and France had a border with Germany. Despite this, it was not to be a clear road through to Germany: even breaking out of Normandy was to prove more difficult than the Allies had first thought.

D-Day was a cataclysmic event: the turning point in the war. It put the Germans under pressure. The code-name 'Operation Overlord' was well chosen. This, at last, was the 'Second Front' that the Soviet dictator Joseph Stalin had been demanding almost since the German invasion of the Soviet Union under the banner of 'Operation Barbarossa'.

The assault was conducted by both air and sea, and the maritime element was so important that it required its own operation and its own code-name, 'Operation Neptune'.

Neptune was the biggest maritime invasion in history. It required almost 7,000 ships to land more than 130,000 men on D-Day alone, the overwhelming majority of those engaged in the invasion, with another 23,000 either parachuted in or landed by gliders. They were part of a massive armada of almost 7,000 ships of all types and all sizes. Most were British, American or Canadian, but there were others manned by the 'Free' forces of France, Poland, the Netherlands and Norway.

Yet, despite the weather, not everyone was suffering. Many were in high spirits, especially aboard the warships. Lord Lovat commanded the 1st Special Service Brigade, and, as always, he was accompanied by his piper, the Cameron Highlander Bill Millin, who stood in the bows of the brigade's landing ship in battledress blouse and kilt and played 'The Road to the Isles'. Two Hunt-class destroyers played 'A-hunting We Will Go' over their tannoys, prompting Free French destroyers to play the '*Marseillaise*' while French *matelots* danced with excitement and waved at the other ships, thrilled at returning home after four years. Aboard other warships, crews were cheering.

Dice and poker games flourished aboard the American landing ships, the men choosing to gamble using the special Allied occupation currency that had been issued, much to the disgust of the Free French leader, General Charles de Gaulle. This was a show of bravado, as one soldier remarked: 'All are tense and all are pretending to be casual.'[1]

Sea power played its part in the invasion, not simply to land troops and tanks on the beaches, or provide covering gunfire, important though that was. First, the Allied navies had to survey the beaches; then clear the mines, right under the noses of the German gun emplacements and immediately before the landing craft and landing ships approached; then guide the assault craft to the shore; and bombard enemy positions so that the invaders had the best possible chance of reaching their initial objectives. The task of the Allied navies did not end with the invasion, as the armies ashore had to be kept supplied and reinforced, so protection from a German naval counter-attack was important. Fuel pipelines, code-named 'Pluto', had to be laid. Two 'Mulberry' harbours had to be towed across the English Channel in sections and assembled, each the size of the important port of Dover, for centuries England's main Channel port for those travelling between the British Isles and the Continent.

Overlord itself, of course, had everything. There was deception on the part of the invaders and delusion on the part of the defenders from the very top, Hitler believing that the Allies would return to Europe via Norway. Hitler was not alone in thinking that the Allied assault would come elsewhere. Given the size of the invasion and the resources devoted to it, it seems incredible that the German generals on the ground thought that it was simply a feint, and that the main thrust would come later through the Pas-de-Calais.

It was not, of course, solely a naval operation. Massive air power was deployed to bomb German defences and cut supply lines that could be used by German reinforcements; to provide fighter cover over the invasion fleet, the landing zones and the landing grounds for the paratroops and air-landed glider-borne troops, and tanks air-landed using the mighty Hamilcar gliders; and, of course, air power was needed in the first place to carry those same paratroops and glider-borne troops. Yet, having said that, not quite everything was deployed, for while the Allied navies provided heavy bombardment to cover the landings, the aircraft carrier, that most important of the Second World War's naval vessels, was absent. Unlike the landings in North Africa, on the mainland of Italy, the south of France and in the Pacific, there was no need for carriers as shore bases were available in the south of England, many of them within 80 miles of the Normandy beaches. In any case, there would have been no room for aircraft carriers to charge around at maximum speed, heading into the wind to launch their aircraft and then recover them as they returned from their sorties.

Planning was beset by competing egos, and by different national priorities. The Soviet leader, Joseph Stalin, whose brutal regime had left his armed services purged of the commanders who could have countered the German invasion of 1941, and who had refused to heed warnings, had pressed his newfound Allies to start a second front almost from the start of the German invasion, ignoring their efforts in the air over Germany, and in the North Atlantic, and even on the Arctic convoys to Murmansk and Archangel, where the weather was as great an enemy as the German *Luftwaffe* and the *Kriegsmarine*'s U-boats. Even the Allied invasions of North Africa, Sicily, and mainland Italy had not impressed Stalin.

The Americans had wanted an invasion in 1943, but this was too soon for Britain's wartime leader, Winston Churchill, whose reluctance and hesitation was born partly from a greater appreciation of the difficulties not just in the invasion but once ashore. Unfortunately, as already mentioned, it was also due in part to the mistaken and impractical belief that invading Italy would provide a path to Germany.

OFFSHORE

The afternoon of 5 June had seen a much more visible Allied naval presence. The fleet of minesweeping flotillas began sweeping from the assembly point, named 'Piccadilly Circus', along the ten channels leading to the Normandy beaches. The 7th US Minesweeping Squadron's USS *Osprey* struck a mine on its way to the US beaches and sank.

Catching a mine was an occupational hazard of minesweeping, but the German offshore barrage of moored mines running down almost the middle of the English Channel was either badly laid, or laid in patches, or had been much reduced by weather and unfortunate vessels detonating some of the mines. As the channels were swept, more than eighty lighted danbuoys were dropped to provide a clear and safe course for the assault forces. All this was happening as the minesweepers had to adjust their courses and their sweeps as the wind and tide changed. Rear-Admiral Alan Kirk, USN, commanding the US Western Task Force, reported that, 'The minesweepers were the keystone of the arch, and their task was one of unprecedented complexity.'[2]

In one sense, the minesweepers were very lucky. By 1940, many of them could clearly see the coast of France, with three hours of summer daylight remaining. They continued their course towards the French coast, expecting at any minute to be engaged by the German coastal batteries, but unable to take evasive action because of the need to remain in the channels being swept. Yet the guns remained silent, even when the 14th Flotilla was so close to the shore, by 2145, that the houses inland from the beach could be clearly seen by the naked eye. It was not for another two hours that any activity could be seen from the Atlantic Wall, and then the target was not the minesweepers but an Allied aerial attack on the fortifications.

The failure of the German gunners to fire at the approaching minesweepers remains one of the great mysteries of the Normandy landings. Some believe that the minesweepers were mistaken for German destroyers – for the RAF made the same mistake a very short time after D-Day.

IN THE AIR

For D-Day, both air-landed troops in gliders and paratroops were being used, and not for the first time by the Allies, as this combination had been used in the landings on Sicily, which were also affected by bad weather. Undaunted, Brigadier James Hill, commanding officer of the 3rd Parachute Brigade, assembled his officers and senior NCOs on the evening of 5 June: 'Gentlemen, in spite of your excellent training and orders, do not be daunted if chaos reigns. It undoubtedly will.'[3]

Meanwhile, the RAF was mounting 'Operation Taxable', which involved tricking the enemy into believing an invasion force was approaching Cap d'Antifer, north of Le Havre, which was also mined, while motor launches towed reflector balloons intended to create an image of large ships on enemy radar. A similar operation was mounted around Boulogne with Short Stirling bombers dropping window.

At 2300 on 5 June, across southern England people ran into the streets in towns and villages attracted by the roar of hundreds of aircraft engines, to see a vast fleet of aircraft silhouetted against the patchy clouds. More than 1,200 aircraft were in the air carrying the British 6th Airborne Division and the American 82nd and 101st Airborne Divisions. The British were headed east of the River Orne so that they could secure the Eighth Army's left flank and safeguard the bridges. The Americans were heading for the Cotentin Peninsula, their main priority being the causeways across the flooded areas behind Utah Beach.

The troops were flown inland, flying over the heavy coastal defences to land before dawn some miles inside enemy-held territory. Many of these were paratroopers, but others were to be air-landed in gliders detached from their towing aircraft or tugs at around 5,000ft. The objective of using airborne troops was to seize vital points such as bridges, to deny these to the Germans either as they tried to send reinforcements, or in retreat, and to ensure that they would be available for the Allied troops, who were expected, somewhat optimistically, to be soon advancing from the coast.

The gliders were towed by a variety of aircraft, but for the British paratroops the most common towing aircraft was the Short Stirling. Originally created as the first of the British force of heavy bombers, it was soon outclassed by the Avro Lancaster and Handley Page Halifax. Someone in the Shorts design office had made the mistake of giving this large aircraft a mid-wing, dividing the bomb bay into two, rather than the high-wing that enabled its rivals to have a single long bomb bay, so when 8,000lb 'double cookie' bombs became available to the Royal Air Force, the Stirling could not carry them. Reputedly the easiest to fly of the British heavy bombers, it was soon relegated to other duties, of which towing gliders was one.

Being towed into action in this way was probably the most comfortable way of reaching Normandy, or perhaps the least uncomfortable. It was not without its hazards, however, although these were probably not apparent to the troops sitting facing each other across the narrow fuselages. The men of the Glider Pilot Regiment, the most short-lived of any British Army formation, were all too well aware of the responsibilities thrust upon them. Once released from their towing aircraft, they were committed to making a landing, with no chance of a go-round for a second attempt, landing on a spot that they had never seen before and which was often not suitable for aircraft, and, of course, all of this was to be achieved in the dark!

Most members of the regiment were sergeants or staff sergeants, and typical of these was Staff Sergeant Roy Howard, whose dilemma was one faced by many others that day. 'My objective was a small corner of a particularly tiny field of rough pasture close to the Orne Bridge,' he recalled later:

If I overshot, I would crush us all against a 14-ft high embankment – if I undershot I would destroy my seven tons of powerless aircraft and its human cargo on a belt of 50-ft high trees. There was simply no room for error. The significance of the two bridges to be attacked by a *coup de main* force was emphasised to us. With the 6th Airborne Division landing to the east of the river, and the whole invasion coming ashore to the west of the canal, it was vital that these troops should be able to cross the two bridges over the Orne and the canal. These two bridges were the only ones where you could do this between Caen and the sea. So it was absolutely vital that we had the maximum surprise element, and the only way to do this was for us to carry out our operation before the rest of the invasion started. So we were going to sneak in just after midnight, and some six-and-a-half hours before the seaborne invasion came ashore.

Someone had made a most marvellous sand-table, a perfect model of what was on the ground in Normandy – even down to the last tree and ditch. The chap who'd made it had put some wires above the area, and slid a cine camera down those wires, filming all the way, and therefore had simulated what a glider pilot would see on his approach. It was incredibly clever, and impressed us all very much. So we were very confident. Each Horsa glider with its 88-ft wingspan was going to carry 28 troops, a mixture of Oxfordshire and Buckinghamshire Light Infantry, plus two or three Engineers – we were also going to carry an assault boat, and numerous other bits of equipment, because it was thought that the bridges might be blown before we got there. We got out onto the airfield about 9.30pm on the 5th June. I think everyone knew on the airfield what was happening except one of the ground staff from the Air Force, who came up to me and said, 'Are you bringing this one back tonight, Staff?' I said, 'No, I don't think so.' He walked away looking dazed.

We'd met the Ox and Bucks lads a few days before and they were a very good bunch. However, on the night they arrived all blacked up, loaded with arms and ammunition, they looked a right bunch of cut-throats. We loaded up, drank a cup of tea, chatted and about twenty to eleven, when it was nearly dark – we had double summertime in those days – we mounted up and when somebody fired the green flare, the engines started and one by one we got under way.[4]

'Twenty-eight troops was a heavy load, not least because they were all fully equipped. We were literally staggering under the weight of the stuff we were carrying,' recalls William Gray, a private with the 2nd Battalion Oxfordshire and Buckinghamshire Light Infantry:

I personally carried four fully loaded Bren-gun magazines plus two bandoliers of .303 ammunition. I had six Mills 36 grenades, two 77 phosphorus smoke grenades, two Norwegian-type egg-shaped stun grenades that just made a bang when you threw them. We carried a twenty-four hour ration pack that consisted of cubes of tea, soup, oatmeal, toilet paper, sweets, matches and some fuel for our little Tommy cookers.[5]

This part of the invasion force assembled at RAF Tarrant Rushton, an airfield in Dorset some 3 miles east of Blandford Forum. It had only opened in October 1943, and was used specifically for glider towing. The make-up of the air-landed force was dictated by the role they had to play once in France.

'It was a *coup de main* operation,' explained Major John Howard, commander of D Company:

Glider-borne to capture two bridges in Normandy and to land soon after midnight ... For this operation I was given two extra platoons and 30 Royal Engineers, so that was 150 infantry, 30 Royal Engineers – a force of 180. We landed in six gliders, each glider containing one platoon of around 25 infantry and five Royal Engineers. Three gliders went for a bridge over the River Orne and three gliders for a bridge over the Caen Canal, now known as Pegasus Bridge. This bridge was much more important; it was much more heavily defended – it was a waterway used for commercial purposes up to the port of Caen. Most of the defences of the two bridges were around this bridge. That is one reason why I went in No.1 glider. We were so thrilled to have this special job – the spearhead of the invasion as it has often been described – that we wanted to get the job done and done successfully, and that seemed to overcome all fear.[6]

His optimism was shared by a junior officer, Lieutenant 'Tod' Sweeney, and again it was a case of feeling that a great honour had been bestowed on him:

At eleven o'clock, we took off from Tarrant Rushton to spearhead the invasion into Europe. It was rather like being picked to play for your country at Lords. The exhilaration buoyed us up and kept us going. We were all scared stiff, of course, but we'd been waiting and waiting for this stage from 1940 onwards, and none of us had even been in action before.[7]

Not surprisingly, many were in fact nervous, or even scared. Hardly any of them would have flown before the war, and while they had been given training in glider landing, it was over friendly soil, and often in daylight. Everyone was issued with a brown paper bag in case of airsickness. 'Suddenly we became airborne,' said Sergeant Henry Clark, who was also in the 2nd Ox and Bucks' D Company:

We could barely see, it was quite dark, there were a few cigarettes going, and there was obviously a tenseness and nervousness because there wasn't the usual idle chatter – nobody was singing and there was almost silence in the glider, but within ten minutes, the usual round of conversation started, people began to sing, the tenseness evaporated and it became just another glider flight.[8]

They flew over the English Channel at around 6,000ft. While the sea had still to abate after the storm of the day before, many recall that the flight was relatively comfortable and one officer recalled that no one in his glider was airsick. The Ox and Bucks' Horsa gliders were towed by Handley Page Halifax bombers – aircraft that normally bore a substantial part of each night's bombing of enemy territory although at first they had suffered from a relatively high accident rate. Flying east of the massive invasion fleet, they crossed the coast near the resort of Cabourg, where there was a gap in the German flak defences.

Released at 5,000ft, the gliders dived, their occupants able to hear the rush of the air over the wings and around the fuselage now that the noise of the towing aircraft's engines was receding into the distance, before levelling off at around 1,000ft.

'It was a hazy moonlit night,' Major John Howard later recalled. 'At 1,000 feet we opened the glider's doors. The most amazing sight was those wonderful Normandy horses and cattle. They were grazing very quietly, as if nothing was happening, although a lot of bombers were going overhead.'[9]

Within minutes they were on the ground. It was just six minutes after midnight on 6 June. The British had returned to France after four years. The Americans and Canadians were arriving for the first time. Now it was time for the bridges to be taken and secured.

NOTES

1. US National Archives.
2. Imperial War Museum Sound Archive.
3. Imperial War Museum Sound Archive.
4. Imperial War Museum Sound Archive.
5. Imperial War Museum Sound Archive.
6. Imperial War Museum Sound Archive.
7. Imperial War Museum Sound Archive.
8. Imperial War Museum Sound Archive.
9. Imperial War Museum Sound Archive.

GLOSSARY

AA	Anti-aircraft
AB	Able seaman
AFC	Air Force Cross
ASH	Air-to-surface vessel radar (US-built)
ASV	Air-to-surface vessel radar (British-built)
Capt	Captain
CAP	Combat Air Patrol
CB	Commander of the Order of the Bath
CCS	Combined Chiefs of Staff
Cdr	Commander
CCGS	Chief of the Canadian General Staff
CID	Committee of Imperial Defence
C-in-C	Commander-in-Chief
CMG	Companion of the Order of St Michael and St George
CO	Commanding Officer
Conning tower	the raised superstructure of a submarine that allows a better view for navigational purposes
COPP	Combined Operations Pilotage Parties
COS	(British) Chiefs of Staff
CPO	Chief Petty Officer
CVO	Commander of the Royal Victorian Order
DFC	Distinguished Flying Cross

DSO	Distinguished Service Order
DSC	Distinguished Service Cross
Dt	detachment
DUKW	open topped amphibious vehicle
E-boat	German MTBs or MGBs
Fin	alternative name, mainly US, for the conning tower on a submarine
Flt	Flight
FUSAG	First United States Army Group
HMS	His Majesty's Ship
HMAS	His Majesty's Australian Ship
HMCS	His Majesty's Canadian Ship
HMNZS	His Majesty's New Zealand Ship
JCS	(American) Joint Chiefs of Staff
KCB	Knight Commander of the Bath
LCA	Landing Craft Artillery
LCI	Landing Craft Infantry
LCN	Landing Craft Navigation
LCT	Landing Craft Tank
LPD	Landing Platform Dock
LST	Landing Ship, Tank
Lt	Lieutenant
Lt-Cdr	Lieutenant-Commander
Lt-Gen	Lieutenant-General
Maj-General	Major-General
MBE	Member of the British Empire
MGB	Motor Gunboat
MTB	Motor Torpedo Boat
MV	Motor Vessel
OBE	Officer of the British Empire
OSS	(American) Office of Strategic Services
PO	Petty Officer
PR	Photo-Reconnaissance
RAF	Royal Air Force
RCAF	Royal Canadian Air Force
RCAN	Royal Canadian Navy
RCNVR	Royal Canadian Navy Volunteer Reserve

RM	Royal Marines
RN	Royal Navy
RNethN	Royal Netherlands Navy
RNR	Royal Naval Reserve
RNVR	Royal Naval Volunteer Reserve
RP	rocket projectile
SANF(V)	South African Naval Force (Volunteer), equivalent of RNVR
SAAF	South African Air Force
SHAEF	Supreme Headquarters Allied Expeditionary Force
SOE	(British) Special Operations Executive
U-boat	German submarine
USN	United States Navy
USS	United States Ship
VC	Victoria Cross

INTRODUCTION:
ASSAULT FROM THE SEA

There is nothing new about amphibious warfare. It was brought to an advanced stage of sophistication during the Second World War, but many lessons had to be learnt during the war years. The Japanese have generally been regarded as the earliest exponents but, in Europe, it dates from before the Battle of Marathon in 490 BC.

There are also records that suggest much earlier attempts at invasion from the sea using what might be described as 'light forces', that is without cavalry, especially by the 'Sea Peoples', originally Phoenicians, who migrated from the Levant in substantial numbers around the shores of the Mediterranean Sea, colonising Cyprus and Malta. Amidst these rare attempts at amphibious assault, there were many more migrations and Doric Sparta and Ionian Athens established colonies or trading posts around the Eastern Mediterranean. Eventually these movements resulted in rivalry leading to war.

In 490 BC, during the Second Persian Campaign, came what is generally regarded as the first amphibious assault, at least in the West, because the Persians' ships were specially constructed to carry horses and cavalry, the troops being carried direct to Attica, the region to the west of Athens, pausing only to take Rhodes and Naxos on their way. These forces landed near Marathon, only to find their way blocked by the Greeks. Rather than attack, the Persians re-embarked, putting their cavalry aboard first, a mistake as the Greeks then attacked the Persian force in strength. Later, in the

Third Persian Campaign, a novel feature was the construction of two bridges across a chain of boats to keep open the route across the Hellespont.

Clearly, even before the Romans, amphibious assault was not unknown and, indeed, there was a degree of sophistication in the ability to land cavalry or to improvise bridges using boats. Records of the numbers involved are few, but when the Athenian trading post at Segesta in Sicily called for assistance, when threatened by Syracuse, which was an ally of Corinth at the time (415–413 BC), the Athenians sent 134 triremes with 25,000 men in their ships' companies, and 6,400 soldiers.

The Greeks and the Phoenicians were the great sea-faring powers of the ancient world, even to the extent that the Persians had to depend on conscripted Phoenician sailors and ships to make progress across the Eastern Mediterranean. Early Rome was not a sea power and it was not until later that Republican Rome began to appreciate the value of ruling the waves, and started to confront the growing power of Carthage in the Punic Wars. The catalyst for this was the need to secure Sicily as part of the Roman Empire. Initially the battles for Sicily were on land, but the need for a fleet soon became obvious and the Romans chose a stranded Punic quinquereme, or *pentere*, as the model for the ships of the fleet. An innovation was the boarding ramp, known as the *corvus*, meaning raven, so that enemy ships could be seized by boarding parties of soldiers. Despite their inexperience in sea warfare, the new fleet enabled the Romans to seize Corsica in 259 BC and then Malta in 257 BC.

Victory required the Romans to seize Carthage itself, and this was to prove another early example of amphibious assault. A fleet of 330 ships was assembled, including troop transports, and engaged the Carthaginians in the naval battle of Ecnomus in 256 BC, where, despite superior Carthaginian tactics, the Romans won having lost just twenty-four ships to the Carthaginians' loss of ninety, of which thirty were sunk by ramming while the boarding ramps enabled the capture of the other sixty.

With the steady demise of Roman might after AD 400, there was a power vacuum in the Mediterranean until the rise of Islam. By the time of the death of Muhammed in 632, the whole of the Arabian Peninsula had become the core of Islam and what followed was a period of expansion that eventually reached as far west as what is now Spain and Portugal, although in the eastern Mediterranean, the successor to the Eastern Roman Empire, Byzantium, held on as a centre of Christian power and many of the Slavic nations also remained unconquered. Throughout the next 900 years, naval warfare remained largely unchanged from that practised by Rome and Carthage, although a primitive flame-thrower known as 'Greek Fire' was invented by a Syrian in Byzantine service, projecting an inextinguishable cocktail of flaming saltpetre, pitch, sulphur and oil onto enemy ships.

Little progress in naval warfare or amphibious assault was made by the Vikings, whose raids and eventual settlement found limited opposition, although they did suffer defeat at the Battle of Stamford Bridge in Yorkshire in 1066.

The Norman invasion of England that culminated in the Battle of Hastings in the same year showed little improvement over earlier practice. The Norman success was due in part to superior tactics, but also to the fact that the defending army led by King Harold had been force marched south from their victory over the Vikings at Stamford Bridge, and were almost certainly less able to fight well than their adversaries.

TOWARDS THE MODERN ERA

The advent of the cannon added a new dimension to warfare at sea as much as on land. Nevertheless, the capture of an enemy ship remained as much part of naval warfare as sinking it. Even at the Battle of Trafalgar in 1805, the British commander, Vice Admiral the Viscount Nelson died from wounds inflicted by a French sniper rather than from cannon fire.

During this period, the threat of a French invasion of England was real. There were few innovations, but a print from the period shows massive *Montgolfières*, or hot air balloons, each carrying up to 3,000 French troops, horses and cannon, across the English Channel. This startling prophecy of what would have been an airborne assault with air-landed forces remained a dream. The technology of the early balloons was simply not up to what was required and, in any case, the unpredictability of the wind over the Channel would have made the operation hazardous. Nevertheless, the concept of an assault using air power could fairly be said to have dated from this time.

Perhaps more of a foretaste of what was to come in the twentieth century came with the Walcheren expedition of August 1809, when the Royal Navy landed what was for the time the considerable force of 40,000 men on the island of Walcheren, using 520 transports escorted by forty-two ships of the line (predecessor of the battleship), twenty-five frigates and sixty smaller vessels under the overall command of Rear-Admiral Strachan. The Dutch port of Vlissingen was captured, but an assault on Antwerp failed and the troops suffered heavy losses before being re-embarked.

There was innovation of a kind in 1830, when the French invaded Algeria with a hundred warships including the first French paddle steamer, and 350 transports landed 38,000 men. This must have been a successful expedition, at least for the French, as the country became a French colony in 1847.

Often at this time, heavy bombardment by ships of the line was used to force the enemy to surrender, a good example being Vice Admiral Stopford's capture of Saint-Jean-d'Acre during the Turko–Egyptian War, after his combined fleet of twenty ships, including three Austrian and Turkish warships, shelled the strong fortress for several hours.

During the Crimean War (1853–56), there were no amphibious assaults as such, but an expeditionary force of around 60,000 men was transported by sea from Varna in Bulgaria to Eupatoria in Ukraine.

Neither the American Civil War (1861–65) nor the Franco–Prussian War (1870–71) involved amphibious assault. As with the Turko–Egyptian War, the Sino–French War (1883–85) saw the use of bombardment rather than amphibious assault to force the Chinese to concede Indo-China to the French. A French squadron brought hostilities to an end with the capture of Mekong.

More amphibious action came with the Sino–Japanese War (1894–95) over the control of Korea. Following a rebellion in Seoul, the Japanese demanded a Chinese withdrawal, but the Chinese reaction was to send a troop convoy with reinforcements. Without a declaration of war, the Japanese attacked the convoy, sinking a transport and damaging a cruiser. War was officially declared on 1 August, during which both countries had to depend on convoys to reinforce and supply their forces in Korea. The landings that mattered most in the war were conducted by the Japanese, landing near Port Arthur in October 1894, and then in January 1895 on the Shantung Peninsula, on either side of the important port and base of Weihaiwei, to which the Chinese fleet had withdrawn earlier, and which was subsequently besieged. When peace was finally negotiated, the Great Powers, which included the UK and the US, forced Japan to return Port Arthur to China.

The Spanish–American War of 1898 saw bombardment used again instead of amphibious warfare. Russian expansion into the eastern parts of Asia and Japanese ambitions for territorial expansion onto the mainland led to the

Russo–Japanese War of 1904–05. The conflict was fought largely ashore, with a short naval action on 9 February at Port Arthur, which Russia leased from China, as the Japanese brought troop transports to Inchon, the port for Seoul in Korea before war was declared, but was also famous for two major naval battles, the Battle of the Yellow Sea on 10 August 1904, and on 27–28 May 1905, the Battle of Tsushima. In both cases, the Russians lost heavily, and the latter engagement was decisive. The war ended formally with the Treaty of Portsmouth (New Hampshire, US) in September, with the Japanese receiving Port Arthur.

Amphibious activity by Ottoman forces was prevented during the First Balkan War (1912–13) by Greek control of the Aegean.

THE FIRST WORLD WAR

The First World War is best remembered in Europe for the protracted offensives and bloody battles on the Western Front, although the Germans and the Russians also had the Eastern Front. However, it was far from being a wholly European War. There were battles on land, on the lakes and offshore in East Africa, and on land and on the rivers in Mesopotamia, present-day Iraq. There were engagements at sea in the Pacific, in the Battle of Coronel, and in the South Atlantic, in the Battle of the Falkland Islands. Another popular memory of the war is what has been variously known as Gallipoli and the Dardanelles, for the war on land and at sea, respectively. This was at the outset a major amphibious operation.

Few now realise that there was a plan for an even more audacious amphibious operation, which would have meant nothing less than the seaborne invasion of Germany herself, with landings on the Baltic coast of Pomerania, the closest point to the capital, just 80 miles from Berlin. Both this aborted plan and the Gallipoli landings had one thing in common: they were attempts to break the stalemate on the Western Front, which saw little substantial movement until mid-1918, and to bring an early end to the war that at first many had thought would be 'all over by Christmas'.

The Baltic operation was the brainchild of the First Sea Lord, Admiral of the Fleet Lord Fisher. Fisher was a brilliant strategist and organiser. He had held the post of First Sea Lord at the Admiralty twice, being brought out of retirement by the new First Lord of the Admiralty, Winston Churchill. On his first appointment to the post in 1904, Fisher had revolutionised naval warfare by commissioning the first 'all big gun' battleship, HMS *Dreadnought*, which rendered all other battleships obsolete. He also warned the naval officers of his day that in future war at sea would be fought in the air above it and beneath the waves, although he actually meant by the airship and the torpedo fired from a surface vessel rather than the aeroplane and the submarine that were to come.

Fisher was almost what today would be termed a 'technocrat'. No engineer, he nevertheless embraced the new technology of his day with enthusiasm. *Dreadnought* could not have been built with piston engines, but the new steam turbines meant that weight was redistributed across the ship, allowing a heavier armament and heavier armour, especially on deck above the engine room, accommodation and magazines.

Fisher's love of technology came to the fore in the plans to invade Germany. He had predicted the date of war breaking out when he realised that the Germans were widening the Kiel Canal so that the largest ships could have a sheltered passage between the Baltic and the North Sea. He knew that the passage of the Norwegian Skagerrak and Swedish Kattegat straits was difficult and shallow, and that the completion of the Kiel Canal improvements would be the earliest date that Germany could start a war.

The idea of invading Germany was first broached in 1909, having occurred to Fisher when he accompanied King Edward VII on a visit to the Tsar a year earlier. Fisher believed that the invasion would pull a million German troops away from the front, although this was more likely to be the Eastern Front. He also expected that many of the troops for the invasion would be Russian.

There were two fundamental flaws to the plan. The first was that the naval power would have to be provided by the Royal Navy, and it would be difficult to get it into the Baltic in sufficient strength in wartime. The second was insurmountable, and concerned the fighting cohesiveness of Russian troops as the country gradually descended into anarchy and eventual revolution.

Churchill was aware of the plan even before he invited Fisher to return as First Sea Lord. He pressed the government to support it and even raised the idea with the Russians. His contribution to the operation was that the island of Borkum, off the North Sea coast of Germany and west of Emden, should be seized first to provide a base for operations on the mainland. Instead of easing the operation, this would have had precisely the opposite effect as

Borkum is not well placed for the Skagerrak, and it would have alerted the Germans to the Anglo–Russian plan. It was unlikely that the Germans would allow the Kiel Canal to be used, and instead of Pomerania, the invasion would have to start with the seizure of Schleswig-Holstein, much further from Berlin. This also meant that Russian troops were unlikely to be available. Despite these drawbacks, David Lloyd George, then Chancellor of the Exchequer but later Prime Minister, supported the plan.

It was necessary to build special shallow draught vessels to enter the Baltic. In all, 612 ships of all kinds were needed, and despite other pressing demands for men, materials and shipbuilding capacity, work had already started on these before the end of 1914. At a time when the country desperately needed men for the frontline, Fisher persuaded Lord Kitchener, Minister for War, to stop recruiting men from the shipyards. Fisher dictated the specifications of the warships, which were to be led by three 'light battlecruisers', an oxymoron, with the first two, HMS *Courageous* and HMS *Glorious* to have four 15in guns in two turrets, while the third, HMS *Furious*, was to have two 18in guns. These were heavy armaments for ships of just 22,700 tons and a shallow draught, and would have made them dangerously top-heavy. To the wits of the Fleet, these three ships were known as 'Helpless', 'Hopeless' and 'Useless'; *Courageous* was also known as 'Outrageous' and *Glorious* as 'Uproarious'! All three were eventually converted to aircraft carriers, the first being *Furious*, which was to launch the first carrier air strike in 1918.

Nevertheless, the idea of attacking behind the fronts gained other adherents, but Turkey was seen as a safer option. Thus the idea of a Baltic operation was dropped in favour of landings in Gallipoli or forcing the Dardanelles.

Behind this decision was the belief that the Turks would surrender when faced with a substantial assault. This was wrong, as events subsequently proved, while Turkish military might was stiffened by the presence of senior German commanders. The Royal Navy had been successful in penetrating the Bosporus and the Sea of Marmara with their submarines, but with heavy coastal artillery batteries on either side of the Dardanelles (known to the Ancient Greeks as the Hellespont), surface units would have much greater difficulty. The other problem was that the operation required the best that the army and navy could offer, but the senior commanders of both services were sceptical about the invasion and neither wanted to lose their best ships or men. Russian involvement was not sought, but instead this became an Anglo–French operation bolstered by substantial numbers of Australian and New Zealand troops. Greek offers of help were spurned.

On 18 March 1915, after bombarding the forts on Gallipoli into silence, a combined force of British and French battleships entered the Dardanelles. It was a disaster from the start. The French pre-dreadnought *Bouvet* struck a mine and exploded, as did the British pre-dreadnoughts *Irresistible* and *Ocean*; more fortunate was the British battlecruiser *Inflexible*, which also struck a mine but was able to limp back to Malta. The attempt to neutralise Gallipoli and the Dardanelles using naval power alone was abandoned.

The fact that so many of the ships deployed were pre-dreadnoughts showed just how little faith the Admiralty had in the campaign. The Admiralty was not alone in this view. The head of the British Army, Sir John French, thought that it was no more than a 'sideshow'. The choice of commander for the ground forces also showed how little hope was vested in the venture. At 62 years of age, General Sir Ian Hamilton was close to retirement, stationed in the UK, and left behind because many senior officers, including French, disliked him. 'My knowledge of the Dardanelles was nil,' he later confessed. 'Of the Turk nil, of the strength of my own forces, next to nil.' Unfortunately, the War Office was unable to improve his knowledge as the available reference material was a good ten years out of date and the maps were even worse, designed for tourists and inaccurate. When the troops were landed, they were to find that, instead of gently sloping gradients, they were faced with rugged terrain with deep ravines cut by many watercourses. Despite the reservations of Sir John French, driving the operation was the Secretary of State for War, Field Marshal Herbert Kitchener. By contrast, the latter was wildly optimistic. 'Supposing one submarine pops up opposite the town of Gallipoli and waves a Union Jack three times,' Kitchener assured Hamilton. 'The whole Turkish garrison on the peninsula will take to their heels and make a beeline for Bulair [the town at the neck of the peninsula].'[1]

No one explained to Hamilton that even the sinking of a major Turkish warship by a British submarine had failed to bring about Turkish surrender.

The one voice of reason and sound ideas was Hamilton's Chief-of-Staff, Major-General Walter Braithwaite, a man who nevertheless lacked diplomacy and was often abrasive. When the two officers met Kitchener to discuss the operation for the first time, Braithwaite proposed that the invasion force should have better air power than the enemy, and aired the possibility of having a squadron of the latest aircraft manned by experienced pilots and observers. Kitchener turned on him, his face red with fury, and barked, 'Not one!'

It was not just air power that was lacking: the expeditionary force also lacked adequate artillery or any hand grenades at all. They did have motor vehicles and armoured cars, but both would be unsuitable on the inhospitable terrain. Mules and stores had to be found in Egypt. The port of Mudros, on the Greek island of Lemnos (the recovery of which was a Turkish war aim), was turned into a harbour to provide a forward base. Jetties and pontoons also had to be assembled. While the effort did not compare with the Mulberry harbour assembled for the Normandy landings, neither did the resources made available, nor the commitment of those in the UK, France or even amongst the British forces in Egypt. Throughout the campaign, those endeavouring to achieve success were to struggle against the odds. General Sir John Maxwell, C-in-C Egypt, another of Hamilton's enemies, only provided support grudgingly when ordered to do so by Kitchener.

Hamilton's own team cannot be completely absolved from any blame at this early stage. The specialists were left behind in Egypt rather than serving as part of Hamilton's headquarters, and those left so far behind included the Quartermaster-General, the Director of Medical Services and the Adjutant-General. It was not until later in the campaign, when it had become bogged down, that an efficient supply operation was created on Lemnos with an experienced general officer in command.

One innovation was the use of floating piers for the landings, designed by an enterprising army officer. Unfortunately, these were supposed to be delivered to the beaches by the Royal Navy, but the job was subcontracted to merchant shipping, and seven were abandoned in the Mediterranean, the one that reached Mudros being abandoned there.

Hamilton assembled 75,000 men, many of them Australians and New Zealanders, who were to prove to be amongst his best troops.

No fewer than five different landing sites were available. One of these was actually in Anatolia, near Besika Bay, and not only offered easy terrain, but had few natural defensive positions for the enemy. Another spot with easy terrain was on the Gulf of Saros, where Gallipoli joined the mainland of Thrace, just 3½ miles wide: this would cut off the whole of Gallipoli, but would mean being under attack from both sides. Gaba Tepe was the next best choice on the peninsula itself, where it was just 6 miles wide and the terrain was relatively easy, with a low valley, which could be protected if high ground on either side was also taken, giving a good defensive position. Cape Helles at the tip of the peninsula was at least within easy range of the guns of the fleet, and meant that fighting would take place on one front. Suvla Bay offered a good beach, with heights nearby which were manageable. There was a large salt lake behind it, which was dry in summer.

Commanding the defences was the German General von Sanders, who only needed eight days to get his forces into position; the Allies gave him four weeks, with the result that he had a force of 84,000 men in six divisions against just 14,000 at the time of the Royal Navy's initial hit and run gunnery raids. The extra time was put to good use, improving communications through repairing and improving the road network. Convinced that the British attack would come in the Gulf of Saros, von Sanders made his headquarters at the neck of the peninsula.

The real flaw had been to allow the Royal Navy to carry out a heavy bombardment, alerting the Turks and their German allies to the possibility of an invasion long before the army was ready to invade. Such a heavy bombardment was needed immediately before the invasion.

On the morning of 25 April 1915, 1,500 men of the Australian 1st Division disembarked from the battleships into small boats, which were towed by small steam pinnaces towards the beach. First light came at 0405, and the pinnaces cast off their tows at 0425, leaving the boats to be rowed to the shore by sailors. It was at this moment that the first fire came from the defenders; initially badly aimed, it became increasingly accurate as the light improved and the boats closed on the coast, but most of the first wave reached the beaches safely.

At Cape Helles, just 1,000 Turkish troops watched the landings by the 29th Division. Many of the men did not encounter opposition, and while two groups did, at one of them, 'X' Beach, it only occurred once they were safely ashore and had advanced half a mile inland, leaving the beach safe for the main body to follow.

Another innovation was the use of an old merchant ship, the *River Clyde*, with doors cut in the sides of the hull so that a large number of troops could land quickly, running across a bridge of lighters. The lighters were towed into place by a tug, but almost immediately began to break away in the strong currents, and were only held together by the prompt action of a commander and an able seaman who dived into the water and held the lashings secure. As the first of 2,000 men of the Munster Fusiliers and the Hampshire Regiment ran through the doors, they were cut down by a well-planned and well-aimed burst of Turkish fire. About half of the men were caught on the pontoon bridge, half remaining inside the ship, whose machine guns mounted in the bows were used to stop the Turks from advancing onto the beaches.

Despite hearing the firing, General Hunter-Weston, onboard the command ship *Euryalus*, failed to take any action. At 0830, the order was given for the main force to land in the face of the fire, led by Brigadier Napier, who ignored the warnings from the officers trapped aboard the *River Clyde*. Within minutes, Napier and his staff were dead. Help did not come until Hamilton, aboard the new battleship HMS *Queen Elizabeth*, ordered heavy supporting fire, but while this moved the Turks from their firing positions, they soon returned once it stopped. Hamilton wanted to divert the troops to another beach, but Hunter-Weston rejected this as interfering with the planned arrangements!

Despite Hamilton being told repeatedly that Turkish forces in the area were weak, no action was taken. Elsewhere, troops who had advanced a short distance inland waited in vain for fresh orders from Hunter-Weston. By evening, Turkish reinforcements had arrived and the two sides had dug trenches and settled into a stalemate, the inevitable outcome of failing to make the most of the initial advance, which, in Hamilton's view, could have 'cut off the enemy troops on the toe of the peninsula'.

At Anzac Cove, the Australians and New Zealanders had remained close to their narrow beach, and were by evening facing determined and repeated counter-attacks by large Turkish forces, whose positions were favoured by the terrain. Evacuation was considered, but rejected out of hand by the Royal Navy as administratively impossible! Instead, those ashore were told to hang on, and supposed to be comforted by the news that the submarine *AE2* had passed through the Dardanelles to sink an enemy ship.

From here on in, the situation deteriorated into a crude resemblance of the trench warfare of the Western Front, but with three differences. One was the lack of water, the second the proximity of the opposing frontlines, which highlighted the third, the lack of grenades, which were so needed that home-made bombs were improvised out of tins. At such close quarters, the hand grenade was the weapon of choice. As on the Western Front, attempts to break the deadlock were costly, wasteful and bungled.

The whole operation could have been a striking success of Allied arms, a relatively easy and bloodless victory putting the Central Powers on the defensive. Instead, within days the whole affair degenerated into trench warfare reminiscent of the Western Front, except that the summers were hotter and drier, and the winters were colder. When air support was provided, under the command of none other than the courageous and colourful Commander Charles Rumney Samson of the Royal Naval Air Service, their reconnaissance reports were ignored or not passed on, and they were restricted to a hundred 100lb bombs per month – a supply they could happily have used within a single day!

Despite a third landing later at Suvla Bay, the entire operation continued to suffer, most of all from poor commanders and a lack of support from the Admiralty and the War Office, so that eventually the Allies had to withdraw and instead of creating a third front that would relieve the pressure elsewhere, had simply wasted resources that were much needed by the troops struggling to contain the Germans in France.

It is usual today to consider the Dardanelles campaign, or Gallipoli, as it was known to the army, an unmitigated disaster. It was a campaign beset by over-ambitious planning with no hope of success. Yet, had the initial landings been better planned and that at Cape Helles pursued with more vigour, the operation could have been a success. The generals aboard the ships seemed too remote from the situation ashore.

There were clearly lessons to be drawn from the Dardanelles. The first was to keep the enemy guessing: the initial bombardment by battleships gave the game away. Next, there needed to be a clear plan, with the armies and navies of both the United Kingdom and France involved in its planning and committed to the project. There had to be good reconnaissance so that conditions on the ground did not come as a surprise when it was too late to do anything about it. The best men and equipment available had not simply to be devoted to the project, but trained and briefed. If the Gallipoli Peninsula had been crossed, cutting off Turkish and German troops, it would have provided a foothold and a new front in the war that really could have eased the burden elsewhere.

THE SECOND WORLD WAR – NORWAY

The first amphibious operation of the Second World War was the German invasion of Norway. The *casus belli* for the war had been the German invasion of Poland. After accepting the German annexation of Austria and invasion of western Czechoslovakia, followed by the occupation of the rest of the country, the Allied response to the invasion of Poland surprised many Germans. It was in any case more of a gesture than a threat since there was no way that an Anglo–French force could liberate Poland, especially as the Germans knew that their project would soon be shared with the Soviet Union.

While the British and French armies, with the airpower of the Royal Air Force and the French *Armée de l'Air*, sat in France, expecting the conflict to follow the pattern of the First World War, still known at the time as the Great War, Germany prepared to invade both Denmark and Norway. It is often said that the reason for these invasions was to forestall an Allied invasion, but while plans were laid for an invasion of ports in northern Norway during the winter of 1939–40, little was done. The Allied invasion would have been made on the pretext of aiding Finland in her war against Russia – the so-called 'Winter War'. In fact, the main reason was to stop supplies of Swedish iron ore reaching Germany: the use of Norwegian ports was vital to the Germans because the Gulf of Bothnia between Sweden and Finland froze in winter, making the direct route from Sweden to German impassable.

The first action came on 16 February, when the Royal Navy was probing Norwegian waters looking for German shipping. That day, the German supply ship *Altmark* was spotted and as she had been the supply ship for the German pocket battleship (or more correctly, armoured ship, *Panzerschiff*) *Graf Spee*, it was probable that there were British prisoners aboard, merchant seamen from many of the German ship's victories. Attempts by a British cruiser and then ships of the 4th Destroyer Flotilla to board the *Altmark* were hindered for several hours by a Norwegian torpedo boat whose commander insisted that the ship was in neutral waters and that there were no prisoners onboard. That evening, one of the destroyers, HMS *Cossack*, went alongside and released 299 prisoners, letting the German ship continue on her way afterwards. This incensed the Norwegian government.

There was no further action until 8 April, when the Royal Navy began mining Norwegian waters to prevent their use by German shipping. The Royal Navy had already begun laying mines in the approaches to the Kiel Canal and the Royal Air Force had dropped mines in this and other German waterways in operations known to the RAF as 'gardening'.

Clearly, the Germans must have been ready earlier to invade both Denmark and Norway as the occupation of both countries started on 9 April. Little could be done to stop the German invasion of Denmark, German forces simply crossed the frontier and, with no resistance, the country was occupied within hours. Norway was different as the Germans had to invade by sea and the inhospitable terrain lent itself to resistance.

While the Germans had carefully planned the operation and allocated substantial forces, troops were landed from the sea at the major ports of Oslo, Kristiansand, Bergen, Trondheim and Narvik, and air-landed troops arrived at the airports at Oslo and Stavanger. For the most part, this operation went according to plan, but the loss of the cruiser *Blucher*, hit by two torpedoes fired from a coastal battery at the Drobak Narrows, protecting the entrance to Oslo Fjord, with the main headquarters staff aboard, hindered the German landings and allowed the Norwegian government and the king to flee the city, and organise resistance.

The Norwegian Army had already started to mobilise, and this encouraged the United Kingdom and France to send troops, assembling an initial expeditionary force of 13,000, supported by air and naval forces, including the dispatch of aircraft carriers. The use of carrier-borne aircraft was necessary because of the limited number of airfields available ashore, and the terrain. Unfortunately, at this time the Royal Navy had no high performance aircraft embarked on its carriers capable of fending off German fighters.

The British and French agreed that the key to holding Norway would be the recapture of Trondheim, from which a counter-attack southwards could repel the invaders. Initially, however, Narvik was seen as being more easily taken and held at the outset. As at Gallipoli, the problem was that a substantial part of the available trained strength of both nations' armies and air forces were stationed in France in anticipation of a German attack, and it was estimated that an army of at least 50,000 troops would be needed to liberate Norway.

At sea, the Royal Navy soon established control. A destroyer action in Narvik Fjord on 10 April saw two German destroyers and some merchantmen sunk, although later two British destroyers were sunk. That same day, an air raid by Fleet Air Arm aircraft operating from the shore station at Hatston on the mainland of Orkney sank the cruiser *Konigsberg*, the first loss of a substantial operational warship to air power. Three days later, the veteran battleship HMS *Warspite* and nine destroyers sank another eight German destroyers in the Second Battle of Narvik.

Aided by these successes, British forces were landed at Narvik on 12 April. These troops, under Major-General Mackesy, were expected to seize the town, using naval gunfire if necessary. It soon became clear that Mackesy had no intention of taking Narvik. At first, this was because he wished to wait for the snow to melt, and for his force to be joined by a half brigade of French *Chasseurs Alpins*, not appreciating that these troops were earmarked for other operations.

While the Germans were left to strengthen their defences at Narvik, British and French troops were being landed near Namsos, further south between Narvik and Trondheim, and expected to move south to Trondheim, a distance of 100 miles, despite 4ft of snow, which hindered movement, and with no protection from German air attack.

Advancing from the north, one British brigade managed to get to within 50 miles of Trondheim by 21 April before the Germans counter-attacked, forcing them back. The northern advance on Trondheim was soon back where it started, at Namsos, from where it was evacuated on the night of 3 May.

Throughout this period, the British and French troops were subjected to heavy bombing by the *Luftwaffe*. Air cover was provided by fighters operating from British aircraft carriers and by RAF Gloster Gladiators operating from a frozen lake at Lesjeshogen, 40 miles from Andalsnes. The Gladiators, the RAF's last biplane fighter, were no match for the *Luftwaffe*'s Messerschmitt Bf109s; at this time, the Fleet Air Arm did not have any high performance fighters. A squadron of Hawker Hurricanes, based at an airfield ashore, were too few and too late to make a difference.

Eventually, on 24 May, it was decided to withdraw from Norway as the German invasion of France and the Low Countries was well advanced. Withdrawal started on 27 and 28 May, and more than 24,000 British, French, Polish and Norwegian troops had left by 8 June, shortly before the surrender of France.

The need to reinforce the British and French units fighting in France was seen as a justification for withdrawal from Norway, but the Battle for France was already lost.

THE BATTLE OF FRANCE AND ITS AFTERMATH

The British Expeditionary Force, BEF, was moved to France on 4 September 1939, the day after the expiry of the Anglo–French ultimatum to Germany over the invasion of Poland. The move was simply a matter of reinforcing the armed forces of a friendly nation. Even so, it was no mean achievement to get 152,000 men across the English Channel, accompanied by an air component of 9,392 RAF personnel and further RAF personnel in what was named the Advanced Air Striking Force. A weakness of the BEF was that it was a purely defensive formation, and even in that role suffered from having very few tanks.

Commanding its 3rd Division was Bernard Montgomery, later to become a Field Marshal and one of his country's top generals. Never one to mince his words, Montgomery described the BEF as 'totally unfit to fight a first-class war on the continent of Europe'.

The BEF was placed between the French First and Seventh Armies on the border with Belgium. Initially, it prepared defensive positions and undertook some very necessary training. Much faith was placed, especially by the French, in the Maginot Line, a strong defensive and fortified line that ran from the Swiss border to that of Belgium, presenting what was believed to be an impregnable line of defence along the border with Germany.

While the German assault on 10 May 1940 was far from being a walkover as in Denmark, the Dutch were forced to surrender on 14 May. Rotterdam was declared an open city, in effect inviting the Germans to enter, but before they did so it was blitzed heavily by the *Luftwaffe*. Paratroops were used extensively by the Germans to bypass the Dutch defences. The rapid suppression of the Netherlands and an advance through the Ardennes caught the British and French armies by surprise and forced them to fall back towards the French coast, and most famously the port of Dunkirk, from which an evacuation, Operation Dynamo, was necessary. Cherbourg was another evacuation port. Using a wide variety of ships, including many small yachts and pleasure cruisers, anything and everything pressed into service, the astonishing figure of 338,226 men were rescued, including French and other troops, and taken to the south of England. This was, of course, far from an amphibious assault, but a withdrawal, and Churchill was quick to point this out.

THE UNSTOPPABLE HUN

The loss of France left the British Empire facing Germany and Italy on its own, plus small numbers of personnel from France, Poland, Norway and the other countries that had been captured by the Germans. With Churchill by now Britain's prime minister and determined to fight on, there was to be no question of a negotiated peace with Germany. Many Germans were disappointed at this, mainly because some, especially in the *Kriegsmarine*, or 'War Navy' had been led to believe that war would not break out until 1943 or 1944, and that the first major naval engagements might not be until 1945, by which time the massively ambitious Plan Z would have been completed.

Designed to produce a substantial balanced navy that could meet the Royal Navy on equal terms, Plan Z foresaw a German fleet with aircraft carriers and a much stronger battle fleet than was the case during the war, as well as many additional destroyers, another weakness of the *Kriegsmarine*. In fact, the only element of Plan Z with any chance of being fulfilled was the late amendment that led to a massive programme of submarine construction. Even so, in 1939, Germany had entered the war with few submarines, and even fewer capable of operating in the North Atlantic.

Having withdrawn from France, at first many among the Allies believed that a possible return to the country could be attempted within a short time. This was wildly unrealistic as not only had the British Army lost all of the tanks, artillery and even lorries deployed to France, the RAF was much weakened and was keeping its best fighters safe, ready for the expected German air assault on the United Kingdom. Worse still, the British did not have anything resembling landing craft or landing ships. Fortunately, the Germans were no better off.

The RAF's Bomber Command was given three main tasks. The first was the wasteful and pointless dropping of leaflets on Germany, which one senior officer described as giving the Germans 'enough toilet paper to last the war'. More useful was the mining of harbours, inland waterways and coastal waters. Most immediate was the bombing of the invasion barges that reconnaissance had spotted being assembled in ports on the French side of the Channel. The fact that the Germans had to rely on using barges showed the weakness in any plan to invade the British Isles, as barges would be vulnerable and there could even be questions over their seaworthiness. This latter fact was ignored, as many British planners were even concerned that the Germans would bypass the south of England and invade via the neutral Irish Free State, despite the lengthy and exposed sea crossing! This led to the supply of fighter aircraft and ships to the Irish.

The weakness of using barges for invasion was demonstrated when the Germans invaded Crete between 21 and 28 May 1941. British, British Commonwealth and Greek troops had been evacuated to the island after the fall of Greece, but as with the withdrawal from France, they had had to leave behind their heavy equipment and, crucially, the communications equipment and anti-aircraft weapons. The main thrust of the German assault had to be by air, using paratroops and glider-landed troops, who suffered such heavy losses that Hitler banned any future large-scale airborne operation. The Germans only won because without radios, lorries and anti-aircraft guns, the defending forces could not organise themselves adequately. Despite the Germans having command of the air, the Royal Navy, at heavy cost, retained command of the seas and inflicted heavy losses on the German barges, or *caigues*, bringing the troops, dispersing the main convoy on the night of 21 May with heavy loss of life.

Many lessons were learnt from these operations in the early part of the war, when the Allies were still on the defensive and the United States had still to enter the war. Naval firepower alone could no longer be counted upon to obtain surrender, but it had to be a vital component of any invasion. Airpower could not be counted upon to obtain surrender either, even though the commander of the RAF's Bomber Command from 1942, Air Chief Marshal Sir Arthur Harris, firmly believed that it could. Air power could not guarantee a successful invasion with air-landed troops or paratroops, but it added an important dimension to any invasion. Only sea power could provide the numbers of men and the quantity of materials required, even though gliders could land a light tank or artillery piece, but the ships had to be able to land all that was needed quickly and as easily as the conditions would allow.

Much work had to be done, in planning, co-ordination and technical development.

All of this might seem obvious; at least with the 20:20 vision of hindsight, yet in the run up to the invasion of Normandy, there was to be rivalry between the generals, especially between Eisenhower and Montgomery.

The situation in the air was slightly better, but only slightly, as 'Bomber' Harris, the controversial commander of the Royal Air Force's Bomber Command, tried to resist transferring his nightly raids from Germany to support of the ground forces. Harris firmly believed that each of these raids was equal to a major sea or land battle.

At sea, the situation was much better, with Operation Neptune in the capable and experienced hands of Admiral Bertram Ramsay, a career naval officer who had returned to the service as war loomed and who had been responsible for the success of Operation Dynamo, which had seen more than 338,000 mainly British and French troops evacuated from Dunkirk and Cherbourg between 27 May and 4 June 1940. This far surpassed the expectations of the British government, and while wars are not won by retreat and evacuation, the loss of so many experienced men would have made the future conduct of the war uncertain, especially at a time when the British Empire was fighting on its own, and in the UK there were still some willing to reach a settlement with Germany. Subsequently, Ramsay had been involved in the Mediterranean landings. No other Allied naval commander had his experience of planning and overseeing operations on such a vast scale. For Neptune, Ramsay required almost 7,000 ships of all types, ranging from humble minesweeping trawlers, through troopships, hospital ships, landing craft and cruisers, to large battleships. There were no less than 277 minesweepers.

Air power was used to keep German E-boats from attacking the invasion force, but on 27 August, well after the landings, British forces experienced their worst-ever 'friendly-fire' incident when an RAF force attacked British minesweepers off the coast having been told that they were German destroyers.

The Allies had already invaded first Vichy-held North Africa, Sicily and the mainland of Italy at Salerno and Anzio by the time the invasion of France started. There had been a number of other invasions, important, but less so, and apart from the US forces' island hopping across the Pacific, British forces had taken Iceland and Madagascar earlier in the war.

One of the reasons for the delay in invading Normandy was the heavy defences created by Hitler's forces in the famous 'Atlantic Wall', which Churchill knew would require a strong assault, even though it was not complete and had its weak points, but, as already mentioned, another reason was Churchill's belief that Germany could be invaded via Italy and Austria, an impractical idea that was soon revealed to be impossible as German resistance in Italy proved to be far stronger than the Allies had anticipated.

Despite the heavy fighting in Italy, the heavy losses suffered in the Allied bombing campaign and the massive effort devoted to maintaining the Arctic convoys to Archangel and Murmansk, Stalin persisted in demanding a direct frontal attack on German forces in France and the scene was set for one of the most audacious amphibious operations of all time.

NOTES

1. Laffin, John, *Damn the Dardanelles! The Story of Gallipoli* (London: Osprey, 1980).

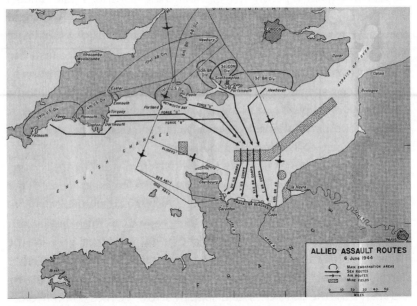

The way to Normandy. Convoys came from all along the south coast of England, and further afield, gathering south of the Isle of Wight at what was known as 'Piccadilly Circus'. All of the invasion beaches were east of Cherbourg and the Cotentin Peninsula, while airborne troops approached from a number of directions. (From an original held in the Imperial War Museum archive)

1

LOOKING FOR A
SECOND FRONT

The fall of France in 1940 left the United Kingdom and the countries of the British Commonwealth, most of which had hastened to the support of the mother country, in a dire situation. Many believed that a German invasion was imminent, and in fact the Battle of Britain arose because this was indeed what Hitler had planned: it was an attempt to gain control of the air over the British Isles. The British had had to abandon the Channel Islands as, being so close to France and south of the Cherbourg Peninsula, they could not be defended. The Germans were able to simply land, after first bombing the defenceless islanders.

The one country that had hesitated to join the rest of the Commonwealth in declaring war on Germany was South Africa. For most of the population in the dominion, this was a war that was far away, a white man's war, and nothing to do with them. These people did not have the vote, however, and the real debate was between the Prime Minister, General Barry Hertzog, who presented parliament with a motion proposing that the country remain neutral, and General Jan Smuts, a junior partner in the governing coalition, who opposed him and won by a narrow majority. There was strong Afrikaner hostility to the war, many of whom were pro-Germany and also pro-Nazi, while others were simply returning to the positions of the Boer Wars. Smuts became the country's wartime prime minister after Hertzog resigned on losing the vote.

What is now the Irish Republic, but was then known as the Irish Free State, was neutral, although many of its citizens volunteered for the British armed forces, as did many of those in Northern Ireland, part of the United Kingdom but outside the scope of conscription. The United Kingdom had by treaty the right to use certain naval bases in the Irish Free States, and certainly these 'Treaty Ports' would have been invaluable during the Battle of the Atlantic, saving the lives of many British, American and Canadian seamen on the Atlantic convoys. The Irish Free State had no intention of allowing its neutrality to be compromised, and it was also felt by the British that a substantial force of troops would be tied down defending the ports from the Irish Republican Army, which had become very active in the years before the outbreak of war.

Standing alone, the United Kingdom soon realised that there could be no early return to Europe. The priority had to be the reconstruction of the British Army as well as absorbing into the British armed forces those from the newly occupied states who had escaped. All this had to be done while the Royal Air Force was under daily attack by a numerically superior *Luftwaffe*, many of whose pilots had gained valuable air combat experience serving with the Condor Legion in the Spanish Civil War. As noted above, even in the UK, there were those who favoured appeasement, and many Germans expected this after the diplomatic victory of Munich, which had allowed Germany to annex the Sudetenland from Czechoslovakia, after the ease with which Austria had joined the Third Reich, and the way in which the remains of Czechoslovakia had succumbed with barely a murmur from the international community in 1939.

Even today, some believe that peace could have left Germany in charge of Europe and with the restoration of its former colonies, lost after the First World War, while the UK and the British Empire would have remained intact. Whether or not this would have been the case is a moot point as, after all, Hitler was planning war, but for 1944, not 1939, and appeasement could once again have simply delayed the inevitable. What is known, however, is that if Germany had invaded and won, the country would have been occupied and transformed. In fact, as late as April 1942, the last year in which Germany had any hope of winning the war, the Reichsminister of Agriculture, Walter Darr, made clear his country's intentions:

> As soon as we beat England we shall make an end of you Englishmen once and for all. Able bodied men and women will be exported as slaves to the continent.

The old and the weak will be exterminated. All men remaining in Britain as slaves will be sterilised; a million or two of the young women of the Nordic type will be segregated and with the assistance of picked German sires, during a period of ten or twelve years, will produce annually a series of Nordic infants to be brought up as Germans. These infants will form the future population of Britain. Thus, in a generation or two, the British will disappear.[1]

While the expectation of land-based warfare in Europe had proved wrong, showing that the Second World War was not going to be an exact copy of the First, one campaign that did repeat itself was that of the U-boats against British shipping, especially in the North Atlantic, while light forces made running convoys along the east coast of England difficult and dangerous, so that once again much of the traffic was transferred to an increasingly overworked railway system. Even the U-boat campaign was to be different, however, as the Admiralty lost little time in organising a convoy system, something which they, shamefully, had failed to do until the closing months of the earlier conflict.

Another big difference was that the Mediterranean was no longer a peaceful backwater. A former First World War ally, Italy's entry into the war in June 1940 meant that the fighting in the Mediterranean and in North Africa was intense while Italy invaded Yugoslavia and Greece, although German help was needed for victory in these countries. The occupation of most of France meant that Germany also had control over the Bay of Biscay, using the bases of the French Navy, the *Marine Nationale*, so that the U-boats did not have to tackle the dangerous waters around the north of Scotland but had direct access to the open sea. This meant, of course, that convoys also had to be escorted through the Bay of Biscay, often dividing at Gibraltar with some ships setting off for Malta and Alexandria, while others headed for Cape Town. This all changed once the Mediterranean became impassable and even British forces in Egypt had to be reached not by the direct route across the Mediterranean via Malta, but via Cape Town and the Suez Canal.

It would be wrong to think that the British could continue the war only in the air and at sea. From 10 June 1940 to 13 May 1943, in North Africa the British Army, with many Commonwealth troops, was locked in battle first with the Italians and then later with the Germans as the Axis powers attempted to reach the Suez Canal.

The colonial powers had a substantial interest in North Africa. France, Spain and Italy all had colonies, while the British effectively treated Egypt as if it were a colony, even though nominally independent and with its own sovereign. The start of the war in the desert, of course, marked the entry of Italy into the Second World War on 10 June 1940. Realising the danger, on 14 June, British armoured units crossed the border from Egypt into Italian-controlled Libya, taking Fort Capuzzo. The Italians in turn marched into Egypt and captured Sidi Barrani in September. British Commonwealth forces launched an offensive, 'Operation Compass', in December, destroying the Italian Tenth Army. This prompted Hitler to send General Erwin Rommel with the *Afrika Korps* to North Africa to prevent an Axis defeat. There was heavy fighting over the next two years, the British suffering a major defeat at Tobruk, and a resounding victory at El Alamein, but it was the Allied landings in North Africa, 'Operation Torch', that eventually saw the Axis forces squeezed between the Allies coming from Algeria and the British Commonwealth forces from Egypt. Even before this, from June 1941, the Axis invasion of the Soviet Union saw German forces in particular diverted away from North Africa and the Mediterranean.

At sea, the initial effort was primarily defensive, protecting shipping. There were attacks on German coastal shipping by light forces and naval aircraft, and in the Mediterranean there was the valiant and highly success-ful attack on the Italian fleet in its forward base at Taranto on the night of 11/12 November 1940, which put three out of the six Italian battleships out of action. This was followed by a successful submarine campaign, with aerial support from aircraft based on Malta, which at times virtually cut off Axis forces in North Africa from their supplies.

In the air, the activity was primarily defensive at first. The Battle of Britain had to be fought and won. A combination of factors enabled this to be done. The German fighter pilots did not stick with the bombers, but instead were enticed away for dogfights with the RAF, and especially the Supermarine Spitfire fighters, so that the RAF's Hawker Hurricanes could attack the bomber formations. British and German fighters were short on range compared to air-craft being developed in the United States at the time, so bombers operating from Denmark against Scotland suffered heavy losses. The biggest problem, however, came when the Germans switched their attention from bombing the RAF's airfields to attacking industry and British cities. This gave the RAF the chance to regroup and rebuild. Initially, night fighters were poor, but as first the Bristol Beaufighter and then the superb de Havilland Mosquito entered service, German losses soared.

Nevertheless, the real change came with the start of Bomber Command's operations against Germany, and also against industrial and military targets in the occupied territories. This was the most obvious means of taking the war to the enemy. At first, the heaviest bombers available were the Handley Page Hampden, known as the 'flying panhandle' because of its shape, and the Vickers Wellington, but true heavy bombers appeared later, first with the Short Stirling, and then the Avro Lancaster and the Handley Page Halifax. The Lancaster, when specially modified, lifted the heaviest bombs of the war, first the 12,000lb 'Tall Boy' and then the 22,000lb 'Grand Slam': huge earthquake bombs that could destroy a submarine pen or other fortification by burrowing beside it before exploding, while convention bombs simply bounced off.

The next stage was to attack in major formations, overwhelming the defences, sometimes with more than a thousand bombers, which reduced Bomber Command's losses to a sustainable level.

There has been much debate over the value of the bombing campaign, even when the RAF and the United States Army Air Force combined, the RAF attacking by night and the USAAF by day. Part of the problem was that the bombers were moved onto new targets too soon, allowing recovery and reconstruction. There was also debate over whether civilians or key industries should be the target – the Americans preferred the latter, but raids on the oil industry in Romania were difficult, involving long flights over enemy territory and heavy fighter attack all the way. Berlin could only really be attacked during the long winter nights for the same reason.

Regardless of the controversy over the morality of bombing and its effectiveness, there can be no doubt that bombing was the most practical means of taking the war to the enemy at a time when few other opportunities existed, and there can be no doubting the courage of those involved. Almost 56,000 RAF Bomber Command personnel were lost during the Second World War.

Equally grim were the losses sustained by the convoys on the North Atlantic and North Sea, with a total of 12.8 million tons of shipping sunk or seized, but mainly the former. Another 570,892 tons were lost in the Mediterranean. This latter figure would have been higher but for the fact that the Mediterranean was avoided by most Allied merchant shipping from early 1941 until the invasion of North Africa in November 1942.

Not for nothing were these theatres of war, North Africa, the Battle of the Atlantic and the Combined Bomber Offensive, regarded by the Allies as akin to fresh fronts in the war.

SECOND FRONT NOW!

There was no call for a second front until after the German invasion of the Soviet Union on 22 June 1941. The operation had been fatally delayed, partly by Germany's need to help her Italian ally in Yugoslavia and Greece, but also because an exceptionally wet spring and early summer had left the ground too soft for large armoured formations and their support vehicles to move with ease. The invasion saw the USSR change sides overnight, having until the assault been an Axis ally supplying Germany with food, raw materials and fuel.

Even today, historians are still amazed at the way in which Stalin refused to accept that Hitler was planning an invasion, despite warnings from his own agent in Tokyo, Richard Sorge, warnings from Churchill, whom he did not trust, and, most blatant of all, German reconnaissance flights over the USSR. He had purged the senior ranks of his armed forces, and insisted on dismantling the USSR's old defensive lines in favour of building new ones to incorporate newly acquired territory – Estonia, Latvia and Lithuania, as well as the eastern part of Poland. This meant that the old defensive lines were broken before the new ones were completed. Like many other leaders, he was amazed and caught off guard by the speed at which the Germans overwhelmed French resistance. He continued to supply grain and oil to Germany right up to the time of the invasion, despite Germany reneging on its supply of machinery. He ignored the requests by his two most senior army officers, Timoshenko and Zhukov, to mobilise in mid-June 1941. He did not use the relief gained by Japan's switch from operations in China to the war in the Pacific to move forces westwards.

Even when German forces surged eastwards across the Bug River on 22 June 1941, Stalin refused to order retaliation, and when he did realise that what was happening was not simply a provocative border incident, he went into a state of shock and even left breaking the news to the Russian popula-tion to Molotov, the People's Commissar for Foreign Affairs, who made the crucial broadcast to a bemused population that believed that Germany and

Russia were staunch allies. Once again, the German advance moved at unbelievable speed, some areas being overrun even before the population knew that they were at war with Germany.

It was not until 3 July that Stalin finally started to broadcast to the population, with a call to arms. Even so, during that month he also sought Bulgarian help to negotiate a truce with Germany, which would involve the USSR ceding some territory, somewhat similar to the Treaty of Brest-Litovsk that had taken Russia out of the First World War. The Bulgarians refused to help.

Once the initial German thrust eased, Stalin's generals were told not to cede any further territory, an order that saw hundreds of thousands of soldiers trapped by a German pincer movement around Kiev. He also decreed that any Russian serviceman taken prisoner by the enemy would be deemed guilty of treason. The punishments would also be extended to the serviceman's hapless family. When his own son Vasili was captured during the war, Stalin dodged the retribution that ordinary families were expected to suffer by simply disowning him.

Over the year following the German invasion, Stalin's representatives were dispatched to meetings with his new allies. Struggling to hold the Germans on the Eastern Front, what Stalin and his advisers immediately latched on was the need for a Western Front, although increasingly this was discussed as a 'Second Front'. By this, he meant that he wanted an Allied invasion of France. This was really another instance of the leaders in the Second World War harking back to the First World War when there had, of course, been an 'Eastern' and a 'Western' front. The geographical terminology was that of the Germans!

Stalin undoubtedly saw himself and his fellow countrymen, and women, as bearing the brunt of the war against the Axis Powers. This was to ignore the fact that the United States in particular, but also the British, Dutch, Australians and New Zealanders were heavily engaged in a battle against Japan, and in so doing had relieved the Soviet Union of any fears of a Japanese attack in the Far East, especially in Siberia. Many Americans wanted the war against Japan to have priority, which was understandable as Japan had launched a massive attack against the US Pacific Fleet in its forward base at Pearl Harbor on the Hawaiian island of Oahu, and worse, done so without declaration of war. The US Asiatic Fleet had also been attacked in the Philippines.

Nevertheless, while pursuing the war against Japan, which of necessity had to be a naval war until bases could be gained that put heavy bombers within reach of the Japanese home islands, the Americans decided that the war against Germany had to be the priority. That meant using the United Kingdom as a base for US bombers operating over enemy-occupied territory. The Americans pursued the war against Germany in the air, and in the North Atlantic, the Arctic and the Mediterranean.

Stalin's desire for an early invasion of France was unrealistic. He had little understanding of maritime matters and no idea of what a successful amphibious operation would take. To some extent, many Americans took the same view, although they expected an invasion of France in 1943. As it happened, the first invasion in the European theatre – if one discounts the British occupation of Iceland* in May 1940, which was handed over to US occupation in July 1942 – was actually just outside Europe, the Anglo-American invasion of Vichy-held North Africa on 8 November 1942, in Operation Torch.

Invading North Africa made a lot of sense. Most importantly, there was no way that the Mediterranean could be secured and Italy invaded until any prospect of opposition from Vichy forces in North Africa had been suppressed. British, Australian and Free French forces had earlier invaded Syria on 8 June 1941, action that was prompted by the Vichy French commander in that country allowing the *Luftwaffe* to use Syrian bases while on their way to support an uprising against the British in Iraq. An attack in North Africa would also relieve the pressure on British and Commonwealth forces that were finally making progress against Axis forces in Libya.

OPERATION TORCH

Clearly, North Africa was a good place to start and to exercise the growing Allied amphibious capability. Without the industrial support of Metropolitan France, Vichy resistance, no matter how determined, was bound to be overcome sooner rather than later. That opposition was likely was demonstrated not just by the Vichy refusal to surrender the French fleet at Mers-el-Kebir and Oran, but by the fact that in May 1941, the Vichy regime had signed the Paris protocols with Germany. These allowed the Germans to use French bases in Syria, which had prompted the British-led invasion of that country, in Tunisia and French West Africa, as well as releasing almost 7,000 French prisoners-of-war for service in North Africa.

For many, this was the 'Second Front', landing almost 100,000 men in French Morocco and Algeria behind the Axis lines. The operation had to take into account that Morocco included Spanish-held territory to the south and east of Tangier. The Allied Naval Commander was Admiral Andrew Cunningham of the Royal Navy, while the Supreme Commander was General Dwight Eisenhower of the United States Army.

The division of territory in Morocco between France and Spain meant that the invasion forces had to be divided into three. The Western Task Force, designated TF34, came from the United States with twenty-three transports to land 34,000 troops commanded by Major-General Patton to the north and south of Casablanca. The force had covering fire from three US battleships as well as the aircraft carrier USS *Ranger* and four escort carriers, seven cruisers and thirty-eight destroyers.

The Centre Task Force came from England and was commanded by Commodore Troubridge, RN, with two escort carriers, three cruisers and thirteen destroyers escorting and then supporting twenty-eight transports and nineteen landing craft, landing 39,000 soldiers commanded by Major-General Frendall at Oran in Algeria.

Near Algiers, 33,000 British and American troops under the command of Major-General Ryder were landed from sixteen transports and seventeen landing craft with the aircraft carriers HMS *Argus* and *Furious*, the world's first two aircraft carriers, three cruisers and sixteen destroyers commanded by Rear-Admiral Sir Harold Burrough, RN.

Good communications are essential in any such operation, but they were more important than ever with the forces divided as they were. Commodore Troubridge had his signals team in the ex-armed merchant cruiser *Large*, which had been converted so hastily that the sleeping accommodation for staff officers, just aft of the bridge, was unfinished and umbrellas provided the only protection from the weather.

The landings all took place on 8 November, starting an hour or so after midnight at Oran and then shortly afterwards at Algiers, while those at Casablanca started at 0430. Many of those involved were very inexperienced, and this told most with the pilots aboard the US ships. The escort carrier USS *Santee* had just five experienced pilots aboard and during the operation she lost twenty-one of her thirty-one aircraft, of which only one was 'just possibly'[2] due to enemy action.

The invasion showed confusion amongst Vichy's leaders. Admiral Darlan, in Oran and in overall command of Vichy French forces, agreed to a cease-fire if Marshal Henri Pétain, the dictator of Vichy France, agreed, but Pétain was desperately trying to prevent German forces from entering unoccupied France. Darlan then decided to change sides and ordered his forces to side with the Allies, but a number of his subordinate commanders disagreed and allowed German forces to enter Tunisia.

Meanwhile, British and American ships attacked the Vichy positions with gunfire and with carrier-borne air power. Several of the British Fleet Air Arm pilots were engaged in air-to-air combat with French fighters. Another was shot down by anti-aircraft fire, but the Vichy French forces surrendered while his captors decided what to do with him, and he was back aboard his ship within two days of being taken. One of the shortest spells as prisoner-of-war on record!

OPERATION HUSKY

Eight months were to pass before the next Allied invasion, that of Sicily, 'Operation Husky', on 10 July 1943. The delay was necessary because Axis forces in North Africa were still capable of fighting and it took until May 1943 before resupply became completely impossible and they surrendered to the Allies.

At this stage, the United States would have preferred to have started planning an invasion of France, but the British saw the taking of Sicily as more important. It would not only lead to the invasion of Italy, through which Churchill hoped to reach Germany, but more importantly it would ease the pressure on Malta and also enable the Mediterranean to be used by convoys once more. The saving in fuel and time of using the Mediterranean and the Suez Canal rather than sailing via the Cape was one consideration; another was that this provided a massive one-off boost in both merchant shipping tonnage, estimated by some to be the equivalent of having an extra million tons of shipping, and naval vessels, all of which could be used to ease the pressure elsewhere.

The decision to invade Sicily was taken at the Casablanca Conference held between 14 and 24 January 1943. Code-named 'Symbol', this was one of the most important conferences of the war, planning future strategy, and was attended by the British and American leaders, Churchill and Roosevelt, as well as Generals Alexander and Eisenhower. There was one noticeable absentee, however: Stalin. The Soviet leader was invited, but he declined because of the critical situation at Stalingrad. It was at Casablanca that the Allies first decided to demand unconditional surrender and also planned a combined USAAF and RAF bomber offensive against Germany. A determined effort was also made to reconcile the different factions of the French armed forces represented by de Gaulle and Giraud, and this led to them forming a French National Committee for Liberation.

Stalin's failure to attend the Casablanca Conference was yet another instance of his lack of logic, especially since he missed the opportunity to demand an Allied invasion of France. The Battle of Stalingrad was almost over, the Germans having been encircled and an attempt to relieve them foiled by the Russians. While final surrender did not come until 2 February, any other leader would have had the strategic perspective and the confidence to leave matters in the hands of trusted military commanders.

Much of the problem lay in Stalin's policy of, in modern terms, micromanaging the war. He knew who was in command and where they were situated, down to middle-ranking officers. His close colleagues, in effect his war cabinet, were constantly harassed and bullied, humiliated in front of their peers. Often, a close member of their family would be held in a *gulag*, or prison camp, usually on rations that were not even at subsistence level. There was no trust, no semblance of being part of a team, just the rule of fear. In short, Stalin felt vulnerable.

Husky was more akin to the Normandy landings than Torch had been, with a combined amphibious and airborne assault. First, on 11 and 12 June 1943, the garrisons on two small Italian islands to the west of Malta, Pantelleria and Lampedusa, surrendered after bombardment by the Royal Navy and raids from Malta-based squadrons of the RAF and Fleet Air Arm.

For some time, the Royal Navy had maintained what amounted to a second Mediterranean Fleet in what was officially known as Force H, based on Gibraltar, while the Mediterranean Fleet had been compelled to withdraw to Alexandria in Egypt from the beginning of 1941. Force H had grown in strength, its successes had included participation in the sinking of the German battleship *Bismarck*. By mid-1943, it had six battleships and two modern aircraft carriers, HMS *Indomitable* and *Formidable*, six cruisers and twenty-four destroyers. Designed to be a fast-moving task force, it did not have escort carriers. Force H was to act as the covering force for Operation Husky. The landings were made by an American Western Naval Task Force and a British Eastern Naval Task Force. There were 2,590 ships altogether, including 2,000 landing craft, such as the new tank-landing ship, or LST, with the intention of landing 180,000 men under General Dwight Eisenhower, who had to face more than 275,000 men in General Guzzoni's Italian Sixth Army.

Besides the sea, the Allies were strongest in the air. The Allies had 3,700 aircraft, mainly operating from land bases in North Africa as well as the three airfields on Malta, while the Axis Powers had 1,400 aircraft.

The Western Naval Task Force was to land the US Seventh Army on the south coast of Sicily, while the British Eastern Naval Task Force would land the British Eighth Army on the south-eastern point of the island. The Americans had to take the port of Licata and the British the port of Syracuse. After this, they had to seize the airfields around Catania.

The assault was launched from North Africa as the forces assembled would have overwhelmed the facilities available on the small island of Malta. On the eve of the invasion, bad weather nearly caused the landings to be postponed. This did at least lull the Axis commanders into a false sense of security, apart from which, many of them expected the Allies to be heading for Sardinia. The result was that the amphibious assault was a great success, but in the high winds, the airborne assault was less so, with many paratroops landing in the seas, while many of the Horsa gliders suffered the same fate, having been released too early by the towing aircraft. More than 250 troops were drowned.

On 11 July, a strong counter-attack was launched by German *Panzer* divisions, but this was broken up by Allied air power and a heavy bombardment from Force H.

Italian resistance virtually ended when Mussolini fell from power on 25 July, after which Hitler dropped his opposition to German troops being withdrawn and some 40,000 German and 62,000 Italian troops crossed the Straits of Messina to the Italian mainland starting on the night of 11/12 August, with much of their equipment and supplies intact.

Only the invasion of Normandy, Operation Overlord, was larger than Husky. More than any other operation, the invasion of Sicily provided the

Allies with vital experience and many lessons were learnt that would prove invaluable later.

OPERATION AVALANCHE

The logical move was for the Allies to follow the retreating Axis forces across the Straits of Messina, and this is what Montgomery's Eighth Army did on 3 September 1943. That same day, the Allies and the Italians signed a secret armistice at Syracuse.

The next step was to cut off as many German forces as possible and also shorten the advance towards Rome. This was done at Salerno on 9 September; the day after the armistice was announced. The landings at Salerno were co-ordinated with a British airborne landing at Taranto to enable the remains of the Italian fleet to escape to Malta. The airborne landing was covered by the guns of the six Force H battleships.

On learning of the armistice, the Germans moved quickly to seize Italian airfields. Salerno was chosen instead of a landing site further north because it was close to Allied airfields in Sicily, but it was only just within range for fighter aircraft, meaning that they could spend very little time patrolling the area, usually no more than twenty minutes, and if combat occurred, they could not return to Sicily. The solution was to deploy aircraft carriers.

The United States Navy provided an Independence-class light carrier and four escort carriers. The Royal Navy once again deployed Force H to cover the landings with HMS *Illustrious* and *Formidable*, as well as creating an escort carrier fleet known as Force V, with the escort carriers HMS *Attacker*, *Battler*, *Hunter* and *Stalker*, augmented by HMS *Unicorn*, a maintenance carrier but here, not for the last time in her career, used as an active fleet carrier launching fighter sorties. Force V provided thirty Supermarine Spitfire fighters aboard each escort carrier and no less than sixty aboard *Unicorn*.

The British ships sailed from Malta as if to attack Taranto, but instead headed north to Salerno. Once off Salerno, Force V was given a 'box' in which to operate, flying off and recovering their aircraft. The trouble was that with so many other ships in the area, the box was too small, giving the carrier commanders great difficulty as they steamed from one end to another and then had to turn. This was nothing compared to the difficulties facing the pilots, trying to land on ships steaming close to one another, and avoid mid-air collisions. Worse still, the weather on this occasion was good – too good. The Seafire needed a headwind of 25 knots over the flight deck for a safe take-off, but in still air conditions the escort carriers could only provide 17 knots. Arrester wires and crash barriers had to be kept as tight as possible. The amphibious assault and the covering force on this occasion were much smaller, at 627 ships.

In contrast to the landings in North Africa and Sicily, the *Luftwaffe* mounted heavy attacks against the carriers and these were sustained until 14 September. The need for air cover meant that the carriers were asked to remain on station longer than originally planned, and their frantic racing up and down with the 'box' meant that fuel began to run low so that they had to resort to using their reserve tanks. In addition to conventional bombing, the German response was augmented by the first use of radio-controlled glider bombs, which damaged two British cruisers and the veteran battle-ship HMS *Warspite*.

The difficulties faced by the carrier pilots meant that deck landing accidents accounted for a higher loss rate than the *Luftwaffe*, with Force V's 180 aircraft reduced to just thirty by 14 September. Meanwhile, the Germans had organised a massive counter-attack between 12 and 14 September.

As the campaign ashore moved slowly, a further amphibious assault was planned for Anzio further up the coast. Shore bases near the Salerno landing site were available for this and carrier air support was not needed, but even in January 1944, the landings at Anzio faced strong German opposition and it took four months for the Allies to break out of their beachhead. While Salerno and Vietri were captured, they remained too close to the German frontline for either to be used as ports.

OPERATION SHINGLE

Convalescing after an illness at Marrakesh in French Morocco, Churchill convened two conferences at his villa to discuss the situation in Italy, where the hopes of a rapid advance on Rome following the Salerno landings had been foiled by strong German resistance. The first was held on 7 and 8 January 1944, with Churchill in the chair accompanied by Lord Beaverbrook, and attended by senior British and American officers. The second was on 12 January, when Churchill and de Gaulle met.

Although the need for a second landing further north had been agreed in late 1943, the initial plan was cancelled in favour of landings at Anzio, code-named Operation Shingle, which was decided at the Marrakesh conferences. Little time was lost in mounting the operation, which took place on 22 January, but suffered accordingly as the force used was too small, simply the 6th US Corps of the 5th US Army. The 6th US Corps was augmented by the 1st British Infantry Division and a British commando brigade, which landed north of Anzio. Other forces landed at the port or to the south. Just 378 ships took part and air support was provided mainly by the USAAF with the Mediterranean Allied Tactical Air Force. The Germans deployed radio-controlled explosive boats and human torpedoes against the ships, but with little effect; German air power was also weak in the area.

There was confusion over the objectives and, instead of exploiting the initial surprise, the 6th US Corps found itself consolidating its position. Bad weather meant that the Allies had difficulty in reinforcing those ashore, and by 26 January, Kesselring, the German commander in Italy, improvised a Fourteenth Army with a core of six divisions. This force surrounded the Allies, and attempts to break through saw both the British and the Americans suffer heavy casualties, 2,100 and 3,000 respectively. As the month drew to a close, 'Ultra' intelligence warned the Allied commanders of a German counter-attack, to which they were able to respond effectively. Fierce fighting in the second half of February saw the Germans suffer very heavy casualties with 5,389 men killed or wounded as the Allies moved heavy artillery and massive air power into position. Nevertheless, Kesselring managed to keep the Allies contained until they were able to break out and link up with the US Fifth Army on 25 May and begin the final advance on Rome.

Anzio was a big disappointment to the Allies. Churchill later wrote that he had 'hoped that the Allies were hurling a wild cat onto the shore but all they got was a stranded whale'. The US Navy's official historian was equally blunt, writing that 'putting such a small force ashore was akin to sending a boy on a man's errand'.

The landings in the Mediterranean were not over until the Allies invaded the south of France in August, and even then there were further minor operations to retake Axis-occupied territory. Nevertheless, Normandy was next and the Allies had learnt much about amphibious operations both in the Mediterranean and in the Far East by this time. Two points were clear. The first was that the Germans might be losing the war, but they were still capable of mounting a formidable defence and still possessed the capability of fighting a highly mobile war so that large and well-equipped forces could be assembled quickly when needed. The second was that any assault had to be meticulously organised and assembled in such force that the defences could be overwhelmed, while the force ashore needed to be sustained and supported, regardless of the weather.

NOTES

1. *Daily Express*, 3 June 2000.
2. Gelbe, Norman, *Desperate Venture* (London: Hodder & Stoughton, 1992).

* The 'invasion' of Iceland was prompted by the fall of Denmark, after which the Icelandic administration declared independence. Churchill was concerned that there could be a coup by Germans already resident on the island, which would make defending the North Atlantic convoys almost impossible. The landing was left to 'Force Sturges', named after its commander, Colonel Robert Sturges, with a total of 815 men plus some intelligence experts. They arrived at Reykjavik Bay on 10 May 1940, and seized key positions without a shot being fired. The German consulate was closed and German nationals interned. The Icelandic government issued a formal protest, but without armed forces and a small population of around 200,000, could do nothing. The population was divided as some had German sympathies, but the island's prime minister described the United Kingdom as a friendly nation and asked the population to treat the British as guests. The Americans were asked to take over in Iceland so that the British troops deployed there could be moved to North Africa.

2

PLANNING AND PREPARATION

The name 'Overlord' was chosen for the Allied invasion of enemy-occupied north-western Europe, while the naval operations, which included the Normandy landings and all associated operations, were code-named 'Neptune'.

As mentioned earlier, the big decisions on the invasion of enemy-held territory were taken at the Casablanca Conference, 'Symbol', held in January 1943. The initial agreement was to establish a joint planning staff, which became known as COSSAC, from the title of the original head of the organisation, Lieutenant-General Sir Frederick Morgan, who was 'Chief of Staff to the Supreme Allied Commander'. Brigadier-General Ray Barker of the US Army was appointed as Morgan's deputy. The supreme Allied commander had still to be appointed, but the Allies realised that it was a matter of urgency that a planning team be established and that this would develop into the nucleus of an operational headquarters for the supreme commander.

It was some time after the conference that Normandy, between Caen and the Cotentin Peninsula, was chosen for the landings instead of the Pas-de-Calais. There were several reasons for this. One was the fact that the German defences were strongest in the Pas-de-Calais and second that there would have been congestion in the narrow Straits of Dover. On the other hand, the Pas-de-Calais had many good ports, and the choice of Normandy meant that two artificial ports would have to be constructed until a major French port could be taken. The decision was taken in June, after which all reference to the operation focused on Normandy.

The conference agreed that the invasion should be carried out during May 1944. Initially, the idea was that it should be a two-pronged assault on the coast of Normandy, and, if possible, this should be coupled with an Allied invasion of the south of France. The tight schedule for building sufficient landing craft and landing ships and training personnel meant that the target date for D-Day was put back to between 5 and 7 June, with 18–20 June as an alternative. H-Hour, the time of the operation, was soon set to be shortly after dawn. The difficulties of finding sufficient vessels for the operation also meant that the Normandy landings could not be tied in with a simultaneous invasion of the south of France.

Well before this, the British Prime Minister Winston Churchill had his mind set on combined operations. He summoned Rear-Admiral Lord Louis Mountbatten, a British naval officer, who was visiting Hawaii at the time. Mountbatten was to be Chief of Combined Operations until October 1943, when COSSAC took over.

RULE BY COMMITTEE

The whole operation was to be overseen by the Combined Chiefs of Staff (CCS). Actually a committee, the CCS was the overall Anglo-American authority, which comprised the American Joint Chiefs of Staff (JCS), and the British Chiefs of Staff (COS). Its role was to provide advice on strategy to Churchill and Roosevelt, and after the latter died on 12 April 1945, his successor, Truman, and then to implement the strategic decisions taken by the British Prime Minister and the US President.

The US Joint Chiefs of Staff Committee was the successor to the Joint Board, which comprised the service chiefs and their deputies, and the heads of their respective air services*, as well as the Head of the War Plans Division. After the Washington Conference, code-named 'Arcadia', in December 1941, it became clear that the US needed a body that mirrored the British Chiefs of Staff, and so the JCS was established in February 1942. The new body was slightly slimmed down, and initially included the General of the Army as Chief of Staff, Admiral Ernest King and Lieutenant-General Henry 'Hap' Arnold, the chief of the USAAF. At first, Admiral Harold Stark was also on the committee, but Roosevelt blamed him for Pearl Harbor and he moved sideways to represent the US Navy in London. Arnold was later promoted to five-star general. The reason for having both King and Stark on the committee was that Stark was Chief of Naval Operations while King was Commander-in-Chief of the US Fleet, but after Stark's departure the two posts were merged.

The British Chiefs of Staff Committee provided advice on strategy and then issued orders to commanders in the field once strategy had been determined. The committee dated from 1923, when it was formed to advise the Committee of Imperial Defence (CID) on strategy. It was later augmented by two sub-committees for planning and intelligence. Other sub-committees were created during the Second World War, but these remained the most important. On the outbreak of war, the CID was replaced by the War Cabinet. In 1939, its members included the ailing Admiral of the Fleet Sir Dudley Pound, Field Marshal Sir Edmund Ironside and Marshal of the Royal Air Force Sir Cyril Newall, with Major-General Hastings Ismay as secretary. These senior officers later changed, Cunningham replacing Pound, Portal replacing Newall and then Dill replacing Ironside before himself being replaced by Field Marshal Sir Alan Brooke. Initially, the members took turns to act as chairman, but Brooke held the post permanently from March 1942. When Commodore (later Rear-Admiral) Lord Louis Mountbatten was appointed adviser on combined operations in October 1941, he attended COS meetings if combined operations were on the agenda, but he became a *de facto* member once promoted to Chief of Combined Operations.

From May 1940, Churchill combined his role of Prime Minister with that of Minister of Defence, and put the COS under his control, sometimes presiding over its meetings, which were held at least once daily. The members of the COS accompanied Churchill to all of the Allied conferences throughout the war years.

Morgan was appointed COSSAC in March 1943 and his headquarters was based in Norfolk House, St James' Square, in central London, although many of the formal meetings were held in Washington. His own staff was drawn from both the British and American armed forces. His instructions were extensive, even including a deception scheme, later code-named 'Operation Cockade', which would keep the Germans on alert for landings during the spring, summer and autumn of 1943. The deception plans will be covered later, but suffice to say that they take at least some of the credit for the Germans having widely varying ideas as to where the Allied assault would come, and, as already mentioned, Hitler believed that the Allies would return to Europe via Norway, while many of his generals believed that the attack would come in the Pas-de-Calais.

One would have thought that the combination of the American JCS and the British COS committees combined with COSSAC would have been enough, but in their desire to ensure collaboration and good co-operation and communication, a further committee was added, the CCS. This was a simple combination of the Joint Chiefs of Staff and the Chiefs of Staff, and was formed as a result of the December 1941 Washington Conference, known as 'Arcadia', and sat in Washington. The British COS was represented by General Dill at first, and later by General Maitland Wilson.

The organisation grew as the war continued, and many sub-committees were established, ensuring effective co-ordination. The main sub-committees covered planning; intelligence; communications; military transport; the assignment of munitions; meteorology, and, finally, civil affairs, the last being formed later than the others, all of which dated from 1942, in June 1943.

The task was difficult as there were many sceptics of a combined approach to the war effort on both sides of the Atlantic. There were national and inter-service rivalries, and different outlooks. One of the main sceptics was none other than chairman Brooke himself, but he was later to describe the organisation as the most efficient 'that had ever been evolved for coordinating and correlating the war strategy and effort of the Allies'.[1]

The main emphasis was the war in Europe and the Mediterranean, but CCS could intervene in any other theatre as it saw fit. Orders to the commanders in the various theatres were usually issued through the chiefs of staff of the country that provided the commander, who then processed the order through the head of the service to which the commander belonged. This prevented confusion and bias.

PLANS AND DECEPTIONS

Meanwhile COSSAC's first task was to draw up an outline plan for the invasion of Europe, into which, as mentioned above, were incorporated no less than three deception plans in an overall scheme code-named 'Cockade' to keep the Germans expecting landings in 1943. One of the more ambitious Cockade schemes was code-named 'Tindall' and called for landings in Norway to be mounted from Scotland. This was the plan that Hitler expected.

Slightly more achievable was another plan for landings on the Brest Peninsula, known as 'Wadham'. Finally, the favourite of the German Army commanders on the ground was 'Starkey', which proposed landings in the Pas-de-Calais. If this was not enough, Morgan and his staff also had to prepare plans for an immediate invasion should the opportunity arise, and these were code-named 'Rankin'.

Each of the deceptions had its weaknesses. Assembling the required forces in the north of Scotland would have been difficult, and the passage to Norway too long, risking not only discovery and attack, but also risking the invasion force's troops arriving in a poor state and exhausted by the long voyage. No doubt southern Norway would have had to be the landing site, since its terrain is easier than further north, but there was the risk of aerial attack from the *Luftwaffe* based in Norway and Denmark, and the risk of being attacked by ground forces on both sides.

The Brest Peninsula plan also involved a longer sea passage, and once ashore the risk of being left cut-off on the peninsula by German forces, which experience in Italy had shown to be still well-led and highly mobile, and still with sufficient equipment to mount a determined resistance followed by a strong counter-attack, despite almost three years of heavy Allied bombing.

Both of these schemes would have resulted in serious resupply problems, and especially difficulties in landing further men and equipment and, of course, also supplying sufficient fuel.

The short crossing across the English Channel to the Pas-de-Calais was, on the face of it, the most attractive. A short sea crossing with good landing beaches to the north of the port of Boulogne. Unfortunately, the port of Dover was so close to the French coast that it was largely evacuated of its civilian population during the war because of the heavy artillery shelling and no invasion force could sensibly be assembled there. Close to France it might be, but the invasion force would not have been able to take advantage of that and would have had to sail along the south coast from Portsmouth or points further west. Again, too much time at sea, exposed to the weather and the enemy.

NORMANDY IT IS

COSSAC prepared an outline plan for an invasion of Normandy for presentation to the 'Quadrant' conference held in Quebec in August 1943. Running from 17–24 August, the conference was largely between Roosevelt and Churchill with their military and diplomatic advisers. Stalin was still not present. Once approved, the detail was left to the respective sea, land and air commanders to prepare. Morgan was given increased powers, and expected to prepare for subversive warfare, intelligence and meteorological intelligence, and post-invasion civil affairs, as well as the preparation of the two Mulberry harbours to be towed in sections across the Channel and assembled, and the installation of cross-Channel fuel lines known as 'Pluto'.

As Morgan was later to write in his book on the planning, *Prelude to Overlord*, the civil affairs brief was to be the most difficult as 'there were plenty of affairs but the difficulty was to keep them civil'.

The invasion was the main item on the Quebec Conference's agenda, but it did not confine itself to the Normandy landings. Decisions were taken on the war in the Far East, and a new South East Asia Command was formed with Mountbatten as its supreme commander. Decisions were taken on relations with Spain, which was to be pressured to cut tungsten supplies to Germany and to withdraw its Blue Division from the Eastern Front. Most significant for the planned invasion, consideration was given to the possibility of bringing forward the invasion of the south of France to coincide with Overlord.

At this stage, there was still some flexibility over the date. The year 1943 had already been ruled out, but the major factor was that the landings should be around the time of the full moon, both to provide light for the convoys crossing the Channel and for aerial attacks, and to coincide with the highest tides, the monthly spring tides, so that the landing craft and ships would have a better chance of being carried over any obstacles the Germans might have placed at the low tide mark.

For the Germans, as would be seen later, an invasion of the south of France while fighting went on in the north of the country was to be a major headache. Quite what would have happened had both invasions been mounted at once is a matter for speculation. The Germans had neither the time nor the resources to build a Mediterranean equivalent of the Atlantic Wall, and so the invasion of the south of France was far easier than that of Normandy. On the other hand, would it have been possible to assemble such a strong force for Normandy with the southern invasion also calling upon the available resources?

As the tempo of planning and preparation stepped up, Eisenhower was appointed supreme commander for the Normandy landings in December 1943, with Lieutenant-General Bedell Smith as his chief of staff and Morgan becoming one of Bedell Smith's three deputies.

Admiral Sir Bertram Ramsay, who had returned to the Royal Navy shortly before the outbreak of the Second World War having retired in 1938, had become the Naval Force Commander as early as 1942, in expectation of an invasion being launched in 1943. When it became clear that this would not happen, he was sent to the Mediterranean to become deputy naval commander of the Allied Expeditionary Force under Admiral of the Fleet Sir Andrew Cunningham and planned the landings for the invasion of North Africa, 'Operation Torch', in November 1942, and then became Naval Commanding Officer, Eastern Task Force, for the 'Operation Husky' landings in Sicily in July 1943. The principal USN officer for Operation Neptune was Rear-Admiral Alan Kirk, who would provide the naval cover for the landings in the American Sector. The two admirals maintained separate offices, Kirk's close to the US Embassy, and Ramsay eventually moved to HMS *Odyssey*, near Portsmouth, but the two men proved a fortunate choice and worked well together, co-ordinating their efforts carefully.

NOTES

1. Alanbrooke, Field Marshal Lord, *War Diaries 1939–1945* (London: Weidenfeld & Nicolson, 2001).

* At this time, the United States had no autonomous air force along British or French lines; the United States Army Air Force was theoretically part of the US Army. Nevertheless, the USAAF had developed itself along the lines of the Royal Air Force, placing priority on strategic air warfare and during the Second World War, the US Army (and the US Marines) had to return to basics to provide aerial observation post capability.

3

THE WAR WITHIN –
BATTLING LEADERS

While well-rehearsed photo-calls for a heavily censored press and radio and film news coverage presented the general public in the United States and the United Kingdom with an image of harmony at the top, there was much disagreement on many issues. The most serious problems lay below the level of the politicians, the generals, admirals and air marshals holding different views, sometimes for reasons of policy, sometimes because of experience, and sometimes because of different national viewpoints.

Added to this was the constantly looming presence of the Free French leader, General Charles de Gaulle, who behaved as if his allies were his to command and control, rather than the saviours of his beloved France, and the baleful presence of the Soviet leader, Stalin, who shrugged off the endeavours, hardships and the sacrifices of the Allies and their personnel to insist on a second front, and a 'second front now', no matter what else was happening in the rest of the world or even just in Europe.

Churchill had visited Moscow in August 1942, at no small discomfort and some personal hazard, to explain to Stalin why an invasion of mainland Europe would have to be delayed. He had flown from England to Gibraltar at night, with all other Allied flying in the area stopped so that any other aircraft picked up by radar would be considered German and attacked. He was flown by William J. Vanderkloot, an American who had joined the Royal Air Force some time before the Japanese attack on Pearl Harbor. Churchill and his party spent the day in Gibraltar before flying south-east and then over the Sahara before turning north to reach Cairo, where Churchill was brought up-to-date with the North African campaign. Before leaving, he was joined by a US special envoy, W. Averell Harriman, who was to represent the ailing President Roosevelt. On leaving Cairo, they flew across Jordan and Iraq to Tehran. At Tehran they were joined by a Soviet special adviser, almost certainly someone who could both interpret and understand Soviet signals, before flying over the Caspian Sea and present day Turkmenistan and Kazakhstan, and then turning towards Moscow.

Small wonder that Winston Churchill once observed that, 'There is only one thing worse than fighting with allies, and that is fighting without them.'

While the United States Army Air Force and the Royal Air Force had developed independently of one another yet sharing a belief in strategic air power, in contrast to the tactical *blitzkrieg* type tactics favoured by both the German *Luftwaffe* and the Red Air Forces, down below matters were very different indeed, especially between the armies.

The Americans were keen to get onto the Continent as quickly as possible, and to use large numbers of men in a frontal assault. The idea was simply to steam roller over the opposition. With much more limited manpower and a long history as a maritime nation, the British did not favour the same tactics. The British strategy was to nibble around the edges as it were, hence the landings in North Africa and then in Italy, beating back the enemy and taking territory in stages suited them very well.

There were other differences as well. British units would be rotated out of the frontline to rest and integrate newcomers before returning to battle. The Americans simply sent new arrivals, usually straight from training, to frontline units, where they naturally suffered higher losses than the more experienced troops. Once in the frontline, an American unit remained there.

There was a certain recklessness and lack of concern for human life in the American attitude. The American military historian Edward Luttwak has described this approach as having an infantry mass of 'disposable sons'.

THE ALLIED MILITARY LEADERS

The importance of the invasion meant that the commanders were very senior indeed, the most senior leaders being of five-star rank, meaning General of the Army in US terms or Field Marshal in British. They were given free rein in selecting their most senior subordinates, but only up to a point, as they had to work with whoever was their opposite number or, not even their opposite number but a subordinate heading a major formation belonging to an ally. It was unlikely, for example, that Eisenhower would have chosen Montgomery, the British commander. Little love was lost between these two men.

The most important military leader was, of course, the Supreme Allied Commander, General of the Army Dwight D. Eisenhower, who had chosen Lt-Gen Bedell Smith as his chief of staff. Lt-Gen Frederick Morgan, another US Army officer who had in fact been COSSAC and headed the organisation of the same name, became one of the three deputies at Eisenhower's Supreme Headquarters Allied Expeditionary Force, SHAEF, which was a logical move as when SHAEF was formed in February 1944, it absorbed almost all of COSSAC's personnel. Eisenhower later paid tribute to Morgan, saying that it was he who had made D-Day possible.

There were other important figures as well. The then General (later Field Marshal) Bernard 'Monty' Montgomery was to command the 21st Army Group, later known as the British 2nd Army, while the 1st Canadian Army was under the command of General Henry Crerar. The two US formations were the Twelfth Army Group under General Omar Bradley and the Third US Army under General George S. Patton. Under all of these officers were many others of what the British would call 'general rank', or 'air rank' in the RAF. Air Chief Marshal (equivalent to a USAAF four-star general) Sir Arthur Tedder was Eisenhower's deputy, while Montgomery was appointed commander of the Allied ground forces.

The United States was given the overall command because, despite its heavy commitments in the Pacific theatre of operations, without US support the invasion could not have been mounted, as Churchill was later to remind de Gaulle. Command of the air and sea forces was given to British officers. At sea, Admiral Sir Bertram Ramsay was the overall commander; in the skies Air Chief Marshal Sir Trafford Leigh-Mallory commanded the tactical air forces.

While this team was at or near the front, others not at SHAEF were also involved. One of Tedder's responsibilities was to co-ordinate the work of the Allied Tactical Air Forces with those of the strategic air forces, including RAF Bomber Command led by Air Chief Marshal Sir Arthur 'Bomber' Harris, and his USAAF counterpart, General Carl A. 'Twoey' Spaatz. Naval forces were under the overall command of Admiral of the Fleet Sir Alexander 'ABC' Cunningham, the British First Sea Lord, the highest ranking British naval officer, and the British Army was under the overall command of Field Marshal Sir Alan Brooke, later Lord Alanbrooke.

EISENHOWER

Although General of the Army Dwight D. 'Ike' Eisenhower was already serving as a major during the First World War, he was retained in the United States despite repeated requests for a posting to France, and given the task of forming the US Army's first tank corps, an interesting task as tanks were the military's big invention of the war.

After spending time at the US Army's Staff College at Leavenworth, and then attending the Washington War College, he was appointed to the staff of General John Pershing, before joining the staff of General Douglas MacArthur in the Philippines. This was an unusual arrangement as MacArthur had been appointed a field marshal in the Philippine Army in 1936 and the following year had retired from the US Army (although he was recalled after the US entered the Second World War). MacArthur considered Eisenhower to be the best staff officer in the US Army, but relations between the two men were far from good, possibly because MacArthur was vain and always hungry for publicity and self-promotion. Eisenhower, anxious not to be overlooked for active service a second time, insisted on returning to the US as soon as war broke out in Europe. After serving as a regimental officer, he became a battalion commander in the US Army, which was by this time expanding fast, and a series of appointments followed, each more senior, becoming chief of staff of the 3rd Infantry Division, then the 9th Army Corps and then of the Third Army, becoming first a colonel and then a brigadier-general, before returning to Washington following Pearl Harbor as deputy chief of the War Plans Division. When this was renamed the Operations Division, he became its head with the rank of major-general. In June 1942, he was promoted again and became commanding general of the European theatre of operations. His lack of combat experience caused alarm amongst many senior British officers at this stage, while his substantive rank remained that of a lieutenant-colonel, even though he was acting lieutenant-general.

While many Americans were anxious to see an early assault on German-occupied France, Eisenhower was soon convinced that the British were right to refuse to invade France in 1942, or even the following year. He also accepted that the assault on North Africa was the first step towards liberating occupied territory and then taking the war to the Germans and Italians. He was put in overall command of the North African invasion.

Eisenhower deliberately set out to create a harmonious working relationship amongst the Allies, especially among the British and the Americans, appreciating that nationalistic fervour would undermine morale. He is credited with once saying that he did not mind someone being called a son-of-a-bitch, but objected strongly to someone being called a British or an American son-of-a-bitch.

His penchant for diplomacy meant that he overcame the problems that surfaced in Algiers after the invasion, especially between the Gaullist Free French officers and their Vichy counterparts, but operations in Tunisia showed the inexperience of Eisenhower and his men, as well as the weaknesses in his command structure. Nevertheless, the Allies eventually won the Battle of the Kasserine Pass; lessons were learnt and incompetent commanders were replaced. Afterwards, in February 1942, he was promoted to four-star general.

Allied caution in both Sicily and at Salerno, which allowed the Germans and Italians scope first to evacuate Sicily and then regroup after Salerno, has often been blamed on Eisenhower. Nevertheless, once a unified command was established for the Mediterranean, Eisenhower was brought back to London and appointed supreme commander of the Allied Expeditionary Forces in January 1944, largely because President Roosevelt felt that 'Ike' was the best politician amongst the military commanders rather than because he was the best strategist.

Political ability, or perhaps good diplomacy, was certainly essential. Churchill often had ideas, some of which were sound but others were known to senior military figures as his 'midnight follies', usually after having had a fair amount to drink. The Free French leader, General Charles de Gaulle, was interventionist and arrogant, treating his Allies as if he was in charge and ignoring the fact that he was a refugee from a defeated nation. Then there were the senior military commanders who had their own ideas of how the war should be conducted.

The most prominent amongst the latter were the bomber leaders: Harris of the RAF and Spaatz of the USAAF. Both of these men were committed to carrying out the instructions contained in the 'Pointblank Directive', which meant the combined bomber offensive against industrial targets, mainly in Germany but also in Italy and Romania, the RAF bombing by night and the USAAF by day. These were also known as the 'panacea targets' because the main industries, such as oil and rubber production, were essential to the conduct of the war. Eisenhower needed the bombers switched from Germany to cutting the lines of communications in France. Railways and road bridges had to be the main targets before the invasion could be launched. This was seen as so important by Eisenhower that he wrote in his diary on 22 March 1944 that if his strategy was not adopted, 'I will request relief from this command.'

Eisenhower won the argument, although not quite to the extent that he wanted. Nevertheless, protests from Harris in particular were overruled by Churchill so that by D-Day, railway traffic in northern France had been cut to a third of what it had been in January 1944. The two Allied bomber commands remained under Eisenhower's overall command for some months afterwards and played a part in the eventual breakout from Normandy in August.

Eisenhower's control was complete. He overruled Leigh-Mallory on the disposition of US airborne troops, and was proven right. He also ensured that once the Allies had broken out from their Normandy beaches, no time was wasted in pursuing the retreating Germans, having learnt the lessons of Sicily. On the other hand, he accepted Montgomery's arguments for a bridgehead on the Lower Rhine at Arnhem instead of clearing the approaches to Antwerp first.

Relations with Montgomery, the senior British commander on the ground, were difficult. Eisenhower always wanted a consensus, but Montgomery was impatient and inclined to see only his side of any argument. It has to be said that at times both Patton and Bradley found the search for a consensus infuriating as well.

Consensus and cheerfulness were the two main threads that characterised Eisenhower's command. Even when the Allies faced a serious reversal, he maintained that there should only be cheerful faces around the conference table or in any press or newsreel opportunities. He was promoted to five-star rank, General of the Army, in December 1944, ironically the same month that the Germans launched their Ardennes offensive, more usually known as the Battle of the Bulge, which he had failed to predict.

The most succinct summing up of his record as Supreme Allied Commander comes from his biographer, Stephen Ambrose:

As a strategist, the highest art of a commander, he was far more often right than wrong. He was right in his selection of Normandy as the invasion site, right in his selection of Bradley rather than Patton as First Army Commander, right in his insistence on using bombers against the French railway system, right to insist on a broad-front approach to Germany, right to see the [Battle of the] Bulge as an opportunity rather than a disaster, right to fight the major battle west of the Rhine. Eisenhower was right on the big decisions. He was the most successful general of the greatest war ever fought.[1]

TEDDER

Air Chief Marshal Sir Arthur Tedder was Eisenhower's deputy from December 1943 until the German surrender in May 1945. Like many British airmen of his rank and generation, he had started his military career in the British Army before transferring to the Royal Flying Corps, where he became a fighter squadron commander. As with other members of the RFC, and the Royal Naval Air Service, he was automatically transferred to the newly formed Royal Air Force on 1 April 1918, becoming a squadron leader. He was promoted to air vice-marshal (equivalent to major-general) in 1937 while Air Officer Commanding, Far East, and the following year returned to London to fill the new role of director-general of research and development at the RAF's controlling government department, the Air Ministry.

In his new role he had to work with the Ministry of Aircraft Production when that was formed in 1940, but he did not get on well with Lord Beaverbrook, the department's political head and a friend of Winston Churchill, so by December he was sent to the Mediterranean to be deputy to Air Marshal (equivalent to lieutenant-general) Sir Arthur Longmore, a former RNAS pilot who had made the first aerial torpedo drop, before taking over from him in May 1941. Churchill tried to have Tedder relieved of his post as he considered his estimate of the RAF strength needed to relieve Tobruk to be far too low, but Tedder was saved when the RAF's Chief of Staff, Marshal of the Royal Air Force (five-star rank, equivalent to field marshal or general of the air force) Sir Charles Portal, threatened to resign.

Portal was right and Churchill was wrong, probably unaware of Tedder's great achievement while AOC Middle East. A major weakness among the Allies was army-air co-operation. Ground forces did not always get the air cover needed, and air power was not used effectively, as many incidents during the Battle of France proved, with the RAF Advanced Air Striking Force taking too long to attack German strong points. Tedder's legacy was to work tirelessly to establish good communications between forces on the ground and in the air, despite his Desert Air Force being composed of squadrons from many different countries. This set the pattern for Allied air operations, not just in Africa but also throughout the European theatre. He was promoted to air chief marshal and knighted in 1942 and was briefly Vice-Chief of the Air Staff before returning to the Mediterranean as Allied Air Commander in February 1943, where he first came to Eisenhower's attention.

Working under Eisenhower for the Normandy landings as Deputy Supreme Commander at SHAEF, his organisation of the Allied air forces was so effective that the *Luftwaffe* was overwhelmed and had no chance of interfering with the landings, and suffered massive problems of resupply and reinforcement in the months that followed. After the war ended, he was promoted to Marshal of the Royal Air Force.

Tedder's contribution was not just the creation of a powerful and well-co-ordinated Allied air control, with the two Allied tactical air forces accompanying the ground forces right through to Germany, but, like Eisenhower, he believed in collaboration, a strong unified command, and consensus, so these two men at least worked in harmony.

RAMSAY

Admiral Sir Bertram Ramsay is best remembered not for invasion but for evacuation, as he commanded Operation Dynamo, the evacuation of the British Expeditionary Force, and other Allied troops, from Dunkirk in 1940. This has done his memory a great disservice as he was also the controlling hand behind the landings in North Africa and Sicily, and he was undoubtedly the right choice for the Normandy landings.

Ramsay was unusual for an officer of such senior rank in that he had returned to active service after retirement in 1938. He had extensive experience during the First World War first with the Grand Fleet and then with the Dover Patrol. He retired in the rank of vice-admiral and retained this rank when recalled in August 1939 as Vice-Admiral Dover. Like many others, Ramsay no doubt expected his duties to be much as those of the earlier conflict, when the Dover Patrol kept the sea lanes open between England and France so that the armies on the Western Front could be kept resupplied and reinforced. Within nine months he was instead organising the evacuation of Dunkirk, and was responsible for the successful recovery of 338,000 men, for which he was knighted.

In April 1942, Ramsay was made Acting-Admiral Naval Commander-in-Chief for the invasion of Europe, which some still expected to occur that year. Nevertheless, the decision was taken to invade Vichy-held French North Africa first and objections were raised to a retired list acting admiral being given control of such a vital operation. This problem was resolved by giving Admiral Cunningham official command, while Ramsay acted as his deputy for both Operation Torch, the invasion of North Africa, and later Operation Husky, the invasion of Sicily, when he commanded the Eastern Task Force. Ramsay's preparations for Operation Neptune started after his return to London in December 1943, and in April 1944 he was returned to the active list with the rank of admiral. His experience of amphibious operations and his knowledge of the waters of the English Channel meant that the naval aspects of the invasion went better than many had expected, including the reinforcement and resupply phase.

This brilliant but modest man was killed in an air accident on 2 January 1945.

LEIGH-MALLORY

Another senior RAF officer who had started his career with the British Army and volunteered for the Royal Flying Corps during the First World War, Air Marshal Sir Trafford Leigh-Mallory had risen to the rank of air vice-marshal by the outbreak of the Second World War and during the Battle of Britain was in command of RAF Fighter Command's No. 12 Group, which defended the Midlands as well as providing reinforcements for groups based further south and east. In this role he was a staunch supporter of the 'big wing' tactic, which was meant to bring overbearing strength down upon enemy formations, but poor communications often meant that this tactic could not be used to best advantage.

Promoted to acting air marshal in July 1942, Leigh-Mallory commanded the air support for the Dieppe raid and in November 1942 he became Commander-in-Chief Fighter Command before being appointed Commander-in-Chief Allied Expeditionary Air Force as an air chief marshal in December of that year. Knighted in 1943, he co-ordinated the tactical air forces from before the invasion and on to October 1944. Sadly, he was killed in an air accident in November while on his way to become Air Officer Commander-in-Chief South-East Asia Command.

MONTGOMERY

Britain's best-known general of the Second World War, General (later Field Marshal) Sir Bernard 'Monty' Montgomery (later Viscount Montgomery of El Alamein) was the victor at the Second Battle of El Alamein, which earned him considerable publicity and public admiration.

Commissioned in 1908, Montgomery suffered serious wounds in 1914 and so spent the rest of the First World War as a staff officer. While this meant that he missed the many battles on the Western Front, it also demonstrated the importance of good planning, the need to ensure that ground troops were properly supported and the importance of winning battles with the minimum cost in human life. Montgomery's stubborn streak and the bungles of many of the early assaults during the First World War also meant that he would infuriate his superiors by refusing to order an advance until he was sure that everything was ready. This caution prevented him from fully exploiting the victory at El Alamein as he failed to mount an immediate pursuit of the retreating Axis forces.

Between the two world wars, he served in India, Egypt and Palestine, eventually becoming a brigade commander. His outstanding abilities were soon appreciated, but this appreciation was undermined by his abrupt and abrasive manner. In April 1939, he came home to become commander of 3rd Division, which became part of the British Expeditionary Force and brought him to the notice of the then Lt-Gen Alan Brooke. After the fall of France, he was promoted to lieutenant-general, and enjoyed a rapid succession of senior appointments. A teetotaller and non-smoker (at a time when most people did smoke), his insistence on training and physical fitness for his men resulted in one overweight colonel protesting that he would die if forced to run 7 miles, to which 'Monty' replied that, in that case, it would cause fewer problems if he died in training than on the battlefield.

Montgomery's big opportunity came in August 1942, when Lt-Gen William Gott died. Gott had been Churchill's first choice as leader of the Eighth Army, at the time caught very much on the back foot in the Western Desert as Axis forces advanced towards the Suez Canal. Given a force with low morale, he inspired his officers and men. His dispositions were right when Rommel attacked at Alam Halfa. Better still, the Second Battle of El Alamein gave him the opportunity for the classic set-piece battle to which Montgomery's tactics were most suited. His victory on 4 November 1942 resulted in a knighthood and promotion to general, and made him a household name in the UK. Most importantly, he earned the support and confidence of Churchill, who later maintained that 'before El Alamein nothing went right, but after El Alamein everything did'. This was typical Churchillian exaggeration for it ignored such triumphs as the Battle of the River Plate and the attack on Taranto, but, as was so often the case with Churchill, it was in line with public perceptions.

Montgomery was the right man in the right place. He was not faultless, and his natural caution adversely affected the Sicilian campaign. A fast-moving mobile war was not his forte, at least not at the time, as he was later to achieve some remarkable advances after the breakout from Normandy. One critic even remarked that 'he always seemed to mislay his genius when he met a mountain'.

As the Allied Land Commander, Montgomery's intervention did much to ensure that the initial assault was successful and some even credit him with avoiding disaster. Montgomery's advance after the Normandy break-out towards Antwerp, which saw his troops covering 200 miles in a single week, was a remarkable success. Yet, in typical 'Monty' fashion, having taken Antwerp, he failed to pursue the retreating Germans further. He also failed to have the Scheldt Estuary cleared so that the port could be re-opened for the Allies; then he launched the airborne assault 'Operation Market Garden' on Arnhem, which was a conspicuous failure despite the heroism and sacrifice of those involved.

By this time, Montgomery's fame seemed to have gone to his head. Instead of the blunt, austere, 'no nonsense' soldier, contrary to Eisenhower's approach, he no longer collaborated as fully as he should with the other Allied commanders. He was promoted to field marshal on 1 September 1944, the same day that Eisenhower took control of all ground forces, and relationships deteriorated rapidly. He made it clear that while he admired many of Eisenhower's qualities, he did not believe him to be a good general in the field. While Eisenhower believed in a broad front approach, 'Monty' favoured a direct thrust into the heart of Germany, and not content with this, pursued the argument almost to the point of dismissal. After the Battle of the Bulge, he claimed to the press that he had defeated the Germans, ignoring the massive effort by US troops in the Ardennes.

Nevertheless, he survived and on 4 May 1945 took the surrender of all German forces in north-west Germany, Denmark and the Netherlands at

Luneburg Heath. Post-war, in January 1946, he was elevated to the peerage as Viscount Montgomery of El Alamein.

Montgomery has been criticised for being vain, conceited and cocky, but while he infuriated and upset his peers, he also had the common touch and could communicate in terms that the common soldier could understand. A phrase he often used was 'We'll hit 'em for six', a cricketing term that needed no explanation to the British, or British Commonwealth, soldier. He believed in keeping strategy simple and robust. His plan for a direct thrust into Germany might well have shortened the war and, no less important, kept much of Eastern Europe from Soviet domination.

BRADLEY

General Omar N. Bradley's early career mirrored that of Eisenhower, even to being in the same class at West Point. Like Eisenhower, he missed active service during the First World War, but his career between the two wars progressed such that by late 1941 he was a brigadier-general commanding the Infantry School at Fort Benning. Promoted to major-general, he commanded two infantry divisions in turn before being posted to North Africa in February 1943 as Eisenhower's 'eyes and ears' and as Patton's deputy at 2nd US Corps, where he succeeded Patton in April. His leadership during the North African campaign led to his promotion to lieutenant-general in June 1943. Further success followed during the Sicilian campaign.

Posted to the UK in September 1943, Bradley was given command of the First US Army, a formation with twenty-one divisions, designated to lead the assault on Omaha and Utah beaches during D-Day. Afterwards, in August, he took command of the new Twelfth US Army Group, which fended off a German counter-attack at Mortain and then with British assistance destroyed the German Seventh Army at Falaise, before advancing towards Paris.

Eisenhower's most trusted general, Bradley was also loyal to his supreme commander, and always supported 'Ike' in quarrels between Montgomery and Eisenhower over strategy and the allocation of supplies. He nevertheless reacted badly when Eisenhower assigned the US First Army to Montgomery during the Ardennes offensive of December 1944, but remained dispassionate and professional enough to order the town of Bastogne to be held and send Patton's Third Army to relieve it. Afterwards, his troops resumed their advance so that by 23 March they were east of the Rhine and linked up with Russian troops around Torgau on 25 April.

Oddly, despite commanding 1.3 million men in four field armies, he was not promoted to full general until March 1945, but post-war he was made General of the Army in 1950.

Bradley has been described as having common sense combined with tactical flair, all aided by an icy calm. No wonder he did not always see eye-to-eye with 'Monty'.

PATTON

Unlike Eisenhower and Bradley, General George S. Patton had seen action during the First World War. A cavalry officer, he competed in the modern pentathlon at the 1912 Olympic Games, held in Stockholm, and in 1916 took part in a punitive raid into Mexico. The following year he was a staff officer to General John Pershing in France, where he rose from the rank of captain to command a tank brigade. He was a major-general early in 1941 and during the North African landings in November 1942, he commanded the Western Task Force's two divisions, with an amphibious assault near Casablanca. He took over the 2nd US Corps after its defeat in the Battle of the Kasserine Pass in March 1943. He rebuilt the 2nd's morale before handing it on to Bradley and starting to plan Operation Husky, the Allied landings in Sicily, where he commanded the US Seventh Army as a lieutenant-general.

A strong-willed and combative officer, his troops took Palermo and then arrived in Messina before the British, even though theirs was supposed to be a secondary role. His career nearly ended when, on at least two occasions, he slapped and abused soldiers suffering from combat fatigue, but Eisenhower regarded him as indispensable and refused to send him back to the US. Nevertheless, Patton spent some time in Sicily without a post until he was ordered to the UK to prepare for the Normandy landings. He also had the role of commander of the non-existent US First Army Group, which was part of the Allies deception plan to protect the Normandy landings.

After the Normandy landings, Patton launched a number of thrusts intended to seize German-held ports, such as Brest, and then took command of the US Third Army, which was four corps strong when formed on 1 August 1944. On 19 August, he was able to put a division across the Seine. The Allies were soon outstripping their supply chain, but Patton nevertheless reached the German border by November.

During the German Ardennes offensive, the 'Battle of the Bulge', Patton's troops made one of the fastest changes of direction in military history, turning north to relieve the town of Bastogne. In March 1943, he crossed the Rhine at Mainz and Oppenheim before advancing into Czechoslovakia and Austria. The following month he was promoted to full general.

Post-war, he became military governor of Bavaria, but was relieved of his command for recommending that former Nazis be employed in the post-war administration of Germany.

He died in December 1945 as a result of injuries incurred in a motoring accident.

Known as 'Old Blood and Guts', Patton was the model of aggression, with highly polished boots and ivory-handled revolvers at his hips. His language was profane and his temperament volatile, but he was also religious, cultured, well-read and sensitive. In short, he was a man of contradictory characteristics.

It has been pointed out that he achieved his fame in just thirteen months of combat.[2]

CRERAR

Commander-in-Chief of the First Canadian Army at the time of the Normandy landings, Lieutenant-General Henry 'Harry' Crerar was a career artillery officer, having served in the First World War, in which he reached the rank of lieutenant-colonel. In contrast to many Canadian officers, he remained in the service when peace returned and, by the outbreak of the Second World War, he was commandant of the Royal Military College of Canada. Crerar was sent to England with the rank of brigadier as a member of the Canadian military staff in London, but was recalled to Canada in 1940 to become Vice-Chief of the General Staff, before becoming Chief of the Canadian General Staff, CCGS, the following year.

As CCGS, he was involved in a number of difficult decisions. One of these was the dispatch of two Canadian battalions to Hong Kong just before the Japanese invasion, which was completed on Christmas Eve 1941. After putting up a fierce resistance, the unfortunate troops became Canada's first prisoners of war. Crerar was also involved in conscription, which was highly controversial in Canada as many Canadians, especially those of French descent, did not want to become involved in another 'British' war, although attitudes had begun to change after the fall of France.

Crerar was appointed to command the 2nd Canadian Division in 1942, and in 1943 briefly commanded the 1st Canadian Corps in Italy; at the end of the year he relieved General Andrew McNaughton as Commander-in-Chief of the First Canadian Army. McNaughton had been relieved of his command for opposing the dispatch of Canadian troops to Italy as he maintained that his men should be kept together as a single fighting unit.

For the Normandy landings, the First Canadian Army was part of Montgomery's Twenty-First Army Group, later the British Second Army. This was an unfortunate pairing as Montgomery was unimpressed by Crerar, but General Sir Alan Brooke, the Chief of the Imperial General Staff, took a different view and said that, 'He [Crerar] has improved that Corps out of all recognition.'[3] On one occasion, when Crerar was unable to attend an important conference, Montgomery threatened to dismiss him, something he was not able to do as such senior appointments were political.

The Canadians played a major part in the advance to the Channel ports and on into Belgium, but early in the battle for the Scheldt Estuary, Crerar was taken ill and had to return to the UK for treatment. He later returned, however, and was promoted to general in November 1944, and remained with his troops for the advance into Germany.

An able administrator, views of his generalship range between 'mediocre' and 'competent'.

Crerar retired from the army in 1946, but continued to serve the Canadian government as a diplomat.

In looking at the generals, it is clear that they varied widely in character, but that the Americans had relatively little experience of warfare. Montgomery could be cautious and slow to grasp opportunities, but he was also wary of repeating the losses in men, and experience, of the First World War. Eisenhower was the diplomat, and almost certainly the right man in the right place at the right time for this reason alone. Comparisons between the air force and navy leaders are more difficult. It is odd that two, Ramsay and Leigh-Mallory, were both killed in air accidents, but air travel was far less safe at the time than it is today, and no doubt in wartime, with so many conscripts, experienced aircraft maintainers were in the minority.

THE GERMAN GENERALS

The Allies faced several German generals, but the two who were most significant and influential were the two *Generalfeldmarschall*s, Gerd von Rundstedt and Erwin Rommel, of whom the former was the more senior. Both were experienced and successful commanders in the field, but Rommel has become the more widely known, in no small part to his time fighting the British Eighth Army in the Western Desert while commanding Germany's *Afrika Korps*.

RUNDSTEDT

Brought out of retirement at the start of the Second World War, Karl Rudolf Gerd von Rundstedt was a fine example of a Prussian officer. Born in 1875, he joined what was then the Imperial German Army in 1892 and served mainly as a staff officer during the First World War. He remained in the army between the wars, reluctantly taking an oath of allegiance to Hitler, before retiring in 1938, by which time he was a *Generaloberst*, or colonel-general, equivalent to a brigadier in the British Army or a brigadier-general in the US Army.

On rejoining in 1939, he acted as commander of Army Group South during the invasion of Poland, a campaign many Germans supported as it was widely viewed as recovering territory taken from Germany after the First World War. He also participated in the invasion of France, after which he was promoted to *Generalfeldmarschall*, equivalent to field marshal or General of the Army, in July 1940. During Operation Barbarossa, the invasion of the Soviet Union, he once again commanded Army Group South, distinguishing himself at the Battle of Kiev in September 1941, where some 600,000 Soviet troops were captured. His success lay in resisting the Fuhrer's interference and supporting his subordinate commanders.

The advance continued even though German supply lines were overstretched, until brought to a halt by the onset of the Russian winter, for which the Germans were ill-prepared, short of food, ammunition, fuel and winter clothing. Although Rostov was taken, the Germans were forced to withdraw by late November, to Hitler's fury. Rundstedt was by this time exhausted and ill, well into his 60s and having suffered a mild heart attack, he offered his resignation, which was accepted by Hitler on 1 December 1941.

Hitler sent Rundstedt a cheque for 250,000 Reichsmarks. This was his way of buying the loyalty of senior officers, which many found offensive, although no one dared refuse. Rundstedt tried to avoid cashing the cheque, until this started to attract unfavourable comment, and eventually did so, giving the money to his daughter, although at his death the money had still not been touched.

Rundstedt was brought back by Hitler in March 1942 to take command of German forces in the west, mainly France, replacing another officer who had fallen ill. He was well equipped for this position as he had a good command of the language and good relations with the Vichy regime. He had no confidence in the Atlantic Wall, comparing it with the failed Maginot Line, and while Hitler pretended to agree with him and his plans for a defence in depth, he sent Rommel with orders to strengthen the Atlantic Wall so that any Allied landings could be defeated on the beaches.

When the invasion came, it was much further west than either Rundstedt or Rommel, who was on leave in Germany, had expected. Both officers demanded reinforcements, which were not available, and Rommel even told Hitler that the battle was unwinnable. In the frantic attempts to reinforce the German defences, the *SS-Panzer-Division 'Das Reich'* was hurried to the front and, in response to French resistance attacks, men in the division murdered more than 600 inhabitants in the village of Oradour-sur-Glane, for which the post-war French government held Rundstedt responsible. Meanwhile, at the end of June, Rundstedt fell foul of Hitler after giving permission for the commander of troops in the region of Caen to withdraw because of the losses being suffered from Allied naval gunfire. Hitler reversed the order. There followed a dispute over whether or not Rundstedt had urged an end to the fighting, but Hitler sacked him once again, although officially this was on the grounds of ill health.

Although Rundstedt was aware of a plot to assassinate Hitler, he had played no part in it, and he did not take action against officers who were involved. He had no liking or respect for Hitler, but believed that a German officer should not be involved in politics.

After the war, he was charged with war crimes, but because of his age and failing health did not face trial. In addition to the massacre in France, he had encouraged his men to take reprisals for resistance activity elsewhere and although he did not encourage his men to take part in anti-Jewish operations, apart from that at Babi Yar, he had endorsed announcements by the German command that were strongly anti-Semitic in tone.

He died in 1953 at the age of 77.

ROMMEL

Erwin Johannes Eugen Rommel was a completely different commander from Rundstedt. He was not a Prussian but a southern German. His *Afrika Korps* was never accused of war crimes; orders to kill Jews, civilians or captured commandos were ignored, and Allied prisoners were treated humanely. Known affectionately as the 'Desert Fox', or *Wustenfuchs*, he was respected by his enemies as well as his own men.

Born in 1891, Rommel joined the Imperial German Army in 1910 having previously considered becoming an engineer. He had built and flown a model glider in 1905, and throughout his life showed considerable technical ability.

He saw active service during the First World War, fighting in France, Romania and Italy, and was awarded the Iron Cross twice and the *Pour le Mérite*, Imperial Germany's highest decoration, but was wounded three times. Rommel established a reputation for being a fearless and decisive commander in the field, able to make quick decisions and exploit enemy confusion. At the Battle of Longarone and the capture of Mount Matajur he took 150 Italian officers and 9,000 men for the loss of just six of his own men and another thirty wounded.

Post-war, he rejected offers of positions on the general staff and preferred to remain a soldier with an operational unit. From 1929 to 1933, he was an instructor at the infantry school at Dresden, where he wrote a manual for infantry officers, which relied heavily on his wartime experiences and also included observations on tactics.

He first met Hitler in 1934 while in command of a mountain battalion. When he realised that a row of SS men would be placed in front of his battalion to protect the Fuhrer, he refused, in Hitler and Himmler's presence, to order his battalion to parade unless the SS men were withdrawn – which they were. Hitler later read Rommel's book with interest and pressed the *Hitlerjugend*, or Hitler Youth, to adopt his ideas, and in 1935 Rommel was assigned to the Headquarters of Military Sports. Promoted to colonel in 1938, he was appointed commandant of the Theresian Military Academy. After the invasion of the Sudetenland, Hitler asked Rommel to command his own personal protection battalion. During this time, Rommel met German Propaganda Minister Joseph Goebbels, whom he impressed, and was often close to the action on the Polish front. Nevertheless, Rommel felt that commanding what was basically an enlarged bodyguard was not the best use of his experience in wartime, and requested a return to active service. He was given a choice of unit by Hitler, and asked if he could take command of one of the new *Panzer* divisions.

Rommel's unit was the 7th *Panzer* Division. During the invasion of France, it moved with such speed that it was often out of contact with headquarters and became known as the 'Ghost Division' because no one knew where it was. He used the *Luftwaffe* as flying mobile artillery, and became one of the leading exponents of *Blitzkrieg*, 'lighting warfare', which, despite its use to describe the German bombing of British cities throughout late 1940 and into spring 1941, was originally coined to describe fast-moving advances by armour supported by air power.

On 20 May, Rommel attempted to cut off the British Expeditionary Force at the Battle of Arras. When the *Panzer* division's guns proved ineffective against the armour of the BEF's Matilda tanks, he turned the highly effective German 88mm anti-aircraft guns on the tanks – the first time this was done – and with another officer went from gun to gun identifying targets for the crews. His efforts were in vain as Hitler ordered the advance to stop while he sought to negotiate with the British, and he then allowed Göring to use the *Luftwaffe* to destroy the BEF on the beaches at Dunkirk, which it failed to do. Rommel was awarded the Knight's Cross of the Iron Cross, the first senior officer to receive it.

Not everyone admired Rommel. There was envy, and also a measure of resentment against this officer who was not of the usual Prussian military caste. His corps commander, Hoth, publicly praised him, but privately reported that he should not be given further command until he had gained in experience and judgement. Many of his superiors were concerned that Rommel took risks, but often this simply reflected their lack of experience of fast-moving warfare, sometimes referred to as 'manoeuvre warfare'.

In February 1941, Rommel was posted to North Africa to lead the *Afrika Korps*, which had been sent to assist the Italians following their defeats at the hands of the British. The German High Command ordered Rommel to defend the frontline at Sirte, but he quickly realised that the position could not be defended, and instead opted to take the offensive at a time when British forces had been weakened by the transfer of many units to defend Greece. The British did not expect Rommel to advance as they had intercepted his orders, but he decided to capture the whole of Cyrenaica (now the eastern part of Libya). This brought him into conflict with the Italian commander in the field, but the situation was resolved when Berlin changed his orders, giving him complete freedom of action.

By April, the major British base and port of Tobruk was besieged. In vain Rommel pleaded for reinforcements so that he could take the port and then press on and even seize the naval base at Alexandria, but the High Command was preoccupied with preparations for Operation Barbarossa and refused. At first, Rommel made many small-scale attacks that had little impact on an enemy who was well entrenched. He actually believed for a while that the British were beginning to evacuate, until he realised that the ships entering the harbour were bringing in supplies and reinforcements. He could not by-pass Tobruk as he needed the port to shorten his lines of communications if he was to advance to Alexandria. The siege lasted two hundred and forty days, before Rommel had good intelligence of the layout of the defences and could bring his forces up to strength and ensure that everyone was trained for the attack. In the meantime, he was given command of the newly constituted *Panzergruppe Afrika* or *Panzer* Group Africa, and supported by Berlin, who believed, with good reason, that German officers should control North Africa.

Eventually, after a number of attacks and counter-attacks, Tobruk was taken on 15 June 1942, with the capture of 33,000 British and imperial troops, marking the greatest British defeat apart from the fall of Singapore. For this, Hitler promoted Rommel to *Generalfeldmarschall*. Nevertheless, Hitler never fully understood or supported Rommel, failing to appreciate why the capture of Egypt was so important. The Fuhrer had provoked a global war without understanding global strategy.

The British Eighth Army fell back on El Alamein, a natural defensive posi-tion where they could not be outflanked, but by the time he reached it, Rommel had just thirteen fully operational tanks. On 1 July, the First Battle of El Alamein was fought, but both sides were exhausted and ill equipped. Rommel himself noted that his 'momentum had faded away'. The British were steadily rebuilding their strength, even though the difficulty of getting convoys across the Mediterranean meant that everything had to come the long way via the Cape of Good Hope. Failure to suppress the defences of Malta also meant that the Axis had their own difficulties with the supply route from Italy to Benghazi under pressure, and even then the supplies had to be moved slowly and expensively across much of what is now Libya.

The British, meanwhile, had placed General Sir Bernard Montgomery in command of the Eighth Army. The Battle of Alam el Halfa started on 30 August, but Rommel's move had been anticipated by Montgomery and by 2 September, Rommel realised that he could not win the battle.

As September passed, two-thirds of Rommel's supplies were being destroyed at sea. Rommel himself was feeling the strain and was sent to Italy to recover. In his absence, General Georg Stumme was in command. Rommel had planned strong defences and was confident that any breach by the Allies could be countered by sending fast armoured reinforcements. The Second Battle of El Alamein started on 23 October, but Stumme suffered a serious heart attack and died early in the battle. Rommel returned immediately, but it took two days for him to reach his headquarters, where he found that the fuel situation was nothing short of desperate. Counter-attacks on 24 and 25 October by two of his *Panzer* divisions had suffered heavy losses due to intense British artillery and air attacks. Another counter-attack on 26 October was too late: the British had already penetrated his defensive lines.

It could have been all over for Rommel had not Montgomery decided on 3 November to wait for more reinforcements and supplies. This gave Rommel the chance to withdraw, his *Afrika Korps* at just a third of its original strength and with just thirty-five tanks left. Thus began a long retreat across North Africa, despite orders not to withdraw which Rommel wisely ignored and thus avoided encirclement. There were several attempts to counter-attack the advancing British Empire forces, but none succeeded.

Once in Tunisia, Rommel found himself fighting British troops in the east and American troops in the west. He was victorious in the Battle of the Kasserine Pass against US troops in February 1943, but on 6 March 1943, he suffered a disastrous defeat in the Battle of Medenine, losing fifty-two tanks after Montgomery turned his anti-aircraft guns on the tanks. He returned to Germany to try to convince Hitler of the seriousness of the situation, but never returned to Africa. His forces surrendered to the Allies in May.

Rommel was next moved to Greece in expectation of an Allied invasion, and when this did not occur, he was moved to France. While Rundstedt believed that it would be impossible to hold the enemy on the beaches because of the devastating naval firepower that could be deployed, as at Salerno, and wanted to keep his main force outside Paris ready for a classic military battle, Rommel believed that the enemy could be held on the beaches, as did Hitler. Nevertheless, Rommel soon changed his mind when he saw the reality of the so-called Atlantic Wall with its uncompleted defences that there was little chance of completing or reinforcing due to the growing shortages of materials. Instead, he planted minefields on the beaches and in the countryside, as well as building tank traps and identifying fields suitable for glider landings and planting poles called *Rommelspargel*, or 'Rommel's asparagus', to prevent their use.

Unlike Rundstedt and most of the general staff, who believed that the Pas-de-Calais area would be the landing site, Rommel thought Normandy was possible, but he also maintained that it did not matter where the Allies landed, only that it was unsuccessful. The bad weather at the beginning of June encouraged Rommel to believe that he could return to Germany to spend a few days with his family, so he was away when the invasion was launched. While he returned to his post there was little that could be done and by July the Germans were on the defensive. On 17 July, Rommel's car was strafed by an RAF Spitfire, and his driver was so badly wounded that he lost control. In the resulting crash, Rommel was thrown from the car and had to be taken to hospital.

Meanwhile, on 20 July a plot had gone ahead to assassinate Hitler. It was unsuccessful, but a witch-hunt inevitably followed as the conspirators were sought. Rommel opposed assassinating Hitler, but three of the conspirators were old friends and they met. They needed his support to give the conspiracy respectability as he was the most popular and well-known figure amongst the German military, but he refused as he did not believe that assassination was right, even though he agreed that Hitler had to be removed. He was prepared to 'come to the rescue of Germany'.

Rommel was arrested and brought before a 'Court of Military Honour', where he faced Guderian and Rundstedt, both men with whom he had fallen out in the past. They decreed that he should be dismissed from the army in disgrace and brought before the 'People's Court', the inevitable result of which would be the death penalty. Hitler knew that having Rommel convicted and executed would be bad for morale, and instead on 14 October sent two of his senior staff officers to Rommel to offer him the chance of committing suicide: if he agreed, his family would be spared shame and would still receive his full pension, while a state funeral would be organised.

Rommel was driven away in a staff car, and he was left alone in a remote location with a cyanide capsule. Within five minutes it was over. The public was told that he had died from a heart attack or had succumbed to the wounds suffered when his staff car was attacked. The promises of a pension for his family and a state funeral were kept, Rundstedt representing Hitler at the latter.

NOTES

1. Ambrose, Stephen, *Parameters* (New York, 1990).
2. Nye, R., *Parameters* (New York, 1991).
3. Alanbrooke, Field Marshal Lord, *War Diaries 1939–1945* (London: Weidenfeld & Nicolson, 2001).

4

SOWING FALSE LEADS

Planning was all the more difficult because of the need for secrecy and the necessity of sowing false leads to make it more difficult for the Germans to defend against and react to the invasion. Those involved in the planning of Overlord were subjected to the strictest security. Plans relating to Overlord and Neptune were only revealed to those officers who were given the security classification of 'BIGOT' and were described as being 'BIGOTed', suggesting that someone somewhere had a sense of humour.

In fact, the plans, including the details of the Mulberry harbours and the exact landing areas, were almost lost. Brigadier Arthur Walker, the British Army's Director of Ports and Inland Water Transport, was taken to lunch at the Naval & Military Club, then still in Piccadilly and usually known as the 'In and Out' because of the signs on its gates, and had the plans in his black civil service briefcase, which he put under the table and promptly forgot.

'I'll never forget the moment,' he recalled later:

> At that moment, I wanted to die. I wanted to be instantly shot ... I rang up the club and the hall porter answered and said: 'Yes sir, a case was left here and I've got it in my cubby hole,' and I galloped the whole way ... to the club and he handed it over to me. It was still locked.[1]

Planning for the invasion of France had started after the Dieppe raid of August 1942. At first, the Allies were uncertain over where the landings should take place. Nevertheless, by June 1943 when a planning meeting was held at Largs in south-west Scotland, sufficient information was available for a decision to be made. The landing areas had to be within range of fighter aircraft if adequate air cover was to be provided and it had to be possible to capture a sizeable port shortly after the invasion had started. Normandy was chosen because of the beaches, its being within range of land-based fighters in the south of England, and because much was known about the area and the German defences. The shortest route across the Channel, between Dover and the Pas-de-Calais, was ideal for peacetime packet ships, but not for the landings in France. The shortness of the distance was in fact a drawback as it would have been too congested and German aircraft and shore-based guns would not even have needed to aim. There was also the problem of having the landing force overwhelm the port facilities at Dover, within range of German coastal artillery, and Folkestone, and the fact that ships coming from ports further west, and even down the Irish Sea, would have further to steam.

The decision was one of the most important of the entire Second World War, and it was also to be one of the best kept secrets. It helped, of course, that the Germans had their own views on the subject – even Hitler had his own opinion.

It was not just the service personnel involved in the preparations who were subjected to restrictions. Civilians were not allowed to travel between the United Kingdom and the Irish Free State, which was probably difficult to enforce given the winding course of the border between Northern Ireland and Eire. Along the coast from the Wash in the east to Land's End in the far south-west, and on both sides of the Firth of Forth, the 10 miles inland became a prohibited zone and only authorised travellers could visit. Travel to the coast in wartime was less attractive anyway, as beaches were fenced off with barbed wire, and piers were partly dismantled with decking removed at the shore end so that enemy ships could not land troops at the pierhead. Until the war, coastal shipping had been in greater use than today and included regular passenger services along the coast as well as those to the Isle of Wight.

These restrictions were over and above the routine wartime restrictions, such as censorship of forces' mail and of newspapers, radio and cinema news footage.

DECEPTION

Both sides resorted to deception during the Second World War. Good deception required as much secrecy as the real thing, and it was also important to see whether or not the enemy had in fact been deceived. One aspect of deception was purely defensive, and that was camouflage, with ships and aircraft painted in dazzle schemes that varied according to the natural colours of the part of the world in which they were operating. In the case of ships, the idea was also to blur the ship's lines not just to confuse her identity but also so that torpedoes would be badly aimed. Major factories and power stations were dazzle-painted so that pilots would have difficulty distinguishing the target and aiming their bombs. Artificial airfields with aircraft built out of wood were one deception, while false gun emplacements were also created and dummy tanks would be parked, 'ready to roll', in the desert.

Probably one of the best instances of deception was the creation of an artificial port on the south coast of England at Hayling Island, which actually attracted a German bomber force that mistook it for the nearby major naval base of Portsmouth early in 1941. Göring claimed a success for the *Luftwaffe*, but in fact just three cows were killed! This was an exception and it helped that Hayling was an island, as is Portsmouth itself (built on Portsea Island).

These deceptions were, of course, different from laying false leads so that the Germans would believe that an attack, or in this case an invasion, would be either coming from a different direction or have a different objective.

In the Western Desert the Allies turned around a number of Axis agents, making them double agents, while wireless traffic was used to simulate extra units on the Allied side, giving the Axis forces the impression that a far larger force confronted them. Not only did the enemy believe that the Allies were half as strong again, but they believed that, in addition to the British Eighth Army, there were also Ninth and Tenth Armies as well. In fact, while some fighting units were assigned so that aerial observation would show extra troop movements, the numbers involved barely equalled a division. The deception even went as far as to lay dummy fuel pipelines across the desert.

The impact of the deception in North Africa was such that Churchill established a special unit, the London Controlling Section, under Colonel J. H. Bevan, which was based under the cabinet war rooms and reported directly to the chiefs of staff. It was not a solely British affair: US officers were seconded to it as required. It also worked closely with a similar section within COSSAC when that was established in March 1943.

Even before this, in January 1941 the British established the 'XX-committee', so called because one aspect of its work was to operate the double-cross system, to co-ordinate the dissemination of false information. The idea was to attempt to control the German espionage system in the UK and to catch new German agents as soon as they arrived. German agents would be supplied with information to pass on to their handlers in occupied Europe. To work effectively, at least some of the information had to be true, and every week consideration was given to what could be released and the advantages of doing so were weighed up against the high probability of losses.

The success rate of German agents was very low, as they were almost all rounded up very quickly. The one exception was Jan Ter Braak, found after he had committed suicide in a Cambridge air-raid shelter in April 1941. Altogether the British secret service, MI5, had 120 double agents. Not all were operating within the UK; some were based in other areas. Those who failed to prove their usefulness were imprisoned and of these sixteen were executed. One captured agent, a Yugoslav, convinced the Germans that a substantial minefield had been laid in the Western Approaches, so keeping the area free from German U-boats. It was in the middle of 1942 that 'XX' started to attempt to deceive the Germans over the plans for the invasion of France. Those involved feared that the Germans would soon discover the deceptions but, as mentioned earlier, many senior Germans remained none the wiser even after D-Day!

It helped enormously that the Allies had broken the German Enigma codes so they had some means of assessing just how well any particular ruse was working, and whether the Germans had seen through it or taken it at face value.

Deception was also tried in the Mediterranean theatre. 'Operation Mincemeat' was the idea of a British naval officer, Lieutenant-Commander Ewen Montagu, and it originated in 'XX'.

Spain had been a close ally of Germany from the end of the Spanish Civil War, in which German and Italian forces helped Franco's Nationalists to victory over their Soviet Union and French-supported opponents, the Republicans. German agents operated freely in Spain during the Second World War, and the narrowness of the Straits of Gibraltar meant that movements of Allied shipping could be closely observed. On 30 April 1943, the British submarine HMS *Seraph* dumped a body off the Spanish coast near the town of Huelva, a spot chosen because the local German consulate was known to be an active spy. The body* was dressed as an officer in the Royal Marines, supposedly killed in an air accident, carrying the papers of a Major Martin and having attached to him a briefcase whose contents included a letter to General Alexander. Dumping the body was no easy task as it had to be in a battered RAF inflatable dinghy, and dropped close enough to the shore to be swept ashore by the tide, but without the submarine herself being detected.

The letter was a false lead, as it gave the impression that the Allies were preparing to invade Greece and that the invasion of Sicily was to be a feint. While the body was handed over to the British consul almost immediately, the briefcase was detained for some days, and tests when it was received in London showed that the letter to Alexander had been opened. By 14 May, Ultra intelligence showed that the Germans had fallen for the deception and the signal was sent to Churchill, who was attending the 'Trident' conference in Washington: 'Mincemeat swallowed whole.'

As hoped, Hitler sent troops to the Balkans and to Sardinia, withdrawing two *Panzer* divisions from the Eastern Front for Greece, rather than for Italy, where they were most needed. As with any good deception, Mincemeat was plausible, especially since Hitler, whose invasion of the Soviet Union had been badly delayed by the need to help his Italian allies out of their ill-fated venture into the Balkans, feared that the whole area could become a quagmire for his forces if an Allied invasion encouraged renewed local resistance.

Seraph was to play a part in Operation Husky, the Allied landings on Sicily. She had to fix herself accurately offshore and lay an acoustic buoy that could be heard underwater by the approaching landing ships. On the night of the invasion, she had to surface and shine a red light out to sea to mark her position. Her commanding officer, the then Lieutenant-Commander (later Captain) Bill Jewell was personally congratulated by the US invasion commander and later awarded the US Legion of Merit.

Deception could sometimes be a dangerous game. In 1941, a senior British intelligence officer, Lieutenant-Colonel Dudley Clarke, was arrested in Spain by the police while dressed as a woman. At the time, Clarke was supposed to be in Egypt delivering top secret material to General Claude Auchinleck, Commander-in-Chief, Middle East. Clarke, who had had most of one ear shot off, was commanding officer of 'A' Force, a strategic deception unit based in Cairo. Nevertheless, he was found by the Spanish police dressed in a floral dress, cloche hat, dark stockings and high heels, a brassiere and wearing lipstick.

When questioned by the police, he initially claimed to be a correspondent for *The Times* newspaper, before changing his story and claiming to be a novelist who wanted to 'study the reaction of men to women in the street'. His luggage contained more women's clothes, a British war correspondent's uniform, and a roll of very fine toilet paper.[2]

This put the British in a difficult position. They wanted Clarke back, and indeed Churchill insisted that if he was released he had to be brought back to London immediately. Yet, they needed to keep his status as a British officer from the Spanish. A wire was sent to the British embassy in Madrid asking that they, 'Wire if he shows signs of mental derangement.'[3]

It was even seen as possible that the story could be published in Berlin to discredit the British government.

Fortunately, while the Germans believed that the whole incident reeked of espionage, the Spanish concluded that this was a homosexual affair and released Clarke.

When released, Clarke explained that he was taking the clothes to a lady friend in Gibraltar and had decided to try them on as a prank, but the clothes actually fitted him. He never really explained what he was doing, but nevertheless rose in the years that followed to the rank of brigadier.

The fact remains that had he been handed over to the Germans, he could have been turned to act as an agent, and it is hard to escape the feeling that someone in his position behaving in such a manner in a neutral capital in wartime was a weak link, especially as many enemy agents were operating freely.

OPERATION FORTITUDE

COSSAC was replaced by SHAEF in February 1944. Everything included in COSSAC passed to SHAEF, including the deception section, known as Ops (B), which was commanded by a former USAAF officer, Colonel H. N. Wild. The main task of Ops (B) was to convince the Germans that the deception plan for Operation Overlord, known as 'Operation Fortitude', was genuine.

Even at this stage, not everything was set in stone. For some time, the commanders were working to an invasion date of 1 May. When Montgomery arrived in London he dined with Winston Churchill on New Year's Eve.

It would not have been a convivial gathering, despite the date, as Churchill loved to drink and was rarely seen without a cigar, while Montgomery neither smoked nor drank, and made no attempt to hide his disgust. Famously, he declared that he was 100 per cent fit because of his abstinence, to which Churchill retorted that he both drank and smoked and was 200 per cent fit![4]

Always late to bed and late to rise, before breakfast the next morning Churchill received Montgomery's initial impressions of the planned Normandy landings:

> The initial landing is on too narrow a front and is confined to too small an area. By D-Day plus 12 a total of 16 divisions will have been landed on the same beaches as were used for the initial landings. This would lead to the most appalling confusion on the beaches, and the smooth development of the land battle would be made extremely difficult, if not impossible ... My first impression is that the present plan is impractical ... The initial landings must be made on the widest possible front.[5]

Montgomery's reservations were not ignored. The biggest difference between the original COSSAC plan, to land on beaches designated as Juno, Gold and Omaha, and that adopted by SHAEF, was that there would be two additional landing sites – Sword in the British sector on the left or east, and Utah in the American sector on the right of the line, or in the west. Churchill supported Montgomery fully in the selection of additional invasion beaches.

Unknown to the planners at the time, the Germans were planning, in case of the landings actually being in Normandy, to flood the Douve River to prevent airborne landings on its banks. While in due course the airborne landings were unaffected, the flooding did slightly delay the joining up of the British and American sectors.

Operation Fortitude was conveyed to the Germans by double agents, but was augmented by false radio traffic that gave the Germans the impression that General Patton was commanding the First United States Army Group, FUSAG, which was based in Kent and Essex. Radio units were deployed in these areas to send heavy radio traffic to make the Germans believe that a substantial force was being deployed and that the landing sites for the invasion would be on the beaches to the south of Boulogne. To make FUSAG seem even more credible, dummy landing craft were built and assembled in the ports of eastern England.

Building dummy landing craft was one thing, but the Allies went even further. Sections of the Mulberry harbours intended for Normandy were temporarily sunk off Dungeness, conveniently situated for Boulogne, to give the impression that a boarding port was being created for the short Channel crossing. Bombing was also intensified around Boulogne, Le Touquet and Calais in the days leading up to D-Day. The English Channel off the coast of these areas was also mined. Nevertheless, the idea that the invasion would be in July was largely propagated through the use of double agents.

Having cracked the German Enigma codes, the Allies were at least able to decode German signals at Bletchley Park. Thanks to these Ultra intercepts, the Allies were able to check that the double agents were in fact working and that the Germans had swallowed the deception.

Convincing at least some of the Germans that Norway might be the invasion site was more difficult. To some extent, the concentration of so much invasion shipping around the coast from Milford Haven in South Wales to Harwich in Essex, at the southern end of the North Sea, helped as it meant that greater concentrations of shipping used more northerly ports. This put the Germans on guard in case something was happening. In fact, Ultra intercepts show that they believed that a 'Fourth Army' existed with a headquarters near Edinburgh and corps at Stirling and Dundee, and that the British Army's Lowland Division (a Scottish formation) was being equipped for an attack on Norway.

This message was reinforced by mining the Kiel Canal and the southern Baltic, the area off the German coast. The Skagerrak and the Kattegat, the channels between Denmark and Norway and Sweden respectively, were also mined. German U-boats off the Danish and Norwegian coasts were also given special attention, being subjected to aerial attack, which not only worried the Germans that an invasion might be coming, but also had the advantage that the U-boats were prevented from sailing south to harass the invasion fleet.

Hitler was convinced that Norway was the likely target area, but most of his senior officers regarded the Pas-de-Calais as more likely. In believing that an invasion would come through Norway, Hitler was showing his usual inability to appreciate strategic realities – any landings on Norway would face the same problems caused by the mountainous terrain and heavily indented coastline that had made the Anglo-French attempt to dislodge the Germans so difficult in 1940. It would also mean that a second invasion would be necessary as the Allies attempted to invade Denmark on their way to Germany. Most senior German officers appreciated this, but another reason so many of the German High Command believed the Pas-de-Calais would be the invasion site was that they thought the British in particular would want to overrun and destroy the sites from which V-1 flying bombs were being fired at London and the south-east of England.

Some senior German officers even suspected landings in Spain, or even Portugal. Neither country would be in a state to resist. Both were backward at the time and the poorest countries in Western Europe. Portugal had a small population and was inclined to favour the Allies, even having allowed the use of the Azores for American anti-submarine operations. Spain was still recovering from the civil war. But, as in Italy, where the Alps posed a problem for a northward advance towards Germany, in Spain the Pyrenees were a barrier to quick and efficient movement into France.

The German High Command was so convinced that the Normandy landings were a feint and that the main thrust would come later through the Boulogne area that there was considerable reluctance to move forces into Normandy for several days after the initial landings. Indeed, by the time large-scale troop movements started on 1 July, Montgomery had a firm bridgehead and could only be dislodged with great difficulty and with far larger forces than could be mustered by the Germans, while Patton was ashore with the Third US Army – a genuine unit this time – and was fighting on the Allied right flank.

One reason for this German belief that further landings were coming was that other deceptions were being mounted at the same time. 'Plan Ironside' was intended to convince the Germans that two weeks after the initial landings, a second invasion would come directly from the United States and the Azores, with troops landing on the west coast of France in the Bay of Biscay. This not only stopped the Germans moving reinforcements to Normandy in the wake of the D-Day landings, but also caused them to destroy four airfields close to the Biscay coast.

If this was not enough, an actor resembling Montgomery was dispatched to Gibraltar and Algiers where he talked about a landing in the south of France.

In fact, the original plan had called for a simultaneous invasion of the south of France, catching the Germans on two sides at once. Despite the massive resources available to the Allies by this time, it soon became clear that this would be stretching resources too far, especially as the demand for landing craft and ships was not solely coming from the European the-atre, for the Allies had already started island hopping across the Pacific towards Japan.

The various deceptions worked as well as the Allies had hoped. On 2 June, Bletchley Park reported that the Germans were giving every indication of having decided that the Allies had completed their preparations for initial landings either in Normandy or Brittany, with a main effort in the Pas-de-Calais to follow.

NOTES

1. Imperial War Museum Sound Archive.
2. National Archive – papers released 22 May 2013.
3. National Archive – papers released 22 May 2013.
4. Montgomery, *Memoirs of Field Marshal the Viscount Montgomery of Alamein* (London: Collins, 1958).
5. Montgomery, *Memoirs*.

* The body was delivered to the submarine while at Holy Loch on the Clyde in the west of Scotland in a container marked 'optical instruments'.

5

DEBACLE AT DIEPPE

While there were some optimists who wanted to return to France as early as 1940, within months of Dunkirk, most in the armed forces and in the British government realised that it would be some time before France could be re-taken. Churchill was adamant that no one was to talk about invasion in the case of France, but use the word 'landings' instead as it was the Germans who had invaded France! In Churchill's mind, Germany, and no doubt Italy as well, could be invaded. In fact, on this Churchill was in line with the French, who regarded the Germans as having invaded, and when discussing the Normandy landings used the term *le débarquement*, 'disembarkment' or 'landing', rather than *l'invasion*. No one underestimated the task, apart from Stalin with his insistence on a second front, and even the Americans when they arrived in force accepted Churchill's arguments in favour of a Mediterranean campaign before any assault on northern France.

As shown earlier, considerable experience was gained by the Allies in the invasions of North Africa, Sicily and then mainland Italy. They had also seen how the Germans managed to invade Norway while the British and French expeditionary force sent to save the country had failed. The Germans had suffered heavy losses in attempting to take Crete and had only won because the defending forces had lost their heavy equipment and, crucially, their communications equipment. The seaborne element had been ruined by the British Mediterranean Fleet despite lacking control of the air. Even with control of the air, the German paratroops and glider-borne troops had taken heavy losses.

Nevertheless, the Allies were soon attracted by the idea of combined operations, and raids on enemy-held territory. There were a number of operations of this kind, of which the two largest were the attack on the naval base at St Nazaire and the Dieppe raid. The former was a great success, designed to destroy the large dry dock and prevent its use by German capital ships. It was mounted on the night of 28/29 March 1942 largely by Coastal Forces, which provided sixteen of the nineteen ships, while the destroyer HMS *Campbeltown* was loaded with explosives and played a sacrificial role. The St Nazaire operation was in effect simply a 'hit and run' exercise, but Dieppe was of far greater significance.

DIEPPE

Plans for raiding forces started to be prepared shortly after the evacuation from Dunkirk. Rear-Admiral Louis Mountbatten, RN, was put in charge of planning combined operations. This was not a happy choice as few senior officers liked him, many regarding him as an upstart, and the Americans may also have disliked his close connections to the British royal family.

The raid, originally known as 'Operation Rutter', was to be launched from five ports in the south of England between Southampton in the west and Newhaven in the east. There would be 5,000 Canadian troops, 1,000 British and fifty US Rangers, supported by 237 ships and aircraft from seventy-four squadrons, of which no less than sixty-six would be fighter squadrons.

Given the complexity of the exercise and the lack of experience amongst the men and their commanders as the first of the Mediterranean landings were still some months away, an exercise was conducted to provide training and also to ensure that the arrangements were workable. This was just as well as the first exercise was a complete disaster. Ten days later, however, all went well with a second exercise. A date still had to be fixed for the Dieppe operation, and it was not until 1 July 1942 that this was decided as 4 July or the first day after that date with favourable weather conditions.

The weather was bad and the operation was postponed on 7 July. Montgomery wanted it cancelled at this stage as the troops involved had been briefed and he feared that security would be compromised. His objections were ignored and planning continued, while he was removed from the operation and posted to Egypt to command the British Eighth Army.

One of the changes made after Montgomery's departure was that of the name, to 'Operation Jubilee'; more serious was the decision to cancel the planned aerial bombardment as it was feared that it could cost heavy French casualties. Instead, eight British destroyers would bombard the port, but battleships, which could have made a difference with their guns of 14, 15 or even 16in calibre, were held back because they would be vulnerable to German shore-based artillery once they were in coastal waters. This was overly cautious as the guns of these ships could easily fire over ranges of 20 miles (32km). Meanwhile, Montgomery's concerns about security were soon justified as French double agents warned the Germans about British interest in Dieppe, while the commanding officer of the 1st Parachute Battalion was later to comment that 'security was abysmal' from the start. In any case, the Germans also detected increased radio traffic and the growing concentration of landing craft in the south coast ports. The next change, as the weather continued to be poor, was that the planned paratroop landings were cancelled since airborne forces were even more vulnerable to the weather. This decision was later reversed.

Mountbatten was anxious to see action and impatient for a landing on enemy territory, although this would be just another 'hit and run' raid. In this he was not alone. Churchill felt that there was much to be gained both in raising morale amongst the Allies, and in showing Stalin that the British were taking the war to the enemy. In fact, by this time Stalin was already on the offensive in northern Russia, and his foremost concern was that the main German thrust had turned southwards towards Stalingrad. The Canadians, who had substantial numbers of troops in the UK, were also anxious to see some action and when the possibility of the Dieppe raid was first raised, they made clear their intention to be involved.

Churchill later recalled:

I thought it most important that a large-scale operation should take place this summer, and military opinion seemed unanimous that until an operation on that scale was undertaken, no responsible general would take the responsibility of planning the main invasion ...

In discussion with Admiral Mountbatten it became clear that time did not permit a new large-scale operation to be mounted during the summer (after Rutter had been cancelled), but that Dieppe could be remounted (with the new code-name 'Jubilee') within a month, provided extraordinary steps were taken to ensure secrecy. For this reason no records were kept but, after the Canadian authorities and the Chiefs of Staff had given their approval, I personally went through the plans with the C.I.G.S., Admiral Mountbatten, and the Naval Force Commander, Captain J. Hughes-Hallett.

Initial planning and control of the operation had originally lain with the then Lieutenant-General Sir Bernard Montgomery, before he was posted to North Africa. Montgomery's South-Eastern Command was to provide the troops, but after pressure from the Canadian government to put Canadian troops into action, the Canadian 2nd Division, commanded by Major-General J. H. Roberts, were selected as the main force.

The initial plan for the attack was an unimaginative frontal assault on Dieppe, but this was developed with the use of British paratroops into an attack on the German artillery positions mounted on the headlands either side of the town and the port. There were plans for an aerial bombardment before the raid to soften up the target.

The special troops who were still assigned to the operation were Royal Marine and Royal Navy commandos, although the idea was that they would follow the main force ashore from motor gunboats and destroy the harbour installations, rather than lead. There was even an ex-burglar on their strength who was supposed to break into a port office and crack the safe, in the hope of finding important documents.

If security was poor, so too was intelligence. Allied air reconnaissance missed the German gun positions imbedded in the cliff faces, while the beaches for tanks were assessed using holiday postcards and amateur photographs. In addition to poor knowledge of the terrain and the defences, there was little knowledge of enemy strength.

Although Mountbatten was in command of special operations, he was not going on the raid; the assault force was led by Major-General Roberts and the naval force by Captain Hughes-Hallett. Mountbatten did, nevertheless, address at least some of the troops before they embarked, as Sergeant George Cook of No. 4 Commando, which was to attack the artillery batteries at Varangéville, recalled:

Mountbatten gave us a lecture – said he wished he was coming with us. Once we realised where we were going, I think 200 blokes thought, 'I wish he were going instead of us.' But yes, very nice talk. We cheered him – off he went.

Then we started priming grenades, drawing ammunition. Our troop were doing the demolitions, so we drew explosives and we'd a fair amount of stuff which we packed up ... Then we had a meal and we sailed – a beautiful evening, as we went down the Solent and past the Isle of Wight.

Suddenly an officer said, 'Oh – they've got all the harbour lights lit.' I looked over the prow of the boat and you could see lights on the shore. The lighthouse at Varangéville was flashing, so I thought, Cor blimey – everybody awake. We're going to have a pretty bad welcome here.

When we landed, there was some barbed wire. We'd a roll of wire netting which we threw over the barbed wire so we could run over it. The Germans were firing tracers from their pill-boxes, and Lord Lovat said, quite casually, 'They're firing too high.' He was about six foot – I'm five foot four – so I thought, 'If they're firing over his head, there's no danger they're going to hit me' – but they did fire their mortars and four or five blokes were killed on the beach.[2]

Cook and his comrades advanced, firing. One of them shot a man out of an ack-ack tower, who 'did a lovely swallow dive off the top', before they reached an orchard accompanied by one of Cook's friends, another sergeant, Geordie Horne, who was almost immediately shot dead, before Cook himself was hit in the face and the shoulder.

Even before the raid began at 0450 on 19 August, the cover was blown completely as a number of the escorting warships had already engaged warships accompanying a German convoy off Puys and Berneval at 0348.

To avoid confusion, the landings were at four beaches, each designated a colour for the operation. One of these, the most easterly, was Blue Beach, where the assault started badly. After leaving the converted Belgian cross-Channel ferry *Princess Astrid*, the 10th Landing Craft Assault Flotilla started off in the wrong direction, and eventually reached the beach sixteen minutes late, as dawn was breaking and the element of surprise had been lost.

The initial attacks were on the coastal batteries. No. 4 Commando led by Lieutenant-Colonel Lord Lovat, one of the great commando leaders, and supported by forty men of the US Rangers, landed at Orange Beach, ready to attack the batteries at Varangéville; the South Saskatchewan Regiment and the Queen's Own Cameron Highlanders of Canada landed at Green Beach and attacked the batteries at Pourville; the Royal Regiment of Canada and three companies of the Canadian Black Watch landed at Blue

Beach and attacked at Puys; and No. 3 Commando attacked the batteries at Berneval, landing at Yellow Beach. The attack at Varangéville was successful, but No. 4 Commando was the only unit to meet all of its objectives during the operation. Their fellow commandos in No. 3 almost missed their assigned positions with just eighteen men landing in the right spot, although they managed to distract the German gunners until superior enemy forces compelled them to withdraw. The Queen's Own Cameron Highlanders of Canada were landed late, but did manage to advance further inland than any other unit that day before forced back once German reinforcements arrived. Most of the South Saskatchewan Regiment was also landed in the wrong place, but it did manage to reach its objectives. Worst off, however, was the Royal Regiment of Canada at Puys, where they were virtually wiped out: just sixty of the regiment's 543 men were evacuated from the beach.

At Puys, the leader of the landing craft flotilla felt his craft scrape the bottom of the seabed even as heavy enemy machine gun fire was sweeping across the craft. 'Down ramp' was called and the men of the Royal Regiment of Canada and the Royal Canadian Artillery dashed into the water, but many were cut down on the ramp, where the bodies piled up, while others were mown down by machine gun fire as they attempted to cross the pebbled beach to the shelter of the sea wall 40ft (12m) away. Out of seven landing craft, just four were operational a few hours later. Out of 545 Canadian troops who attempted to come ashore on Blue Beach, 485 were killed, missing or wounded.

At 0520 the main assault started, led by the Essex Scottish Regiment and Canada's Royal Hamilton Light Infantry, with armour support provided by twenty-seven Churchill tanks of the 14th Canadian Army Tank Regiment. Most of the tanks lost their tracks on the shingle beach, while those that reached land were stopped by concrete tank traps. They were easy targets for German anti-tank guns, while the infantrymen were mown down by intense machine gun fire. In contrast, the fire from the guns of the destroyers offshore was too light to have any effect.

Offshore, Major-General Roberts could not see what was happening ashore because the ships covering the landings had laid a dense smokescreen. This did nothing at all to protect those involved in the landings, but made command and control difficult. Unaware of the true state of affairs on the beaches and on the headlands, Roberts ordered in his two reserve units. When Les Fusiliers Mont-Royal became bogged down under the cliffs on their way to the town centre, Royal Marine commandos were ordered in to help them, which required them to pass through Dieppe and attack batteries on the east headland. This was necessary, but not in the original plan, and their Royal Marine CO, Lieutenant-Colonel 'Tigger' Phillips, had to transfer his men from the motor gunboats, brief them on the new mission, and put them into landing craft.

In the ensuing chaos, most of the landing craft carrying the marines were hit by gunfire on the run-in and the few men who reached the shore were killed or taken prisoner. In an attempt to regain control and end the suicidal mission, their CO stood up in the stern of his craft and signalled to those behind that they should turn back, before he was killed by German gunfire.

The RAF had allocated aircraft to the operation, including many fighters, but Squadron Leader 'Johnnie' Johnson, leading No. 616 Squadron, recalled that there was supposed to be a headquarters ship, HMS *Calypso*, with radar and RAF controllers aboard directing air operations. At no point during his four sorties over Dieppe that day could he establish communications:

> We could see very little except for a bloody great pall of smoke over the town, and lots of shelling going on down below. But we could do nothing about it because the attackers and defenders were all within a hundred yards of each other. We couldn't help the army. When we got home after the first patrol, we knew that the whole thing had been a disaster, but there was nothing we could do to help them.[3]

Withdrawal began at 1100 as the heavy fire continued. It took until 1400. When it left, the assault force left behind 3,367 Canadians who had been killed, wounded or taken prisoner, as well as 275 RM commandos. The Royal Navy lost a destroyer and thirty-three landing craft, and 550 men killed or wounded. The RAF lost 106 aircraft. Compared to this, the Germans lost 591 men killed or wounded, and forty-eight aircraft.

The surviving landing craft had been ordered to the main beach at Dieppe at 1030. When the first landing craft arrived there, it was met by a solitary soldier, and it was only after he had been handed a Lewis gun with which to defend himself that someone realised that he was a German soldier attempting to desert. Once the withdrawal started in earnest, the few landing craft were overcrowded and in danger of being swamped. One of them was hit by a shell and capsized, but the crew managed to get their passengers aboard another landing craft.

In the inevitable enquiry into what went wrong, many tried to blame Mountbatten, but as there was no reprimand and he remained in post, it seems that it was not his fault, and he did not act alone, although there is no written record of the operation being given the go-ahead. General Sir Alan Brooke was abroad at the time and many believe that had he been at home in the War Cabinet, he might have persuaded Churchill to cancel the operation, but this is conjecture.

Some believe that the disaster at Dieppe was necessary so that lessons could be learned in time for the Normandy landings, but, even so, there were many avoidable failings. There should have been a heavy aerial bombardment before the operation, or it should have been called off. Some form of reconnaissance from the sea was necessary and would have noticed the gun positions in the cliff face, and could have assessed whether the shingle on the beach would have damaged the tank tracks. This would have required reconnaissance parties to land on the beach and take samples, without being noticed. Much heavier naval firepower was needed and it had to continue right up to the moment the landing craft hit the shore.

It also became clear that a variety of different weapons would be needed, especially different types of tank for use by engineers to clear mines or overcome obstacles while still protected by armour. There would be many of these in due course, some called 'Hobart's Funnies' after Major-General Percy Hobart, Commanding Officer of the British 79th Armoured Division.

Some credit the Dieppe raid with improving air-ground co-ordination, which led to the creation of the two Allied Tactical Air Forces, but this development took place in the Western Desert and was subsequently applied to the invasions in Sicily and Italy, so that by the time of the Normandy landings, air-ground co-ordination had reached a stage of perfection.

NOTES

1. Churchill, *The Second World War* (London: Cassell, 1950).
2. Imperial War Museum Sound Archive.
3. Johnson, Group Captain 'Johnnie', *Wing Leader* (London: Chatto & Windus, 1956).

6

DISASTERS ON EXERCISES

In wartime nothing is certain, and every movement is vulnerable. The skies over the United Kingdom, and especially southern and eastern England, were so vulnerable to marauding enemy aircraft that as far as possible flying training was moved abroad. The Royal Air Force had the benefit of the Empire Air Training Scheme, with aircrew trained in Canada and Southern Africa, where the better weather was another advantage. The Royal Navy's Fleet Air Arm had the welcome opportunity of the Towers Scheme, training at the massive USN flying school at Pensacola in Florida.

The seas were no safer. Apart from aerial attack, there was the ever-present risk of mines, even in the narrow waters of the Solent, between Portsmouth and the Isle of Wight, and of fast-moving E-boats, German motor gunboats and motor torpedo boats.

The Germans had planned a substantial and balanced fleet before the war, with first 'Plan X', then 'Plan Y' and eventually 'Plan Z'. Even the last of these was further modified. It called for a balanced fleet with aircraft carriers, more battleships than in fact the Germans had during the war, as well as destroyers and cruisers. The modification made to Plan Z was to create a strong ocean-going submarine force. This was a cause of friction between the German Navy's head, *Grossadmiral* or Grand Admiral Erich Raeder, and his submarine commander, the then Commodore Karl Doenitz, who was later to succeed him. Raeder believed that the emphasis on submarines was wrong as detection systems had improved so much since the First World War, but Doenitz believed that the U-boat still had a major role to play and that limitations on manpower and competition between the German armed forces for scarce raw materials and fuel meant that only submarines could be built and manned in large enough numbers to make an impact.

What neither man had expected was that war would break out on 3 September 1939. Both had been assured by Hitler that war would not come until 1944 or even later, and that there would not be a major set-piece battle between the Royal Navy and the German *Kriegsmarine* until 1945. So it happened that war broke out before the German Navy was ready, and doubts remain to this day over whether the massive cost and the demand for raw materials implicit in Plan Z could ever have resulted in the plan being fulfilled.

Germany thus entered the war with very few ocean-going submarines, very few destroyers, no aircraft carriers, and one battleship being completed while another was still being built. The destroyer situation became much worse after the invasion of Norway when ten ships were lost in the two naval battles at Narvik. On hearing the news that war had broken out, Raeder was visibly shaken and had to excuse himself from the meeting he was attending, concluding that his men 'would only be able to show that they knew how to die with honour'.

Where Germany had an advantage was in the eventual size of her submarine force, and, once bases close to British waters were obtained, in her force of fast-moving E-boats. The term 'E-boat' was an Allied invention as it meant 'enemy boat', but to the Germans these were *Schnellboote*, or 'fast boat', and included both motor gunboats and torpedo boats.

On 9 February 1944, General Eisenhower sent a note to General George Marshall, the US Army's Chief of Staff and therefore his immediate chief: 'I am just a bit uneasy about our failure to get a greater leaven of combat experience amongst our formations.'[1]

The landings in North Africa, Sicily and then mainland Italy had shown that despite the advent of the landing craft, training was still an issue. Troops with little or no experience of amphibious assault needed first-hand experience. It was also important that they come under live fire so that they might become used to the sounds, sights and even smells of explosives. The rapid expansion of the Allied armies, and especially those of the United States, meant that a substantial proportion of those involved had no combat experience. Troops who had experienced amphibious assault were, of course, by this time heavily involved in the fighting in Italy. This had to be remedied, and so Operation Tiger was born.

OPERATION TIGER

The final decision to use Normandy for the landings was taken in June 1943. COSSAC, which by this time had developed into SHAEF, considered a major training exercise was essential. Slapton Sands, some 10 miles from the peacetime seaside resort of Torquay, was chosen as the beach characteristics were similar to those of Normandy, and especially Omaha and Utah beaches. Slapton Sands was also close to the established British training area on Dartmoor. Other beaches to the east of Portsmouth were used to simulate the British landing zones of Gold, Juno and Sword beaches.

While landing exercises commenced in December 1943, a major exercise, Operation Tiger was scheduled to run from 22 April until 30 April 1944, the highpoint being a landing at Slapton Sands. The troops would be subjected to live firing and no less than 30,000 men were to be put ashore using nine LSTs.

The initial part of 'Tiger' consisted of marshalling and embarkation exercises. When loading any type of landing craft, but especially a large LST, careful planning was needed so that the items likely to be needed first were embarked last, a technique sometimes known as 'combat loading'. This took until 25 April. On the evening of 26 April, troops boarded the ships intended to carry the first wave and set sail. When it became clear that many of the troops were not hardened seafarers, an attempt was made to simulate crossing the English Channel by taking the ships around Lyme Bay so that they could arrive at Slapton Sands at first light the following morning.

The landing was preceded by a live firing exercise to accustom the troops to the sounds and smells of gunfire. As the landings on D-Day would be covered by heavy fire from warships positioned astern of the landing ships, so too at Slapton Sands. The heavy cruiser HMS *Hawkins* was to shell the beach using live ammunition from 0630 to 0700, known on the day as H-60 to H-30 with 'H' hour being the time of the landings at 0730. Between 0700 and 0730, beach masters had to inspect the landing area to ensure that it was safe. As several of the LSTs were late, the officer in command decided to postpone H-hour by sixty minutes to 0830. The live firing exercise would also be delayed by an hour. This signal was received aboard *Hawkins*, but not by all of the LSTs. This meant that at 0730, while troops were landing on the beaches, the live firing started. Although a white tape was placed across the beach as a further safety measure intended to stop troops from crossing into the live fire target zone, many US soldiers ignored the tape and pressed on.

This was the first major tragedy to affect Operation Tiger.

SLAPTON SANDS

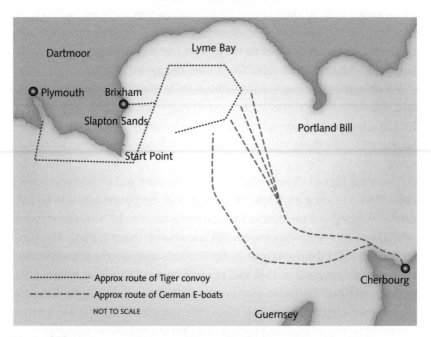

The laudable desire to conduct an exercise so that fresh troops would not only experience a beach landing, but do so under live fire, resulted in 'Operation Tiger'. The 'invasion convoy' was inadequately protected and was the victim of a surprise attack by German E-boats, which happened upon it by chance.

Of course the Germans would be aware that Allied activity in the English Channel was increasing. All that could be hoped was that the level of activity would confuse the enemy and that the real invasion site would remain a mystery. The fear was of German aerial attack, although by this time Britain's air defences were in good shape, or attack by U-boats or E-boats. The latter posed the bigger threat, being small and fast moving, and there had been many running battles between British motor gunboats and E-boats. In late February, four ships had been sunk by E-boats based on Guernsey, and the Free Norwegian-manned destroyer HMS *Eskdale* was sunk on the night of 13/14 April. Intervention by larger German ships was extremely unlikely as the capital ships had been ordered home by Hitler, although the giant battleship *Tirpitz* was moored in a Norwegian fjord.

The E-boats were commanded by *Kapitan zur See* (naval Captain) Rudolf Petersen from his base at Wimereux, a few miles north-east of Boulogne, from which he controlled all E-boat activity in the English Channel and North Sea.

By this time, the German E-boats were 115ft (35m) in length and had three Daimler-Benz diesel engines driving three shafts. Most had a maximum speed of 35 knots, but those of the 5th and 9th *Schnellboote* flotillas, with six and three boats respectively, had been supercharged to provide a maximum speed of 40 knots. With a crew of twenty-one men, each E-boat had two 21in fixed torpedo tubes with two reloads, and most had two or three 20mm cannon, though some had a heavier 37mm cannon.

The convoy for the assault on Slapton Sands, known as 'Red' Beach, was code-named T45. It was drawn from part of Force 'U', the American force assigned for the landings on Utah Beach on D-Day. Convoy T45 sailed from Plymouth at 0945 on 27 April. There should have been two warships as escorts, but the elderly destroyer HMS *Scimitar* had been holed above the waterline the previous day and it was decided that she should remain in port. This left just the Flower-class corvette HMS *Azalea* as escort and she headed out to sea with the leading ship of the convoy, LST 515, 2,000yd behind and the remaining four LSTs following at 700yd intervals. The decision to keep *Scimitar* in port for repairs was not passed up the line of command to the officer in charge of the operation, Commander Force U. It was not until 1930 that the weakness of the convoy escort became known and a sister ship of *Scimitar*, *Saladin*, was ordered to take her place, and left Start Bay at 0137 on 28 April.

In addition to what might be described as the close escort, other defences included three British motor torpedo boats stationed off Cherbourg to stop E-boats heading across the Channel. Nevertheless, the nine boats of the 5th and 9th *Schnellboote* flotillas managed to slip past the British MTBs at 2200 on 27 April. They crossed the Channel at 36 knots and maintained radio silence, evading patrolling warships off Lyme Bay. Meanwhile, another three LSTs sailing from Brixham had joined the convoy as it moved west of Torbay and headed north by north-west before turning towards Slapton Sands.

The E-boat commanders seldom knew what their target would be and most often looked for targets of opportunity. Nevertheless, at 2317 Petersen in France radioed the bearing of a possible target and the six boats of the 5th Flotilla divided up into pairs, or *Rotte*. In the dark, it was impossible to be certain of the nature of the targets, but at around 0130 the third pair of E-boats spotted what they believed to be two destroyers at 2,000m. One of the E-boats fired both tubes at the stern of the ship to starboard and the other fired its tubes in turn at the other. Both E-boat crews saw explosions just over a minute and a half later. The second pair also fired both tubes, but no explosion resulted, leading the *Rotte* commander to conclude, correctly, that his targets were shallow draft landing craft. The first formation saw what they thought to be a tanker ablaze, and both E-boats fired at a target and were rewarded with an explosion after seventy-six seconds.

Attracted by the explosions and tracer shells, the 9th Flotilla headed for the area. Two of the three E-boats fired their torpedoes at the same ship, while the third boat broke away to attack what its commander thought were small escorting vessels, but which in fact were small landing craft infantry.

Those aboard the ships in the convoy could not at first see their attackers in the darkness and the confusion of the action. The convoy had been joined by a British fighter and a naval direction tender from Portland, whose role was to provide radar and communications for the convoy, but was ordered to make port 'all haste' just as the attack started. In the hours that followed, the scale of the losses suffered by the convoy became apparent. Two LSTs, 507 and 531, had been sunk, with the loss of 202 and 424 men respectively, out of a total of 943 US Army and US Navy men aboard. LST 289 was damaged with a loss of thirteen men, while LST 511 had been hit by fire from LST 496's defensive weapons, with eighteen of those aboard wounded.

The total death toll has since been put at 946 killed, with another 200 wounded. Two LSTs were sunk and another two badly damaged. These losses were in addition to those suffered on Slapton Sands in the 'friendly fire' incident.

Afterwards, in his report on the incident, Rear-Admiral John Hall, RN, had to offer a sincere apology to the Americans. Under the pressures of war with operations against enemy surface vessels and other actions planned, communications had broken down. Nevertheless, an attempt was made to draw lessons from the action, including using larger escort forces and having rescue craft standing by as well as having lifeboats and life rafts ready to be lowered. Improving the exchange of information was another recommendation, aided by ensuring that all involved used the same radio wavelength, and reminding all involved in any such action not to look towards fires or flares as this would impair their night vision. It was also recommended that small arms should be more widely available aboard landing craft as the guns on warships or the larger LSTs could not depress sufficiently to attack the E-boats. It was also decided that training be given in using the kapok life preserver rather than the CO_2 type as the former was more effective in keeping heads above water, even though it took up more space aboard ships. Bootlaces were also to be loosened so that boots could be kicked off more easily once in the water.

No official statement was issued and the disaster remained a closely guarded secret. Those in the know were warned not to say anything on pain of court-martial. Of the many burns cases and other wounds and injuries received by the military hospital at Sherbourne, the personnel were ordered not to ask questions, again on pain of court-martial.

Of greater concern to the Allies, ten of those posted as missing were 'bigoted' officers, that is, they knew the location of the invasion beaches, even though, as with everyone else, including Eisenhower and Montgomery, they did not yet have the date. A thorough and exhaustive search of Lyme Bay was conducted for fear that the men might have been picked up by the Germans, and all ten officers were found.

Amongst those searching for survivors and then for bodies was Ordinary Seaman Jack 'Buster' Brown serving in the fleet minesweeper HMS *Kellett*:

On 28th April 1944 our captain received the signal to proceed to Slapton Sands where German E-boats had attacked a fleet of US landing craft who had been rehearsing for the D-Day landings. I remember the dozens of corpses covered in oil floating in the sea, and our ship's boats being lowered to recover them. We had about 70 brought aboard, but only one was still alive, and he died shortly afterwards. The flotilla returned to our base at Portland where the dockland abounded with ambulances, but there was not much that could be done for the poor blokes ...[2]

The failure of the exercise was largely down to bad luck, but the failure to provide adequate close protection was inexcusable and must have done much to weaken American confidence in their British allies at a crucial point of the war. One corvette at the head of a convoy was no defence at all from E-boats attacking from the seaward side. Even had both warships been in position, it is unlikely that the outcome would have been much different. This should have been realised even before the exercise started, as a Royal Canadian Navy officer, Lieutenant Albert Morrow, commanding *MTB726* recalled afterwards:

> An American torpedo boat under the command of Commander Buckley has arrived at Dartmouth amidst talk of an operation to try out landing craft in advance of D-Day. Lots of officers had tried to give Buckley advice about how the German E-boat tactics worked but his attitude had been, 'Oh, we don't need that advice.' His skippers had wanted it – but he didn't. And then one night in April 1944 they carried out an operation called Operation Tiger. They were to do a landing at Slapton Sands – and Jerry sat out there torpedoed these ships. It was exactly what we had warned Buckley about. So this is one of those things – no matter who you are or where you are, it's foolish not to take any advice when it comes to enemy tactics. It was a tragedy that could have been averted if only he'd listened.[3]

In short, the best defence against an E-boat attack would have been a close escort of motor torpedo boats or gunboats.

NOTES

1. Dwight Eisenhower Papers, Vol. III.
2. Imperial War Museum Sound Archive.
3. Imperial War Museum Sound Archive.

7

INVENTION – THE KEY TO SUCCESS

With the debacle of Dieppe behind them, the Allies had learnt some harsh lessons. They had to review their planning and find solutions for many problems. Securing a major port was essential, but would be difficult. In any case, no one could expect the Germans to hand over a port without first sabotaging the installations so that it would take some time to restore it to use – time that would not be available to armies facing strong and well-co-ordinated counter-attacks.

Many of the problems had been foreseen, and Churchill had recalled Rear-Admiral Lord Louis Mountbatten from Hawaii to start preparations as early as late 1941. Mountbatten recalled:

In October 1941, I was recalled from Pearl Harbor to take up the job in charge of combined operations by Mr Winston Churchill. The very first day I reported to him, he said, 'You are to prepare the invasion of Europe for unless we can land and fight Hitler and beat his forces on land, we shall never win this war. You must devise and design the appliances, the landing craft and the technique to enable us to effect the landing against opposition and to maintain ourselves there. You must take the most brilliant officers to plan this great operation. You must take bases to act as training establishments where you can train the Navy, Army and Air Force to work as a single entity. The whole of the south coast is a bastion of defence against the invasion of Hitler. We've got to turn it into the springboard for our attack. There are three conditions for a successful invasion. First, obviously, to get ashore against no matter what opposition. Secondly, having got ashore to stay ashore no matter what the weather conditions. Thirdly, to stop the enemy from building up his forces against you quicker than you can, otherwise he'll throw you back into the sea.[1]

Mountbatten later recalled that they needed landing ships and landing craft, but these simply were not available in 1941. Apart from the issue of designing such craft, building them would be a problem in its own right as the nation's shipbuilding yards were busy constructing ships for the Battle of the Atlantic. With Churchill's support, many were built in British yards, but production only really gained momentum after Pearl Harbor, when US yards became available. The availability of sufficient landing ships and landing craft also had a bearing on the earliest date that landings in Normandy could be managed.

LANDING CRAFT – AND MORE

The wide variety of landing ships and landing craft also included ships with a floodable rear dock from which landing craft, already loaded, could float out. This was much faster and safer than having to scramble down the sides of a troopship and into a landing craft. Today, such ships are known as LPD, landing platform dock, but in the 1940s ships were still ships and not 'platforms'.

Landing craft were not always used for landings. The relatively cheap mass production of these vessels and their capability to operate in shallow water led to many variants. Many were fitted with rockets to provide a massive intensity of fire as the assault force neared the coast. Others carried guns: basically artillery fixed into position. These landing craft were known as landing craft, gun, large, or LCG(L).

Such heavily armed landing craft complemented the work of the coastal monitors, which were relatively small ships with a heavy armament of battleship calibre although with a single turret.

PORTS AND PIPELINE

Once ashore, the troops would need fresh supplies of all kinds and rein-forcements, but they would also need fuel, especially once the two tactical air forces had aircraft based ashore in temporary airfields. It was vital that a port was available, and in due course it was decided that not one but two ports, each the size of the port of Dover, a cross-Channel port that had been developed over several hundred years, would be necessary to the suc-cess of the campaign. Fuel was a problem in a league of its own. A steady stream of tankers would be required, each vulnerable to attack from the air or the sea, even once German artillery was safely bypassed, and each needing time to unload in France, and still at risk when taking on cargo in the south of England.

The solutions to these problems were both practical and elegant. The two ports would be the Mulberry harbours, prefabricated ports that could be towed across the English Channel in sections and assembled, while the vital fuel supplies would be delivered continuously by the 'Pluto' oil pipe-lines laid beneath the sea and safely out of sight.

As early as May 1942, before the ill-starred assault on Dieppe, Churchill had written to Mountbatten regarding the possible use of floating piers in any landings in France. Mountbatten's Combined Operations Headquarters, COHQ, had already started to research ways of reinforcing and sustaining troops once ashore, and this work intensified.

The planners at COHQ realised as early as 1942 that the landings would soon come to a halt if dependent on supplies moved over the Normandy beaches. Beach landings were exposed to the weather regardless of posi-tion, but at Normandy there was the added complication that the tidal range was no less than 25ft, and supplies could only be discharged for a certain period of time either side of high tide. It was clear that something would have to be built to handle supplies.

Amongst the possibilities being investigated by COHQ were floating piers known as Whales with adjustable legs known as Spuds to allow for the inevitable variations in depth, and these were to be protected by large num-bers of hollow concrete caissons up to 200ft long and 60ft high, displacing 6,000 tons, known as Phoenixes. In turn, to provide a sheltered anchorage in deeper water, 200ft long floating tanks known as bombardons were also to be provided at the 10 fathom, or 60ft (just over 18m) depth line.

As work continued, the age-old use of blockships, known as Corncobs, was also considered to provide smaller harbours known as Gooseberries, so that small craft could be sheltered and unloaded once the Gooseberries were in position. Five Gooseberries were built, two of them forming the basis of the Mulberry harbours and the other three were used to provide smaller sheltered harbours.

It was decided that two Mulberries were required and combined they were made up from 400 units with a total weight of 1.5 million tons. Such a massive project would have overwhelmed even the largest shipbuilder of the day, so they had to be built around the UK before being towed to the south coast of England where they were submerged to avoid detection by the *Luftwaffe*. They could not be towed across the English Channel until after the Normandy landings, when that exercise required no less than 10,000 men and 132 tugs. The Mulberry for the British and Canadian forces in the Eastern Sector was moored at Arromanches, while that for the US formations who comprised the Western Sector was moored at Saint-Laurent-sur-Mer.

For those handling the sections of the Mulberries, their first sight of them came as a surprise.

'We arrived at what seemed like a huge office block without windows, sixty foot high,' recalled Kenneth Bungard, a seaman on one of the tugs,

> We were told to clamber up on top, not knowing at the time that this lump of concrete was actually floating and when we got to the top we found that it was just a huge hollow concrete box. Next to it was a tug ... and the tug towed us away ... on top of this thing ... We just had to sit there while we were towed along at four knots, which isn't very fast, and as the dawn began to break we found ourselves in a bay by Dungeness where we promptly went down inside this concrete box, opened the sluices and sunk on the sand and wondered what the hell we were doing ... We soon realised why they asked for volunteers, because these things had never been taken across an ocean ... it was like trying to drag a brick across the Thames.[2]

The sinking at Dungeness was a ploy to make the Germans believe that an embarkation port was being built ready for an invasion of the Pas-de-Calais. It was also a means of utilising the Mulberry harbours until they were needed in Normandy.

Despite prefabrication, assembly of such massive projects on the Normandy coast could not be done overnight, and on 19 June, when they were nearly completed, a severe gale blew up and drove no less than 800 craft ashore and damaged the Mulberry at Saint-Laurent so badly that it was decided to abandon it. This left the Arromanches Mulberry as the sole port for some time, handling up to 11,000 tons of supplies daily, and though it was originally intended to last for just ninety days, it remained in daily use until December.

Although at first everything had to pass through Arromanches, before long the one vital item in the supplies needed by the Allies that did not need the Mulberry harbour was oil. At first, oil was piped in from tankers moored offshore using buoyed pipelines in an operation code-named 'Tombola', to a British terminus ashore at Port-en-Bessin and an American one at Sainte-Honorine-des-Pertes.

Once again, Mountbatten's COHQ was to the fore and as early as 1942 was experimenting with ways of pumping petrol across the English Channel using flexible pipes. This work led to Pluto, or 'pipe line under the ocean', and successful trials were conducted with a pipeline laid across the Bristol Channel.

Once the port of Cherbourg was captured, four Pluto pipelines were laid from the Isle of Wight to Cherbourg, with tugs towing large drums known as Conundrums across the Channel. This in itself was never going to be enough as the size of the Allied forces increased, and in January 1945 another sixteen pipelines were laid from Dungeness in Kent to Ambleteuse in France. As with so much else, Pluto amazed those who first saw it, including Lieutenant William Jalland, a platoon commander in the 8th Battalion, Durham Light Infantry:

> As the preparations for D-Day gathered pace, I remember being open-mouthed at some of the equipment that was being assembled. Part of Pluto that looked like an enormous bobbin floated about in Southampton Water. We didn't know what it was. We saw pieces of Mulberry, some with cranes, some without. Again, we'd no idea what they were. We saw the crabs, the scorpions and the flails. We didn't know what any of it was, but we knew we'd be on our way very soon.[3]

HOBART'S FUNNIES AND OTHER TANK CREATIONS

While the Mulberry harbours were part of a grand scheme, Dieppe had shown that landing on a beach was far from easy, especially for heavy armoured vehicles. Today, combat engineering vehicles are part of every major army's equipment, but at the time there was much to learn and many problems to be overcome. In effect, these were more mobile, adaptable and modern descendants of the siege engines used in the Middle Ages.

There were many ideas floating around, and of the more practical several came from either the British 79th Armoured Division or from the Royal Engineers, many known as 'Hobart's funnies' after the 79th's commanding officer, Major-General Percy Hobart. After the Commander-in-Chief of the British Army, Field Marshal Sir Alan Brooke, decided to create new units to overcome the many obstacles that would lie in the path of an invading force, Hobart was placed in command.

Not everything was new and untried. During the desert campaign in North Africa, a modified Matilda tank, known as the 'Scorpion', had been invented with revolving flails mounted in front of it to clear mines; the USSR also had T-34 tanks with mine rollers. The Scorpion's weakness was that it had been conceived and constructed in haste, so only limited success was achieved. Other armies had developed bridge laying tanks. The efforts for the Normandy landings resulted in the largest collection of specialised armoured support vehicles at the time.

Before the landings, Eisenhower and Montgomery were treated to a display of various tanks, including tanks that were fully amphibious, tanks that could clear mines, known as the 'Crab', flame-throwing tanks, and engineer tanks. Eisenhower liked the amphibious tank, but left the decision to General Omar Bradley. While Montgomery wanted the US Army to make use of the tanks, few were accepted for service, largely because most of the 'funnies' were based on the Churchill tank, which meant adding training and support, including spares, for another tank to the US Army's already crowded inventory. The Churchill was also regarded as slow, even though cross-country performance was good. Nevertheless, later, before the landings, the Americans did adopt some of the ideas using the Sherman tank as the basis for the specialised vehicles.

Getting a Sherman tank ready for amphibious operations took some time. The crews were supplied with large tins of Compound 219, consisting of grease with so much fibre in it that it handled like putty. This had to be applied to any crack or crevice found in the Sherman tank to make it watertight for beach landings. The engine inspection doors were sealed with it, and so too was the escape hatch on the floor of the tank through which the driver and co-driver could escape – although presumably not while the tank was wading ashore!

Making the gun barrel watertight was especially tricky as the gun might need to be used immediately. The solution was to place a seal over the barrel and the gun mantlet, but with a small explosive charge behind it, with a wire to detonate the charges running down the barrel and into the tank. In theory, once ashore, the explosives could be detonated leaving the gun barrel clear and the gun turret able to rotate freely.

The most commonly used and successful of the 'funnies' included the AVRE, or 'Assault Vehicle, Royal Engineers', which carried a crew of six, a driver from the Royal Armoured Corps and five Royal Engineers. The main gun was replaced by a 'Petard mortar', which fired a 40lb (18kg) high-explosive projectile known as the 'flying dustbin', up to 150yd (137m), to destroy roadblocks and bunkers. A weakness was that the mortar had to be reloaded externally, exposing the NCO sapper, who also commanded the tank, while this was being done. Another feature was the use of side hatches so that the crew could dismount to place 'Wade' demolition charges. The AVRE also used a demolition method called the 'Double Onion', which consisted of two large demolition charges on a metal frame that could be placed against an obstacle or a wall and detonated safely from a distance.

The AVRE was a versatile vehicle. It could also carry a 'Bobbin', a reel of 10ft (3m) wide canvas reinforced with steel that could be laid in front of the AVRE on soft ground so that it and following vehicles would not get bogged down. Another useful load was the 'fascine', a bundle of wooden poles with a metal pipe in the centre to allow water to flow through, that could be laid to fill a ditch. Alternatively, a small box girder could be carried so that a gap of up to 30ft (9m) could be closed in thirty seconds.

There was also the 'Bullshorn Plough', which was a large plough carried ahead of the AVRE to excavate the ground and expose landmines.

Not all of the tanks had roles that were primarily defensive or engineering. The 'Crocodile' was a Churchill tank with a flame-thrower in place of the hull machine gun, and an armoured trailer towed behind with 400 imperial gallons (1,800 litres) of fuel. This could throw a mass of flame more than 120yd (110m), which was far further than a man-portable device, and was very effective at clearing beaches and fortifications as it had an unnerving effect on the enemy.

Another means of discomforting the enemy was the so-called 'canal defence light', an extremely bright light hidden inside a tank intended to dazzle and blind the enemy. This was not available until some time after D-Day.

Getting off beaches and over other obstacles needed the ARK, or 'armoured ramp carrier', which again was a Churchill tank but with the turret removed and extendable ramps front and back so that other vehicles could drive over it and surmount obstacles.

There were also 'DD' tanks (duplex drive, meaning that they had marine propellers as well as tracks) which were amphibious, usually Shermans although Valentines were used for training, which could be launched off-shore to provide support for the first wave of infantry. These used large canvas floatation collars, which looked like a canvas and metal fence, and displaced enough water to provide buoyancy once in the water, and in addition to their tracks, they had propellers at the rear. There was also the 'Buffalo', a British amphibious landing vehicle. Such tanks were also useful for river and canal crossings.

One problem with the amphibious tanks was that they needed more space aboard the LSTs than conventional tanks because of the large flota-tion collar. Typically, an LST that could carry nine Sherman tanks could only carry five amphibious tanks. There were also limitations to their amphibious capability as they had only been tested in waves a foot high (0.3m); on some beaches the waves were 6ft high (1.8m) on D-Day. Most were fitted with enough air to allow the crew to survive for five minutes under water and thus have time to escape, but life rafts were also carried aboard the tanks.

Another Sherman-based tank was the 'Crab', which used a mine flail mounted ahead of it.

Broken down or war damaged tanks could be obstacles in themselves, so another Sherman 'funny' was the BARV, 'beach armoured recovery vehicle', which was a Sherman M4A2 tank with waterproofing and a tall armoured tower in place of its turret. This could operate in 9ft (2.7m) of water and was designed to remove vehicles blocking access to the beach. The BARV fleet was operated by the Royal Electrical & Mechanical Engineers, REME, as one would expect given their role in handling breakdowns.

Ashore, the work of the BARV was complemented by armoured bulldozers, based on the Caterpillar D7, which could not only remove obstacles but also fill in bomb and shell craters. The 'Centaur Bulldozer' could undertake a similar role and was based on the Cromwell tank, again with turret removed. The idea was that these would be able to keep up with fast-moving armoured divisions, but again the Centaur was not available for some time after D-Day.

GETTING THE DETAILS RIGHT

No matter how good the aerial reconnaissance, when briefing those preparing for the invasion it is important to give them a good idea of what they will see. Photographic interpretation is a rare skill, even in the armed forces and in wartime.

The planners resorted to building models. Mention was made earlier of the sand model prepared for the glider pilots with a wire and movie camera so that they were able to watch a film showing just how their landing would be. Something also had to be done for those aboard the warships.

The model for the warships providing heavy fire off Omaha Beach was made of rubber in sections about a foot square; it was sent to the commanding officers of the ships and had to be assembled onboard. Once assembled in a large shed or hangar, they were able to sit and look at it, getting a view of what Omaha Beach would look like from the sea in the cold, grey light of a summer morning. One of those involved recalled that, 'You saw the exact beach, including the background, as we would see it on the day. The security was intense, and even if a man went sick, he was sent to a special hospital ... which was under guard, and was not allowed to be removed.'[4]

Not everything was so advanced or sophisticated. During the two years prior to the landings, the British government had been assembling a vast collection of holiday postcards and photographs having asked for snapshots of beaches from Spain to Norway. The broad spread of locations was intended to ensure that no one knew where the invasion would take place. It meant that unit commanders were each given a sandbag in which they had copies of photographs showing families sitting on beaches, even building sandcastles, with important details such as seawalls behind. There were also recent aerial reconnaissance photographs and maps, with details such as the height of the seawall, the nature of the beach, whether it was sandy or pebbled, flat or sloping, the kind of artillery the Germans were believed to have, telephone lines, and the location of minefields and barbed wire.

NOTES

1. Imperial War Museum Sound Archive.
2. Imperial War Museum Sound Archive.
3. Imperial War Museum Sound Archive.
4. Imperial War Museum Sound Archive.

8

UNDER THE NOSES OF THE GERMANS

There is an old British Army adage that 'time spent on reconnaissance is never wasted'. For D-Day, the formal reconnaissance had to be provided for the army by the Royal Navy and the Royal Air Force. The army was helped by the French resistance, which was aided and armed by the British Special Operations Executive, SOE, and the American Office of Strategic Services, OSS. The French resistance was a substantial organisation, and in May 1944 its strength has been estimated at 100,000 personnel ready to take orders from General Koenig, head of the Free French Forces of the Interior, as well as between 35,000 and 45,000 *marquis*, who were armed, although many only had sufficient ammunition to fight for a day. The mainstay of the resistance's work was sabotage, frequently disrupting the railway system and communications.

RESISTANCE AND SABOTAGE

There were other forms of resistance and sabotage. One of these was the eighteen 'Cooney' teams, each comprising three uniformed French Special Air Servicemen who were parachuted into Brittany on the night of 7/8 June 1944 to cut railway links with Normandy, which prevented the German 3rd Parachute Division being moved to Normandy by train.

Teams of three seemed to be the ideal; there were also the 'Jedburgh' teams, unusual in that they, too, were all in uniform, each of which consisted of an Englishman, an American and a Frenchman. These were first dropped into France at the time of the Normandy landings, but follow-up teams were also dropped in France over the next ten weeks.

The members of the Jedburgh teams were drawn from the SOE and the OSS. Their role was to co-ordinate the work of the French resistance and the *marquis*, ensure that they worked towards fulfilling the Allied aims, and also act as a 'staff' for the resistance groups. This was important as there was considerable rivalry between resistance groups with differing political outlooks. The teams were kept supplied with arms and each included two officers and a sergeant wireless operator. Each member was trained in guerrilla warfare and sabotage. A total of ninety-three teams were dropped, and of the 279 personnel involved, twenty-one were killed.

A third element in gathering intelligence was the 'Sussex' teams, each of two men who were run by the Bureau Central de Renseignements et d'Action, OSS and the British MI6. The members were recruited from French forces who switched to the Allies after the invasion of North Africa and were trained by MI6. The first team was dropped in February 1944 and by the end of May there were thirteen teams, all of whom transmitted information about German movements around the time of the Normandy landings. In contrast to the Cooney and Jedburgh teams, the members of the Sussex teams did not wear uniform.

Before the landings, the main means of passing information and orders to the French resistance was through the news broadcasts from the British Broadcasting Corporation, BBC. In France, and indeed all of the occupied territories, only the elderly and children would be at home, with men and women expected to work as normal. Listening to the radio was banned, but families took turns and radios were hidden. Initially, it was the evening news bulletins broadcast at 1800 and 2100 that carried the information, but then shortly before the Normandy landings the message was received that they should listen in to the broadcasts twenty-four hours a day.

One family who had an SOE operative living with them and working on their farm installed a small radio in their hayloft in a farm outbuilding. As D-Day approached, the SOE operative and the family were reminded to listen in, and to wear working clothes, but also to make arrangements for those left behind, ensuring that they had enough food and could look after the farm animals. When the message was received that the armada had sailed, the villagers knew somehow and a small crowd assembled outside the farm outbuilding. The SOE operative and her comrades assembled and cleaned the weapons that had been hidden in beehives, waiting until the morning to allocate weapons to those they knew they could trust. Then the villagers went out to blow up railway lines and bridges, and to fell trees to block roads.

ON THE COAST AND OFFSHORE

Despite the inventiveness of the Allies, getting ashore safely also depended on having a thorough knowledge of conditions offshore – shallows, rocks and reefs could all pose a threat to the best-prepared landing force. In addition to these natural obstacles, there was always the possibility of coming across man-made obstacles, which could include minefields or structures placed under the sea to impede any seaborne assault. The problem was not new, not unique to Normandy nor even to the Second World War. During the First World War, the landings at Gallipoli had suffered because the British battleships were wary of drawing too close to the shore for fear of German mines.

In the attack on Dieppe discussed earlier, not the least of the problems facing the landing force was poor knowledge of the conditions ashore. Earlier in the war, half of the British and French shipping losses in the Norwegian campaign had been due to hitting rocks or floundering on shoals in uncharted waters.

For the Normandy landings, the solution was the creation of teams known as Combined Operations Pilotage Parties, or COPPs, whose members were sometimes known as COPPists. Their role was to find out as much as possible about conditions offshore and on the shore. Of necessity, the work had to be done in advance of the landings with the risk of detection by the Germans and, of course, that also meant blowing the landings' cover, alerting the enemy to where the assault would come.

Earlier experience in the war had shown that using a submarine for reconnaissance inshore was not enough. It could not detect tides or currents, or sandbars close to the beaches that could leave a landing craft, let alone an LST, stuck offshore, the vehicles and troops inside vulnerable to enemy fire and unable to wade ashore, or, even worse, driving or leaping off expecting to find shallow water only to sink beneath the waves. Would the beaches be able to bear the heavy weight of armoured vehicles? Would there be marshy areas? Samples of sand or shingle would be needed for analysis.

One of the first known attempts to handle this form of reconnaissance thoroughly was made in 1941, when the British were planning an assault on Rhodes. The navigating officer for the raid was Lieutenant-Commander Nigel Clogstoun-Willmott, RN, who quickly realised that surveying the beaches through a submarine periscope was insufficient. He went ashore and started to conduct a more thorough survey using a compass and a torch. His wanderings faced opposition, from the British Army, whose commanders were concerned that his reconnaissance would alert the Italians to the planned raid. Months of planning would be wasted and there would be a risk of heavy casualties or of soldiers being captured.

Nevertheless, Brigadier Laycock, the eponymous leader of Layforce as the raiding group was known, had on his team a Captain Roger Courtney, an army officer, and member of the Special Boat Section. Courtney trained Willmott in use of the Folbot canoe, a frail craft that could be folded. They set out in the Folbot from their mother ship, the submarine HMS *Triumph*, taking with them Tommy guns, grenades, infrared signalling equipment, and a flask with coffee laced with cognac. They paddled the canoe until it was a hundred yards offshore, at which point Willmott slipped over the side and swam ashore to survey the beaches and identify the sentries' placements. The first thing he discovered on reaching the shore was that rocky outcrops rendered the proposed landing place unsuitable for tanks. Altogether, despite having to lie low at times due to patrolling sentries, he gathered information on four landing sites and discovered a sandbar 15yd from the shore that could have proved a fatal trap for tanks as they rolled off the LSTs. On the fourth night, Courtney went ashore.

It must have been a big disappointment to the two men when the raid was abandoned, not because of any obstacles they had found but because of the German advance into Greece. Nevertheless, the exercise had not been in vain as their superiors were impressed by their work and after Combined Operations were established, in September 1942, Willmott was recalled to the UK to set up a training programme for future operations.

This was no small order. Willmott's first task was to train men not for Normandy but for Operation Torch, the Allied invasion of Vichy French-held North Africa. This was scheduled for November, leaving him with just eight weeks to select and train sufficient men. Their initial training ground was

Hayling Island, just to the east of Portsmouth on the Hampshire coast, but they were later moved to Largs in the west of Scotland. At first, the training was based on Willmott's experience in Rhodes, but over the next few months, with increasing experience and major invasions planned, the range of equipment and the variety of tasks expected of the reconnaissance teams grew.

By mid-1943 the range of equipment included a wet suit with reinforced elbows and knees so that the wearer could crawl when necessary. The suit also had buoyancy control and pockets and pouches. Rope-soled fishermen's boots were also worn. Equipment carried on each mission included a waterproof torch with a blue lens and a compass as well as a revolver in a holster and a fighting knife in a scabbard. A chinagraph pencil was attached to the waterproof suit by a short line and a matt white slate was provided for writing under water. There was a weighted line for measuring the depth of the water and a fishing line on a reel to measure the distance from the shore. For communication, there was an infrared signal lamp and a grenade that could be used to signal with an underwater explosion and a 'bong stick', a metal box containing a metal hammer attached to a rod, which could make a sound detectable by Asdic up to 12 miles away and which was more reliable than the signal lamp, which could be obscured by high waves.

There were also auger tubes for taking samples from beaches, and sometimes trowels were carried for the same reason, as well as bags for shingle, flares, emergency rations and a flask of brandy.

By June 1944 the COPPs had a total strength of 174, and apart from the HQ staff of fifty-seven personnel, there were nine parties with eleven or twelve men each. Not all of the parties were involved in the Normandy landings.

No. 1 COPP conducted beach surveys on the Normandy coast throughout the winter of 1943–44. On D-Day, its members led the British 1st Corps to Sword and Juno beaches, and crewed the X craft (midget submarines) mentioned in the preface as markers for the landing ships. No. 2 COPP manned landing craft navigation, LCNs, as part of the Normandy surveys. No. 6 COPP guided in AVREs to the designated beaches. No. 9 COPP manned a marker boat off Sword Beach on D-Day.

The remaining COPPs were not having an easy time while these units were engaged in preparing for or supporting the D-Day landings – they were deployed elsewhere, in the Mediterranean and in the Far East. D-Day did not mark the end of the line for the COPPs as they were also used for major river crossings, including the Rhine in 1945.

AERIAL RECONNAISSANCE

Aerial reconnaissance was not new – it dates from the Battle of Mauberge on 2 June 1794, although in truth this was more an air observation post providing information for commanders on the ground from a captive or tethered balloon. The American Civil War saw similar activity. True aerial reconnaissance really dates from the First World War. It was used by both sides. During the Second World War, it became clear that the ideal reconnaissance aircraft was a small, fast fighter, and special versions of the Supermarine Spitfire were used by the RAF. Later versions had a pressurised cockpit so they could fly higher and thus cover a wider area. By 1944 the best photographic reconnaissance aircraft was the de Havilland Mosquito, not a light fighter but a versatile twin-engined aircraft that had the speed of a fast fighter, but when used as a bomber could match many medium bombers for warload despite being much smaller. It was built of wood – a non-strategic material, and as a result was often known as the 'wooden wonder'. It was known to the USAAF as the F-8.

Having a good aircraft with excellent cameras was only part of the story. Aerial photographs had to be examined by highly trained photographic interpreters who could 'read' the images and assess what was happening on the ground or at sea. Photographic interpreters would hope to be able to identify decoys as well as the real thing.

Well in advance of D-Day, frequent photo-reconnaissance missions were flown over France, initially by the RAF but later also by the USAAF. Their work helped the Allies decide where to land, and what the obstacles were likely to be, as well as German defensive measures. Although special attention was paid to Normandy in the run-up to D-Day, it could not be the only area to receive attention as it was still important that Germans believe that the landings would take place in the Pas-de-Calais area. It was also important to cover the areas behind the beaches to see what reserve forces the Germans could move forward after the landings, and to identify targets for bombing or sabotage in an attempt to hamper the German response to the landings.

Of course, aerial reconnaissance was not one-sided, which is why it was so important that dummy landing craft were positioned around the south and east coasts of England to mislead the Germans.

1. 'Into the Jaws of Death' is the official caption for this image. The 16th Company of the US 1st Infantry Division head ashore to what became known as 'Bloody Omaha', the D-Day landing beach that saw the worst fighting and, of course, the heaviest casualties. The weather was still poor, and there was some way to go before reaching dry land. (USCG)

2. Preparations for Operation Overlord, the Normandy landings, involved the assembly of large numbers of landing craft of many different types, as this view of the quayside at Southampton shows. (IWM A23731)

3. The splendid frontage of Southwick House near Portsmouth, which became the headquarters for the planners as they prepared for the landings. It was the scene of many fraught discussions, not the least of which concerned the weather. (Wikimedia Creative Commons, photograph by Amber Kincaid)

4. Almost certainly Nazi Germany's best-known general and certainly one of the ablest, Rommel was given the poisoned chalice of having to fight off any invasion. Here he inspects part of the so-called 'Atlantic Wall' defensive system with other officers. He was to find much of it in poor condition. (German Federal Archive)

5. An official portrait photograph of *Generalfeldmarschall* Karl Rudolf Gerd von Rundstedt, the German C-in-C in the West. Rundstedt despised Hitler, calling him a 'Bohemian corporal' behind his back, but obeyed him and was accused of war crimes against civilians, and only escaped prosecution because of his age and poor health. (German Federal Archive)

6. General of the Army Dwight D. 'Ike' Eisenhower was renowned for his diplomacy and was seldom happier than when talking to his troops. This was a staged event, what would be called a 'photo call' today, showing him addressing American paratroopers early in the evening of 5 June. (Library of Congress)

7. For a man who could be a stickler for discipline, Montgomery frequently ignored the British Army's uniform dress codes, as can be seen here, but he also did so even on formal occasions. He is seen here after the advance from Normandy with his pet dogs, 'Hitler', left, and 'Rommel', right; in the background, by his caravan, is a cage of canaries. (Imperial War Museum)

8. General George S. Patton, known as 'Old Blood and Guts' to his men, seen here as a lieutenant-general, was one of the few American senior officers to have had frontline experience in the First World War. A highly valued commander, he was nevertheless highly controversial and at least twice came near to disciplinary action for striking soldiers suffering from shell shock. (US Army)

9. General Omar N. Bradley was Eisenhower's most trusted senior officer and acted as his 'eyes and ears' while Patton's deputy. Always loyal to Eisenhower, Bradley later took over from Patton. (US National Archives)

10. An official portrait image of Lieutenant-General Henry 'Harry' Crerar, the most senior Canadian officer in Europe at the time of the Normandy landings. Opinions of Crerar were mixed: Montgomery did not like him, but the Chief of the Imperial General Staff, General Sir Alan Brooke, later Field-Marshal Lord Alanbrooke, thought that he had done much to improve the Canadian forces in Europe. (Library & Archive of Canada)

11. Although not used at Normandy, *X-24* shows just how small the X-Craft midget submarines were. Two of these played an important role guiding landing craft to the beaches in the British sector, but the Americans turned down an offer of similar help. (Royal Navy Submarine Museum)

12. Actually in the water and running on the surface, this shows how little protection was given to the crew members on the hull, which was necessary if they were to 'con', or navigate, their craft. Not surprisingly, most of those responsible for navigational and guidance work off the Normandy beaches were swept overboard at least once. (Imperial War Museum)

13. A soldier's eye view of the approach to the beaches at Normandy. Clearly, the landings have already started. Obstacles on the approach to the beach can be seen, while it looks as if the landing craft has engineering equipment aboard, possibly an armoured bulldozer. (Imperial War Museum)

14. A packed landing craft approaches Juno Beach with soldiers from the Winnipeg Rifles aboard. Their troopship can be seen in the background. (Library and Archives of Canada)

15. In many cases, the approaching landing craft and disembarking troops were met with heavy fire. This German *Panzer* IV turret at Omaha Beach is just one example of the German defences. (German Federal Archive)

16. A convoy of LCIs, landing craft infantry, approaches the Normandy coast. Towed barrage balloons provide protection from enemy air attacks, but there is little protection from the weather, although the sea seems to have calmed somewhat, or from the dreaded German E-boats. (United States Coast Guard Service)

17. As the war progressed, the means of landing invasion forces became more sophisticated. This is HMS *Eastway*, a dock landing ship with a floodable stern to enable the launch of landing craft. (IWM A20411)

18. A Centaur IV tank, possibly operated by Canadian troops, crosses Juno Beach towing a 'Porpoise' sledge carrying additional ammunition. (Library & Archive of Canada)

19. An amphibious Valentine DD tank. The canvas skirts were supported by metal poles to enable the tanks, often known as 'floaters', to have sufficient buoyancy to reach the shore. The 'DD' meant that they had duplex drive, with a transmission system that enabled them to switch between using propellers in the water or tracks once on dry land. (Imperial War Museum)

20. An aerial shot of the battleship USS *Arkansas* underway. By this stage of the Second World War the battleship had been displaced in naval warfare by the aircraft carrier, but their heavy armament still proved useful in softening up enemy defences before an amphibious assault, and made it difficult for enemy forces to re-group afterwards if within the 20-plus mile range of the battleship guns. (United States Navy)

21. Fuel was essential, and the 'Pipeline under the Ocean', or 'Pluto', was one of the great achievements of the war. In fact, this is not Pluto at all, but a 'Conum Drum', around which the pipeline was wound and played out as it was towed across the Channel. There were two pipelines, known as 'Dumbo' and 'Bambi', running from Shanklin Chine on the eastern side of the Isle of Wight, initially carrying almost 4,000 imperial gallons (18,160 litres) of fuel daily. (Imperial War Museum)

22. Amphibious operations really needed amphibious vehicles, of which the American-built DUKW, usually known as the 'Duck', with six-wheel drive, was the most successful of the war years. Too small to act as a proper landing craft, it was nevertheless invaluable for crossing rivers. (Imperial War Museum)

23. Another amphibious vehicle was the Canadian 'Buffalo', described by one of those present as being like a tank without a turret. This photograph shows the 'Water Buffalo' carrying US Marines to land on the beaches off Tinian Island, near Guam, July 1944. (US Marine Corps)

24. After the landings and before the completion of the Mulberry harbours, this is the build-up of reinforcements and supplies. The landing ships could unload quickly, but lacked the capacity of conventional cargo vessels and also needed supplies to be on wheels for efficient landing. (Public Domain)

25. The view from the first wave of landing craft heading for Omaha Beach. This was the most fiercely contested of all the beaches in the Normandy landings, with defences that had been relatively unscathed by Allied bombing and German reinforcements inland not far from the beach. (Public Domain)

26. US troops struggle ashore on Utah Beach, by far the easier of the two beaches in the American sector. At this stage, they were not only at risk from enemy fire, or of blundering into deeper water if the seabed was uneven, but of being run over by their own landing craft as it became lighter and was swept forward by the sea. (Public Domain)

9

SOUTHWICK HOUSE – THE NERVE CENTRE

While the initial planning was conducted in London at Norfolk House, close to the main service ministries, the Cabinet War Rooms and the US Embassy, as preparations became more advanced, it was also essential to be close to the main ports. Southwick House in Hampshire had become the wartime home of HMS *Dryad*, the Royal Navy's School of Navigation at Portsmouth in 1941 after the dockyard area had been heavily bombed. In late 1943, it was chosen as the Advance Command Post of the Supreme Headquarters Allied Expeditionary Force and from early 1944 it was occupied by the leaders of the Normandy landings. Here worked Allied Supreme Commander General 'Ike' Eisenhower with his Naval Commander-in-Chief Admiral Bertram Ramsay, and the Army Commander-in-Chief General Bernard Montgomery, each with their own staffs.

Southwick House was convenient for Portsmouth, but not so close that it would suffer air raids; by early 1944 the heavy blitzes were past in any case and Portsmouth was sufficiently far west not to be troubled by the V-1 missiles that were landing haphazardly in London and Kent.

The Royal Navy obligingly moved HMS *Dryad* out of Southwick House and into the grounds, acquiring additional land from the owners.

THE COMMANDERS GATHER

With so much to prepare and the need to keep in touch with the Allied leaders, Eisenhower did not move to Southwick House until 2 June, taking residence in a large trailer caravan parked in the grounds and hidden by camouflage nets. He described it as 'my circus wagon'. His rare moments of relaxation consisted of reading westerns while lying in his bunk and smoking up to four packets of his favourite Camel cigarettes daily.

He also visited the troops. In general, he made a favourable impression, even on British troops, but not always. Hearing that there was friction in Southampton between British troops and their better paid, better fed and better clothed American counterparts, he addressed the British. All went well until he agreed that the American troops were indeed 'overpaid, over-sexed and over here' and followed this by saying that when the Americans got across the Channel, they would show the British troops how to fight. By all accounts, that night the blood flowed in Southampton!

Churchill was behaving in an eccentric manner at this time. In between flashes of brilliance and periods of leadership, in which he showed his ability to say the right thing at the right time and inspire, he would propose ideas that were simply eccentric. Some of these were his 'midnight follies', inspired, allegedly, by his late nights and considerable consumption of alcohol. He had had a special train formed for his own use, which he regarded as his 'advance headquarters', and moved around the Portsmouth area in it. This caused considerable problems for the Southern Railway's operations in a busy area. Portsmouth is just under 75 miles from London, and while regular trains were less frequent and much slower in wartime, the regular electric service from Waterloo still took under two hours, so Portsmouth could hardly be described as inaccessible. More important, there were many extra trains running for although the regular scheduled services used by ordinary travellers were reduced, many specials were run for the armed forces, as well as goods trains carrying fuel, supplies and equipment.

Eisenhower's famed diplomacy was to be put to the test. Churchill had famously described the 'Cross of Lorraine', referring to the Free French symbol and its leader, General Charles de Gaulle, as being the 'greatest cross he had to bear'. De Gaulle had proved to be extremely difficult for the British and Americans to work with. The Americans had tried to bypass him believing that after liberation he could turn out to be a dictator, and President Roosevelt had refused to discuss post-liberation civil government with him. Relations were inflamed further when de Gaulle discovered that the British and Americans had decided that civil administration would be carried out by the 'Allied Government of Occupied Territories', AMGOT, as elections could not possibly be held for some time after liberation. De Gaulle and his associates, meanwhile, had formed the *Comite Français de Libération Nationale*, CFLN, in Algiers, which on 3 June announced that it was to be the *Gouvernement Provisoire de la République Française*. Roosevelt forbade Eisenhower from dealing directly with de Gaulle, and he was permitted to work only with General Pierre Koenig, whom de Gaulle had appointed as commander of the French Resistance, which the Free French had named the *Forces Françaises de l'Intérieur*, or FFI. Eisenhower was also ordered not to trust Koenig with details of the invasion.

Churchill knew that he had to present a common front with Roosevelt, but had also urged him to work with the CFLN as the Allies would need the help of the French Resistance in the landings. It was also Churchill's view that the French 2nd Armoured Division, equipped by the Americans, should play a part in the invasion. Roosevelt agreed and the division was moved to England under the command of General Philippe Leclerc. It eventually formed part of General Patton's Third Army although it was not part of the Normandy landings.

The French leader had to be invited to the UK to be briefed on the D-Day landings for, as Churchill explained to Roosevelt, it would be 'very difficult to cut the French out of the liberation of France'. He sent two Avro York passenger aircraft (developed from the Lancaster bomber but with a different fuselage, unlike the post-war Lancastrian conversions) to fetch de Gaulle and his staff to London. Even at the last minute, de Gaulle almost refused to make the trip, despite Churchill sending a representative, Duff (later Sir Duff) Cooper. It was all done in great secrecy, but when they arrived at RAF Northolt, west of London after an overnight flight at 0600 on 4 June, a large RAF guard of honour was waiting and an RAF band played the *Marseillaise*.

No doubt de Gaulle carried the humiliation of French defeat with him throughout the remainder of the war, but he was also a difficult individual. The Allies suspected that the Free French harboured many Vichy spies, but it was also the case that time and time again de Gaulle had acted prematurely with little regard for security.

On stepping down from his aircraft and inspecting the guard of honour, de Gaulle was handed a gushing letter of welcome from Churchill, inviting him to lunch aboard his special train, skulking in a siding in a small station near Portsmouth, after which they would both go to Eisenhower's headquarters. Duff Cooper accompanied de Gaulle to see Churchill, thinking that the concept of an advance headquarters was 'perfectly absurd'. Churchill would certainly have been better at the heart of things in London. Possibly his reluctance to authorise a cross-Channel invasion (although he always insisted on using the term 'landing'), and then his excessive over-optimism once plans were laid, made him nervous and keen to be close to the scene of action. He actually wanted to watch the landings from a British cruiser, HMS *Belfast*, until King George VI pointed out that, as sovereign, he was commander-in-chief of all the armed forces and he had been told that he should not go, so Churchill could not go either!

Duff Cooper was dismayed when on arrival at the train he found that Churchill was accompanied by Field Marshal Jan Smuts, the South African general turned politician* and a Francophobe.

Churchill explained to de Gaulle that he wanted him to make a speech on the radio, but de Gaulle wanted to discuss the civil government of France. De Gaulle made clear that he was infuriated by Roosevelt's refusal to recognise de Gaulle's provisional government. What made matters worse was the Allied occupation currency produced by the Americans was not recognised by de Gaulle, a matter that the British and American governments had ignored, and which made the currency worthless. In fact, American troops referred to the poor quality banknotes as 'cigar coupons'.

Churchill enquired how de Gaulle could expect the British to act independently of the Americans, pointing out that the British could only liberate Europe because of the Americans: 'Every time we have to decide between Europe and the open sea,' thundered Britain's wartime leader, 'it is always the open sea that we shall choose. Every time I have to choose between you and Roosevelt, I shall always choose Roosevelt.'[1]

After that, the argument cooled down and they lunched. Churchill started by proposing a toast, 'To de Gaulle, who never accepted defeat,' to which de Gaulle responded with the toast, 'To Britain, to victory, to Europe.'[2]

After lunch, Churchill took de Gaulle to meet Eisenhower and Bedell Smith at Southwick House. It was important that Eisenhower and de Gaulle met, but the Supreme Commander, although his usual charming self, was preoccupied, not knowing whether to go ahead or delay because of the increasingly poor weather. Taking up Churchill's idea that de Gaulle should make a broadcast, Eisenhower showed the Frenchman the speech he was to make. Eisenhower had amended Roosevelt's suggested draft, but even so it meant that de Gaulle was to tell the French people to obey the Allies and not mention his provisional government. De Gaulle wanted to make changes, which initially Eisenhower agreed to consider, but on returning to London he was told that there was no time to make any amendments as the Joint Chiefs of Staff would need to agree them. De Gaulle then refused to address his people on the radio the next morning. He went further, and ordered the French liaison officers attached to British and American formations not to accompany them. Churchill received the news during a meeting of the War Cabinet and immediately exploded into a rage.

Anthony Eden, Churchill's Foreign Secretary, and de Gaulle's associate, Pierre Viénot, undertook negotiations between the British and French leaders, but to no avail. De Gaulle declared that Churchill was a 'gangster' and Churchill accused de Gaulle of 'treason at the height of battle', and even proposed to fly de Gaulle back to Algiers 'in chains if necessary'.

TO KILL, OR NOT TO KILL

One of the big questions that surfaced while preparations for the Normandy landings were in hand at Southwick House was that of assassinating key figures in both the German armed forces in France and amongst the Vichy French government. Obviously, German officers such as General Erwin Rommel and Field Marshal Gerd von Rundstedt were on the list, but so too were logistics experts who would control the movement of German reinforcements and supplies after the invasion. A list was drawn up at Eisenhower's request by his intelligence staff.

'The Chief of Staff has asked me to look at this,' wrote Charles Peake, a British political officer on Eisenhower's staff. 'And to advise him about suitable candidates to whom suitable attention might be paid, prior to, on and after "D" Day. On the German side, Stulpnagel, Rundstedt and Rommel look likely, but there may be some Vichy collaborators whose removal from the scene would assist.'[3]

Someone added a handwritten note to the document suggesting that while it might be an advantage if prominent Vichy figures were 'bumped off', it should be left to the Free French to decide what to do. Another senior figure, in this case from the British Foreign Office, Peter Loxley, thought that leaving the Free French to assassinate senior figures in the Vichy regime would be 'plain sailing', but advised against targeting senior German officers:

> If the proposal is that the Allies, if and when they capture Rommel should have him speedily put to death, rather than treat him as a prisoner of war, all sorts of large issues, such as our policy in regard to war criminals, at once arise. I am having the political issues urgently examined here.[4]

The British intelligence service's chief, Stewart Menzies, known at the time simply as 'C', made known his dislike of the plan and it was abandoned two days later by Victor Cavendish-Bentinck, the chairman of the Joint Intelligence Committee.

One of the Allied leaders' concerns was that the assassination of German officers could lead to reprisals against the French civilian population, possibly disrupting the French resistance cells at a time when they were most needed. There was also the very real fear that Allied prisoners-of-war could be targeted as a tit-for-tat response. 'C' also felt that the effect of the assassinations of German officers would not be worth the gamble, writing: 'We do not believe, however, their removal will have much, or indeed any, effect on the efficient functioning of so widespread and highly organised a machine.'[5]

The legality of such action was another point that weighed on Allied minds. So late in the war, with the end in sight at least in Europe, they did not want to be accused of being war criminals and find themselves classed as no better than the enemy. If the French resistance wanted to do something that rebounded badly on their fellow countrymen, so be it, but it was not for the Allies to be involved in what many regarded as an unpleasant way of fighting a war.

THE BATTLE OF THE WEATHER

No one can reside in the British Isles for any length of time, or indeed visit, without being unaware that the weather is unpredictable. Officially, it is described as a temperate maritime climate, but many might doubt the use of the word 'temperate'. The war had started with what many described as the worst winter on record, that of 1939–40. Such conditions inevitably spilled over into the near continent, and especially northern France, at its closest point is just 22 miles away from the south coast of England.

Late May had been hot, with temperatures of up to 100 degrees Fahrenheit (approximately 37.7 degrees Celsius) in southern England on the 29th. The meteorological team at Southwick House knew it couldn't last. The chief meteorologist was Dr James Stagg, a tall Scot who had been given the rank of group captain in the Royal Air Force. He had taken up his appointment with the not altogether welcoming Lieutenant-General Sir Frederick Morgan: 'Good luck, Stagg. May all your depressions be nice little ones, but remember we'll string you up from the nearest lamp post if you don't read the omens aright.'[6]

Eisenhower had been demanding that Stagg and his team produce three-day forecasts each Monday that were checked against the actual weather conditions as the week progressed. On 1 June, the network of weather stations showed deep depressions forming over the North Atlantic. Bad weather in the English Channel could be severe enough at any time, but the shallow draught landing craft would be especially vulnerable and *mal de mer* was a well-known hazard for cross-Channel travellers. But these travellers were not holidaymakers who could rest and recover once on shore; they were soldiers who would be fighting for their lives from the moment they left the landing craft or landing ships.

The planners were not just concerned about those at sea. The gliders and paratroops would be extremely vulnerable and could be blown off course by strong winds, while the necessary air cover and air strikes also depended on good weather, perhaps to an extent not always appreciated today.

Stagg's role was made more difficult by the presence of American meteorologists in his team, who were considerably more optimistic than their British counterparts, who knew the uncertainties of the British weather all too well. Mid-morning on Friday, 2 June, Stagg had to brief the assembled Allied commanders, including the newly-arrived Eisenhower, on the weather, and provide an update later in the day at which he would be expected to forecast the weather over the weekend so that those assembled could decide whether or not to postpone the invasion.

Late afternoon and early evening, Stagg was on the telephone contacting weather stations around the British Isles and beyond to Newfoundland on the other side of the Atlantic. He found, as he expected, that none of the experts he consulted could agree on the weather for the next twenty-four hours, let alone the agreed five day forecast sought by the supreme commander. His task was made all the more difficult because it was a beautiful evening, with what would be regarded as a late sunset, due to wartime double summertime.

Accompanied by his American colleague, Colonel D. N. Yates, Stagg addressed the meeting in the library at Southwick House at 1930.

'The whole situation from the British Isles to Newfoundland has been transformed in recent days and is now potentially full of menace'[5], he told Eisenhower and the other commanders. This seemed strange to many of those present given the beautiful evening. Eisenhower pressed further, wanting to know what the weather would be like for the paratroops and the glider-landed troops. When pressed for the likely conditions for 6 and 7 June, Stagg was forced to say that he could only guess, not advise. After the meeting, the two meteorologists were told that there would be no change of plan for the next twenty-four hours.

Early on Saturday 3 June, any optimism evaporated. Stagg's well-founded pessimism was justified when a weather station in the west of Ireland reported that the barometer was falling rapidly and the wind was already at force six. Yet, the meteorologists were still analysing the data to come up with different conclusions. Stagg had once again to address the supreme commander and the commanders in chief with their staffs at 1930.

'Gentlemen, the fears my colleagues and I had yesterday about the weather for the next three or four days have been confirmed.'[7] He then presented a detailed forecast through which Eisenhower sat motionless, his head slightly to one side, staring at Stagg. When Stagg had finished, Eisenhower recommended a provisional twenty-four-hour postponement, despite it being a calm, clear night in Hampshire.

At this moment, the strong security and censorship that had prevailed unravelled when Associated Press in the US issued a story that the Allies had landed in France. It was retracted twenty-three minutes later, but not before CBS and Radio Moscow had broadcast.

The news that the operation had been postponed for a day because of the weather had an impact on the men waiting to board the ships. The news reached Private Peter Fussell of No. 1 Commando at 1600 on Sunday:

We were given the reasons, the weather had broken and it was unlikely we would be landing for the next twenty-four hours. We were told that a decision would be made by midday on Sunday. After that, every man Jack, whatever your religion, went to church. It didn't matter what denomination you were, agnostic, atheist, Church of England, Roman Catholic, Presbyterian or Jewish, you stood in some church and someone blessed you.[8]

As the momentum picked up, there was a further meeting at 0415 on Sunday. The 24-hour postponement was confirmed. The convoys were cancelled and, leaving nothing to chance, those landing craft that could not be contacted by radio were rounded up by destroyers and sent back to shelter off the south coast.

Yet, as the morning passed, the clear skies continued, leaving poor Stagg unable to face his fellow officers at breakfast. It was with relief that he noticed the clouds coming in during the afternoon.

For the planners and, most of all, their commanders, the situation was on a knife-edge. Postpone for too long and the tides would be wrong. If the landings could not be mounted within forty-eight hours, a two-week delay would be necessary, and that would mean unloading the men from the ships. It would be impossible to maintain secrecy. Morale would plummet.

GO!

It was during the afternoon of Sunday 4 June that the meteorologists first noticed that the deepening depression in the Atlantic was slowing down. A gap was opening in the weather sufficient for the landings to go ahead. Just as the news of the impending bad weather contrasted with the calm and clear conditions prevailing in the area around Southwick House, the news about a break in the bad weather contrasted with the wild conditions as Eisenhower opened a further meeting at 2130 that Sunday. Rain was beating against the windows while a strong wind shook the trees in the grounds.

Landing craft and landing ships offer few creature comforts; they are far worse than a troopship and not meant to be occupied for long. A ship at anchor has a very uncomfortable motion, with the constant jerking of the ship's motion being checked by the anchor, and needs to be under way at slow speed to have any chance of competing with the sea conditions. Many of those at the conference, and especially the sailors amongst them, were well aware that conditions aboard the invasion fleet were far from ideal.

Against these conditions, Stagg had to tell his audience that the weather had suddenly changed again. It would improve on Monday afternoon, albeit briefly, but it should be long enough for the landing to go ahead. He was questioned about this.

The Naval Commander-in-Chief of the Naval Operation, Admiral Bertram Ramsay cut the discussion short by telling those assembled that if the operation was to go ahead on Tuesday, he had to issue a provisional warning within the next half-hour, on the condition that 'if they do restart and have to be recalled again, there can be no question of continuing on Wednesday'.

The Air Commander-in-Chief was concerned about visibility being good enough for his bombers and tactical strike aircraft. Eisenhower turned to Montgomery, asking if he saw any reason why they should not go ahead. 'No,' replied Montgomery. 'I would say – *Go.*'[9]

The decision had been so touch and go, so much in the balance, that the staff officers waiting outside with sheaves of orders each had two sets, one for go and another for a further postponement, to be signed by their commanders.

To Stagg's relief, early on Monday 5 June further meteorological reports confirmed that there would indeed be a break in the weather. At the morning conference, he was able to confirm the previous day's forecast. He noted in his memoirs that Eisenhower's smile returned. There was some further discussion, but not much, as once the decision was confirmed those present had other matters to attend to.

Before lunch, Eisenhower went to see the last troops embarking at South Parade Pier at Southsea, the resort area of Portsmouth in peacetime, its shingle beaches now closed off by barbed wire and concrete tank traps. Later, he was to go to RAF Greenham Common in Berkshire to see the US 101st Airborne Division board its aircraft, and for a photo opportunity for the press. Even while he was doing this, with his usual charm and ease with the ordinary soldier, Eisenhower must have been aware that the optimism of the meteorologists had not been shared by Leigh-Mallory, who was predicting 70 per cent casualties for the US paratroopers' dropping zone.

Yet, the die had been cast – it was too late to postpone the operation.

NOTES

1. Churchill, *The Second World War* (London: Cassell, 1950).
2. Churchill, *The Second World War*.
3. Assassination Priorities for Overlord, Public Record Office, Kew.
4. Assassination Priorities for Overlord, Public Record Office, Kew.
5. Assassination Priorities for Overlord, Public Record Office, Kew.
6. Stagg, J. M., *Forecast for Overlord* (London: Ian Allan, 1971).
7. Stagg, *Forecast for Overlord*.
8. Stagg, *Forecast for Overlord*.
9. Imperial War Museum Sound Archive.
10. Stagg, *Forecast for Overlord*.

* He was also the man who at the request of the First World War British government had investigated British air power and proposed an 'air service' in his report, which led to the formation of the world's first autonomous air service, the Royal Air Force, RAF on 1 April 1918.

10

CONFUSING THE ENEMY

All that had been done to mislead the Germans (*see* Chapter Four) about the location and the timing of the invasion could have been wasted had the Germans managed to locate the vast invasion fleet. With almost 7,000 ships of all kinds, this was the largest amphibious assault in history, and difficult to hide even in the open seas let alone in the far more confined space of the English Channel. This was in fact a very good reason for choosing Normandy rather than the even more confined waters of the Pas-de-Calais, which at its narrowest was just 22 miles wide. The Germans had radar, but no less important, the Allies had several ruses that would confuse the Germans until the landings actually started.

The first and most basic precaution was to prevent the *Luftwaffe*'s aircraft from spotting the invasion fleet. By this time, the RAF's night fighter operations had reached a degree of sophistication that would have been almost unimaginable at the beginning of the war or during the dark days of the blitz on British cities. The de Havilland Mosquito night-fighter was fast and equipped with radar, and capable of staying airborne for several hours, in contrast to the famous Supermarine Spitfire which was noticeably short on range, as, fortunately, were its German opponents. Mosquito squadrons were sent on patrol along the French coast ready to intercept and shoot down any German aircraft that might have taken advantage of the break in the storm to get airborne.

At sea, the fear was that German U-boats would mount a massive attack on the landing fleet from their bases in Brittany. Both the RAF and the

Royal Navy mounted anti-submarine patrols, the main force being that of 19 Group, RAF Coastal Command operating Short Sunderland flying boats and Consolidated B-24 Liberator maritime-reconnaissance aircraft. The group included Australian, Canadian, Czech, New Zealand and Polish squadrons alongside those of the RAF, and their patrol area stretched from the southern coast of Ireland down to the Brest Peninsula.

For some weeks before the invasion, another high performance British aircraft, the Hawker Typhoon, optimised for ground-attack using rockets, had patrolled the coasts of France and Belgium attacking German radar sites as far west as Brittany. This also helped to confuse the Germans over where the landings would be.

The RAF also mounted major radio jamming operations so that the frequencies used by the *Luftwaffe*'s night fighters would be unusable.

Next, the RAF and the Royal Navy simulated an invasion fleet approaching the French coast. Part of the RAF's contribution to this was Operation Taxable, in which the famous 617 Squadron, the 'Dam Busters', dropped 'window' (fine strips of aluminium) from their Avro Lancaster heavy bombers to simulate a large convoy on enemy radar screens approaching Cap d'Antifer, north-east of the major port of Le Havre. This is easier said than done, as the aircraft obviously could not remain in the air at shipping speeds, they had to fly back and forth to create the effect of shipping creeping towards the coast rather than aircraft approaching at around 200 miles per hour.

Squadron Leader John Shannon of No. 617 Squadron recalled Operation Taxable afterwards:

The object was for eight aircraft to fly in rectangular orbits at a steady speed of 200 mph at 3,000 feet, dropping out bundles of 'window' ... which once released into the air, gave a blip on German radar. Intelligence sources had calculated that the radar blips appeared every 12 seconds, so we had to drop our bundles of 'window' every 12 seconds. We would fly for 32 seconds ahead, turn onto a reciprocal course and fly for 30 seconds and turn again and fly ahead on a forward course for another 32 seconds and then turn again and fly 30 seconds back. The effect was that we were slowly, very slowly, moving forward. We had to fly line-abreast eight aircraft with something like a mile distance between them ... All the timing was absolutely synchronised so that we all got on our positions and started at the same time. In each aircraft were two pilots and two navigators, because the work was so concentrated that we had to have a break every so often. We had three additional people in the aircraft with stop watches, dropping window out at 12-second intervals – they'd drop a bundle out and as soon as it hit the airstream it would scatter and the blips would start coming through on the German screens. The operation tied up a tremendous amount of German reserves in that area. We would tell that they thought something was happening because we watched their guns on the French coast firing into the Channel, in the belief that they were lobbing shells into the middle of a landing force.[1]

The other part of the RAF plan was 'Operation Glimmer', in which Short Stirling bombers dropped window, this time off Boulogne.

At surface level, the Royal Navy had motor gunboats and motor torpedo boats towing reflector balloons, again off Cap d'Antifer, to simulate large ships approaching the coast.

There were other means of jamming radar, as Sergeant Jack Nissen, an RAF radar-jamming expert, recalls:

Two hundred ships were each equipped with two or three kilowatts of Mandrel jammers, which were used on that 'one-night-only' basis. When Eisenhower said 'Go', everybody on board their ships, wherever they were, threw this big master switch. Nobody had been told what the switch was but when it was thrown, the German radar operators saw some hash on that bearing. Hash can be caused by a faulty valve and I can imagine the German radar people on that night – they'd be sitting in their tiny ops rooms, cut off with just a telephone, dawn approaching, when all of a sudden the front end of their receiver goes on the blink. When that happens, you'd normally just give it a tap. If that didn't work and you were tired out and fed up and wait-ing to go off duty, you might say forget it for tonight, wait till the mechanic comes on duty, he'll replace the valve and everything'll be fine. If that's what the German radar people did say, they made a fatal mistake. Because at first light on the next morning, all the capital ships were in position, lying four or five miles offshore with their big guns. And by then it was too late.[2]

The other fear was that of a massed attack by U-boats based at Brest, which required the Royal Navy and the RAF to mount intense anti-submarine patrols. That such precautions were necessary was beyond doubt. Perhaps the best proof of this came from 19 Group, RAF, whose aircraft attacked no less than forty U-boats. A Canadian, Flying Officer Kenneth Moore, sank two U-boats within twenty-two minutes on the night of 7 June. The approved technique was for the aircraft to dive towards a surfaced submarine, the front gunner firing at the conning tower to disable the submarine's anti-aircraft defences and attempt to delay a crash dive, while the bomb aimer prepared to drop depth charges that would cripple or even sink the submarine. This could be dangerous, and it was not unknown for aircraft to be shot down by a U-boat's AA defences.

NOTES

1. Imperial War Museum Sound Archive.
2. Imperial War Museum Sound Archive.

11

THE GERMANS PREPARE

For the German soldier based in France, life was easy. Possibly only those based in the Channel Islands had a more comfortable war, except for the final months when they were cut off and food became very scarce – one German soldier in Guernsey maintained that he thought that he had been posted to a garden. Some described life in France after Dunkirk as being a 'conqueror's paradise', to the extent that officers on leave from the Eastern Front tried to get passes to visit Paris rather than spend their leave in Berlin, or any other German city, where the RAF and later the USAAF had become very active, the former bombing by night and the latter by day.

Industrial and military targets in France were not immune from attack, but life in the major cities was not so different from peacetime as the Allies did their best not to inflict civilian casualties. It was certainly better than living in a German city.

As shortages of luxuries and then necessities became more widespread, the Germans found it easy to acquire many items in France that had disappeared from the shops at home. One wartime photograph of a young naval rating from the battlecruiser *Scharnhorst* about to depart home on leave shows him burdened with parcels. Personnel going home to Germany on leave often carried boxes of fresh food, including meat, for their hungry families.

One reason for this relative abundance was that, despite the efforts of the resistance, many French people simply tried to get on with their lives as best they could. Most German commanders played their part by demanding that

their men behaved correctly. The irony was that, as the Allied air forces gradually gained control of the air and communications became ever more badly
disrupted to the point that farmers could not get their produce away to the
markets in the major cities, the German garrison took over as a major market.
Sometimes payment was in occupation currency, sometimes in cigarettes.

Many Germans in France from the Eastern Front thought that the troops
based there had grown soft. One senior officer noted that the troops had
done nothing other than send food home. He regarded France as damaging
the men's fighting spirit with its pleasant climate, wine and women.

Of course, everything depended on which arm of the forces one
belonged to. For *Luftwaffe* pilots flying from French bases over southern
England, life was as dangerous as in any war zone. The U-boat crews, who
had the advantage of the open seas once they took over French naval
bases, had to face the growing competence and strength of the Allies
in anti-submarine warfare, especially once they had broken the German
'Enigma' codes and could identify the position of the U-boat hunting packs.
For both these groups of men, life was precarious and could be measured
in months, if not weeks or even days.

Not all Germans were happy with the comfortable life in occupied France,
an occupation that by this point extended to the whole of France since
Vichy territory had been invaded when the Germans saw how quickly Vichy
resistance had crumbled in the face of the Allied landings in North Africa.
General der Artillerie Erich Marcks was the very model of a Prussian officer,
even to the extent of having a scar across his nose and neck. He was also
the commander of LXXXIV Corps, which defended the Normandy sector.
On one occasion at dinner in the mess, he waved away the whipped cream,
saying, 'I do not wish to see this again as long as our country is starving.'[1]

But Marcks was an exception.

EXPECTING AN ALLIED ASSAULT

The Germans may have been fooled about the exact landing spot, but it
was increasingly clear that an Allied assault would come sooner rather than
later. Although he still seemed to favour Norway as the Allied route into
Germany, even Hitler could not ignore the growing signs that something
was happening on the Channel.

Unrealistic as usual, Hitler was confident and hoped the Allies would come soon. He was certain that the Allied landings would be held by the Atlantic Wall, and smashed there, bringing the war in the West to an end, allowing him to transfer his forces to deal with the growing pressure on the Eastern Front as the Russians gained in confidence, competence and strength. Propaganda minister Joseph Goebbels encouraged his leader as well as the German population by taking the line that, 'They are supposed to be coming. Why don't they come?'[2]

Hitler remained willing to believe his own regime's propaganda, throughout the war. This may have been an inherent character flaw, or it could also have resulted from the fact that, apart from some well-publicised visits to the French coast and to Paris, he did not travel as extensively as the three Allied leaders, especially Churchill. He was also determined to hold on to as much territory as possible, so when his generals proposed making a strategic withdrawal, he resisted and was quick to accuse them of treachery or cowardice, if not both! Erwin Rommel, for example, one of his best generals, on realising that the German Army would be under pressure simultaneously in the west, in the east and in the south, in Italy, actually wanted Germany to withdraw from Italy to allow a better concentration of air and land forces on the other fronts. Rommel's view was shared by the Commander-in-Chief West, *Generalfeldmarschall* Gerd von Rundstedt, who also believed in Frederick the Great's policy that 'he who defends everything defends nothing'.

Many other officers, including Rommel, also knew that Hitler himself had written in his autobiography, *Mein Kampf* (*My Struggle*), that, 'When the Government of a nation is leading it to its doom, rebellion is not only the right but the duty of every man.'

THE ATLANTIC WALL

Like many Germans, Hitler believed that the so-called 'Atlantic Wall' stretched from Norway to the border between France and Spain. This was far from being the case. Apart from anything else, Germany did not occupy all of France until November 1942, by which time the resources for building massive new fortifications were in short supply. There were indeed strong fortifications in Normandy and the Pas-de-Calais, as well as around

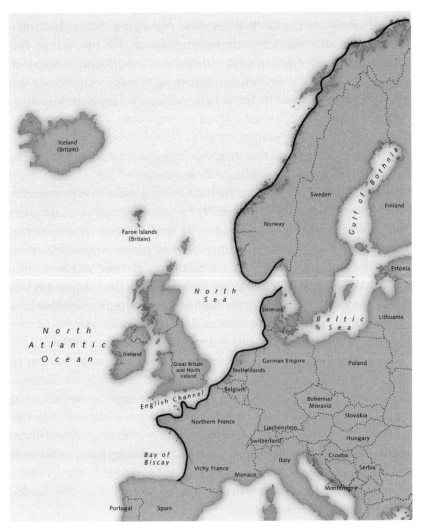

The Atlantic Wall as German propaganda liked to believe it to be. In fact, the Biscay coast of France was not occupied until late 1942, and Iceland was by this time garrisoned by the United States. The Germans lacked the manpower, materials and industrial capacity to have created a defensive system as comprehensive as this suggests. (from an original in the German Federal Archive)

key ports such as Cherbourg and Brest, but despite pleas from the army for much enhanced coastal defences, Hitler preferred instead to build massive new U-boat shelters. Like the French Maginot Line, the Atlantic Wall could be bypassed. Von Rundstedt viewed the Atlantic Wall as a cheap bluff and felt that Germany was mistaken in keeping so many troops in Norway, which, he believed, could be better defended by the navy given the heavily indented coastline and the difficulty of moving troops over the mountainous terrain. Others also wanted troops to be withdrawn from the Channel Islands, but Hitler believed that these would be immediately re-occupied by the British and used as a springboard for an assault.

In fact, much of the Atlantic Wall was nothing more than propaganda. When Rommel was given responsibility for preparing Germany's defences for the long-expected Allied invasion, he discovered many weaknesses, including much work that was incomplete. Manpower and materials were part of the problem, but so too were the effects of Allied bombing, which left much damage to be repaired. The famous raid on the Ruhr dams in May 1943 by the RAF's 617 Squadron, the 'Dam Busters', caused damage that took 7,000 workers to repair. These workers, and the materials used, could have been put to better use enhancing and completing the Atlantic Wall.

One of the best examples of Hitler's poor grasp of strategy was that he held to the concept of 'fortresses' which should be held to the last man, taking unnecessary losses. In Eastern Europe, as the Soviet armies advanced, the main fortresses were the capital cities, ports and major river crossings. In France, the fortresses were the main ports on the Channel and Biscay coasts. Dunkirk, Calais, Boulogne, Le Havre, Cherbourg, Brest, La Rochelle and Bordeaux, were all viewed as 'fortresses to be held to the last man'. Hitler had refused to allow any flexibility to his generals when they needed it most, fighting defensive battles.

The ugly truth was that Germany had overreached herself under Hitler. She lacked the manpower to fight a war on so many fronts, and lacked the industrial capacity, fuel and raw materials essential to all-out war. Generals in the field were constantly assured that as many as a thousand jet fighters would help to turn the tide of the war, and new rockets would bring British surrender. The generals were too wise and realistic to believe any of this.

DISILLUSIONMENT

Many of Germany's senior officers were by this time completely disillusioned with Hitler. When he had first come to power, many in the army viewed him with disdain. Although loyal to the regime in the sense that he did not believe he should be involved in politics, Hitler's Commander-in-Chief, West, *Generalfeldmarschall* Gerd von Rundstedt, referred to Hitler to his closest aides and friends as 'that Bohemian corporal', whom they regarded as an upstart. By contrast, Hitler had been warmly welcomed by the officers and men of the navy and, when it was unveiled in contravention of the Treaty of Versailles, which had banned it, by the *Luftwaffe*. Under Hitler, the navy ceased to be the *Reichsmarine*, or 'state navy', and became the *Kriegsmarine*, the 'war navy'.

Unlike Stalin, Hitler did not suddenly turn on his closest associates, and never felt the need to imprison their families to ensure loyalty and, most important, unquestioning obedience. Yet, his persistent interference and the refusal to take the advice of experienced and capable military commanders undermined their loyalty. Perhaps the most important point of all was the fact that many of them knew that defeat was inevitable while others realised that victory was no longer assured. They knew how crippling and humiliating had been the conditions imposed at Versailles, and not only did they not want to see the experience repeated, they dreaded what the vengeful Soviets would do. Hitler's rise to power had been given impetus by the fear of many Germans that the Bolshevik Revolution would spread to their country. They were not alone in this, as the same concerns were felt by many in other European countries, including the United Kingdom. But, unlike the UK, Germans had seen attempted Communist take-overs, not least in the post-war navy, where attempts had been made to establish workers' communes in a number of bases. In short, by this time many senior officers were fearful about the outcome of the war and the fate of their country and its people.

Even so, Hitler was not alone in being over-confident. The debacle at Dieppe may have taught the Allies many useful lessons, but it also gave many German officers the impression that they could repel any invasion. More widely, many German officers were simply anxious to be fighting again, to face the enemy and settle the matter once and for all. The more junior the officers, the more confident they were. For them, defeat in the previous conflict was history, a vague memory for some, but a wrong to be righted in the eyes of many. When Hitler had invaded Poland, many saw it simply as a case of restoring Germany's ancient lands.

Charged with improving the Channel Defences, the only part of the 'Atlantic Wall' that came near to meeting the requirements, Rommel knew that these defences could still be further improved. Once loyal to Hitler, Rommel had seen, and his morale had been undermined by, Allied air power in action in North Africa. It had been in North Africa that Allied air-ground co-operation came to maturity and achieved a hitherto unmatched level of efficiency and effectiveness. The same organisation had developed into efficient air cover over Italy, and Rommel suspected, rightly, that this would be seen again in the campaign for France.

Like most senior German officers, Erwin Rommel, by now a *Generalfeldmarschall*, expected the landings to be in northern France, within easy reach of air bases in the south of England. But where? The Pas-de-Calais was his favourite because it gave both the shortest sea route and then provided the shortest route into Germany, less than 300km (187 miles). It would also mean an early capture of the V-1 rocket launching sites and, if handled properly, offered the prospect of cutting off German forces from Normandy to Brittany and beyond.

The German Fifteenth Army was stationed in the Pas-de-Calais, the Seventh Army in Normandy. Rommel based his headquarters in the Château de la Roche-Guyon, between his two armies and overlooking the River Seine. A humane, cultured man, Rommel allowed the owners to retain apartments on the upper floors.

When he diverted his attention from Norway in the face of increasing evidence that France was the target, Hitler stubbornly argued that both the Pas-de-Calais and Normandy could expect landings, so that, whatever the outcome, he could insist to his generals that he had been right. While Hitler is believed to have suspected that Normandy was most likely, the *Kriegsmarine* ruled this out as they believed that landings could only be made at high tide.

Certain defensive measures were put in place in Normandy. These included the flooding of the River Douve to prevent airborne landings on its banks. In due course this would make it difficult for the Allies to link up the British and American sectors after the Normandy landings, but once over-come and bypassed, the flooding was to make it difficult for the Germans to reinforce their troops in the Cotentin Peninsula.

Rommel spent little time at his headquarters, leaving after an early breakfast on tours of inspection with just one or two officers. Briefings were held on his return in the evening, after which he dined with his chief of staff, *Generalleutnant* (Lieutenant-General) Hans Speidel, and his naval adviser, *Konteradmiral* (Rear-Admiral) Friedrich Ruge.

Though Rommel had a naval adviser, co-ordination between the German armed forces was poor. Indeed, there had been rivalry throughout the Hitler period, and constant attempts to catch the leader's ear. Steel that could have been used for warships was earmarked for 'tropical barracks', while Goering famously persuaded Hitler that he could finish off the retreating British at Dunkirk using air power alone, with the result that the tanks were held back until it was too late. Pressed by Rommel to bring all three services in France under a centralised control, Hitler refused. He was supported in this by Goering and Doenitz, heads of the *Luftwaffe* and the *Kriegsmarine* respectively. In any case, he preferred to be the one in control, which meant maintaining organisations that were rivals rather than collaborators. This is what was meant by the term 'the Fuhrer system'.

Speidel was a member of the resistance movement, led by *Oberst* (Colonel) Claus Schenk von Stauffenberg, who believed that Hitler's assassination was the only way of saving Germany. Many others, including Rommel, simply wanted a new leader.

DEFENDING FRANCE

The arithmetic of the German defences in France was as follows: the army had 120,000 troops in the north, while the *Luftwaffe* had around 350,000 ground staff. Despite this, the *Luftwaffe* could not defend the ground forces from Allied aerial attack, and would not let its anti-aircraft batteries defend army targets. These were Rommel's troops. His commander, von Rundstedt, led 1.5 million members of the *Wehrmacht*, but despite being 'commander-in-chief', he had no authority over the *Luftwaffe* or *Kriegsmarine*. Of his 1.5 million men, 850,000 were actually soldiers. This force included thirty-six infantry divisions, of which less than half had transport and mobile artillery and were given the role of providing coastal defence. By this stage in the war, quality varied considerably, and even included soldiers who had suffered serious wounds that would have seen them discharged or put on rear echelon base duties in the Allied armies. After five years of war, many of the infantry units had suffered heavy casualties and the spread of conscription to older and younger age groups meant that there were a high proportion of older and less fit men, and younger immature soldiers.

Faced with a manpower crisis within Germany itself, recruitment, which really meant conscription, had been boosted by troops from Luxembourg and the territories of Alsace and Lorraine, which had a history of being ruled by Germany or France depending on who had won the last war. The territories seized in the late 1930s and after the war began had also been scoured for those of German ancestry, the *Volksdeutsche*, from a wide swathe of territory from the Baltic States and Poland to the Black Sea. So '*Deutsch*' were these '*Volks*' that many did not speak German! There were also *Osttruppen*, Russian troops who had volunteered to escape the prisoner-of-war camps, and Poles, who were forcibly conscripted. These two categories represented around 20 per cent of the troops in the Seventh Army in Normandy.

This assortment, and especially the Russians, may have been officially *in* the German Army, but they were definitely not *of* the German Army and were still treated as inferiors, *Untermenschen*, subhuman, and often given tasks such as operations against the French resistance. Rommel certainly did not have a cohesive fighting force under his command as comradeship and team spirit were both lacking. It was not surprising that a number deserted and joined the French resistance, while others surrendered as soon as they could. German officers feared being shot in the back, especially in the heat of battle.

As a result of the selection of the best troops for the crack units, the *Panzer* and *Panzergrenadier* (mechanised troops) were strong and well manned. They were led by experienced officers, seasoned veterans of the war in North Africa. Only at the Battle of Kursk were the Germans able to mount a stronger *Panzer* force than that the British were to face at Caen.

It did not help that the best soldiers were absorbed by the *Panzers* or the SS, or by the *Luftwaffe*, which uniquely controlled Germany's paratroops. Even the *Panzers* could not be used without Hitler's approval.

This left Rommel in a difficult position. He wanted a forward defence to attack the Allies as they landed and before they could establish a bridgehead. A different view was taken by *Generaloberst* Heinz Guderian, inspector-general of the *Panzer* forces, and *General der Panzertruppen* Leo Freihe Geyr von Schweppenburg, both of whom believed in a strong armoured counter-attack. The *Panzer* units would be kept hidden in the forests north of Paris before the attack, meaning that the Allies would be able to establish themselves before the assault. Rommel believed that Allied air supremacy meant the *Panzers* would fail to have any impact on the battle.

In fact, with his experiences in North Africa and Italy behind him, Rommel was the most clear-headed of the German generals in northern France. He believed that the outcome would be decided within two days. He inspected the coastal defences and the coast, noting that one long curving bay was similar to that at Salerno, and in fact he had correctly identified the site of Omaha Beach. To augment the defences, the turrets of captured French tanks were fixed on top of concrete bunkers, where they were known as 'Tobrouks'. Rommel's asparagus were erected in areas identified as being most suitable for glider landings.

Nevertheless, there was one serious flaw in all of this activity. Improving the defences was given priority over training. Frequently poor German marksmanship was to be one of the pleasanter surprises awaiting the Allies.

Meanwhile, the *Panzer* units assembled in Normandy to support the Seventh Army included *Generalleutnant* Heinrich Freiherr von Luttwitz, whom Rommel trusted and who would, he believed, negotiate with the Allies given the chance. *Generalleutnant* Fritz Bayerlein commanded the *Panzer-Lehr-Division* and was also well known to Rommel having served in North Africa. There were also a number of SS *Panzer* units, including the 1st *SS-Panzer-Division 'Leibstandart Adolf Hitler'* and the 12th *SS-Panzer-Division 'Hitlerjugend'*, which were later joined by the 9th *SS-Panzer-Division 'Hohenstaufen'* and the 10th *SS-Panzer-Division 'Frundsberg'*, both of which transferred from the Eastern Front, doubtless to the great relief of the men involved. While the 12th *SS-Panzer-Division 'Hitlerjugend'* comprised fanatical young men prepared to die for the Fuhrer, the opposite was true of the 21st *Panzer-Division* commanded by *Generalleutnant* Edgar Feuchtinger. This was the unit closest to the Normandy coast, yet it had the obsolescent Mark IV tank rather than the newer and more capable Panthers and Tigers, also, a sixth of its personnel were *Volksdeutsche*, who, it was claimed by their commanding officer, 'could hardly understand orders and could hardly be understood by their NCOs and officers'.[3]

Feuchtinger was a known philander and a hard-line Nazi, disliked by his fellow officers. On the night of the invasion he was not at his post, but in Paris with his mistress.

INVASION!

Feuchtinger was not the only one absent on the night of the invasion. Ruge discounted an imminent invasion because of the weather and the Germans, lacking weather stations on the Atlantic, were told by their meteorologists that they could discount an attack until 10 June. Rommel therefore decided to return to Germany to see his wife and to visit Hitler to seek two more *Panzer* divisions.

History was repeating itself: Rommel had also been absent for the Battle of El Alamein, though on that occasion it had been because of illness.

Many others had the sense that something was coming. The increase in activity by the French resistance did not go unnoticed, and increased Allied aerial activity in France rather than over Germany was another sign that something was happening, or about to. Interrogation of a captured member of the French resistance also drew an admission that an invasion would begin within a few days. Of course, even the Germans must have realised that their often brutal interrogation methods would draw false information as the victim tried to appease his tormentors.

Despite the growing realisation that something was likely to happen, the *Kriegsmarine* did not send out patrols on the night of 5/6 June, largely due to the bad weather. The Allied minesweepers, proceeding abreast towards the Normandy coast, went unnoticed and unchallenged.

Yet another clue came when one of the so-called 'personal messages' broadcast by the BBC in code to the resistance aroused German suspicions. Rundstedt's headquarters sent out a general warning at 2115, but only in the Pas-de-Calais, Fifteenth Army territory, was an alert implemented. At the Château de la Roche-Guyon, Speidel and Ruge were throwing a dinner party.

Just as Speidel was getting ready for bed at 0100 on 6 June, he received the first reports of paratroops landing.

NOTES

1. Foreign Military Studies, United States Army Military History Institute.
2. European Theater Historical Interrogations, United States Army Military History Institute.
3. *Generalleutnant* Edgar Fuchinger, Foreign Military Studies, United States Army Military History Institute.

12

THE NAVAL ACTION

Operation Neptune was the largest ever undertaken by the Royal Navy. The largest maritime invasion in history required almost 7,000 ships of all kinds to land 75,215 British and Canadian troops and 57,500 US troops, a total of 132,715 men, plus armoured vehicles, artillery, motor vehicles and supplies, on the first day.

Some say that to those aboard the ships in this massive armada it *seemed* to stretch to the horizon, but the truth is that it almost certainly did, as once assembled at the rendezvous point at 'Piccadilly Circus', actually some miles to the south of the Isle of Wight rather than the centre of London, the assembled fleet covered 5 square miles of sea. There were more than 4,000 landing ships and landing craft, preceded by 287 minesweepers abreast clearing the English Channel ahead of the invasion fleet. Escorting the convoys, but not the landing ships and craft, were six battleships; four monitors, shallow draft ships with a heavy armament who would join the battleships in giving naval gunnery cover; twenty-two cruisers; 104 destroyers and another 152 escort vessels such as corvettes and frigates; eighty patrol craft, including anti-submarine trawlers and gunboats, and 360 motor launches. No less than 79 per cent of the warships were British or Canadian, while 16.5 per cent were American; the remaining 4.5 per cent were manned by crews from France, Greece, the Netherlands, Norway and Poland. The US contribution consisted not just of United States Navy warships, but also those of the United States Coast Guard, which in wartime passed from the

US Department of Transportation to the USN, although today its peacetime home is the Department of Homeland Security.

Even though the strength of the Royal Navy, Royal Canadian Navy and the United States Navy had increased massively since the outbreak of war, assembling such a vast armada was no easy task, and operations elsewhere were seriously affected. The most obvious change was the decision to postpone the invasion of the south of France until August, but less obvious was the suspension of a number of convoys for the Soviet Union. The navies concerned were stretched to the limit, especially as the war in the Pacific moved steadily towards Japan. Perhaps Stalin did not appreciate that this would happen when he insisted on a 'second front', but naval strategy was never his strongpoint.

THE ROYAL NAVY IN 1944

The period between the two world wars had not been good for the Royal Navy as, like most industrialised nations, the United Kingdom struggled through the years of the Great Depression. There were other factors at work. Before the First World War, the Royal Navy had been the largest in the world, although its vast colonial responsibilities meant that it was spread very thin in places. After the war, the Washington Naval Treaty of 1922 placed upper limits both on the total tonnage of warships allowed each nation, but also limits on each type of warship, such as battleships and battlecruisers, aircraft carriers, cruisers and small vessels. The Royal Navy suddenly found that the United States Navy was, officially and legally, to be its equal.

Unlike the British Army and the Royal Air Force, the structure and command of the Royal Navy was different, the Admiralty being both a government department and an operational headquarters, which would not simply pass instructions down the line through its various commands but which could, and when necessary did, communicate directly with the commanding officers of individual warships. Nevertheless, there was a fleet structure, the most important being that of the Home Fleet, successor to the famous Grand Fleet of the First World War, followed by the Mediterranean Fleet, which had been based on Malta until withdrawn to Alexandria when Italy entered the war. As the Mediterranean had effectively been cut in two when Italy entered the war, there had also, until the Italian surrender, been Force H, based on Gibraltar and which ranged freely between the North Atlantic and the western Mediterranean as required. There had also been squadrons based in the Caribbean and South Atlantic, as well as India, while the China Station, which became the Eastern Fleet in December 1941, had been eliminated by Japan's entry into the war. Nevertheless, as the Battle of the Atlantic eased, the Royal Navy had established its most powerful fleet, and the most balanced in terms of types of ships, in the British Pacific Fleet, which helped the United States Navy carry the war to Japan.

There were six home commands: Orkney and Shetland; Rosyth, on the northern shores of the Firth of Forth in the east of Scotland; The Nore, in the Thames Estuary and based on the naval port and dockyard of Chatham; Dover, the newest, dating only from October 1939; Portsmouth; and, at Plymouth, Western Approaches. The latter was moved to Liverpool, partly because of the difficulties of operating out of Plymouth under attack from the *Luftwaffe* and E-boats, and partly because it was more central with many convoys heading to and from the Bristol Channel ports, Liverpool, or Glasgow.

Dover, which not only guarded the Straits of Dover but was also responsible for the evacuation of British and French troops from Dunkirk under Operation Dynamo, and then controlled the Normandy landings, was subjected not so much to German air raids as artillery fire. Many of its peacetime population was evacuated, but without the cross-Channel ferries, on which so much of the town's employment was based, their peacetime occupations would also have disappeared.

Despite the economic difficulties of the 1920s and 1930s, the Royal Navy had 129,000 men, of whom 12,400 were Royal Marines, in 1939 and this could be augmented by a further 73,000 men from the Royal Naval Reserve and the Royal Naval Volunteer Reserve. By mid-1944, the Royal Navy had reached its all-time peak strength of 863,000 personnel, of whom 73,500 were members of the Women's Royal Naval Service.

The size of the Royal Marines grew rapidly during the war to form a division of three brigades as well as anti-aircraft batteries and the Royal Marine Fortress Unit. All of this was belated. After the First World War, the Royal Marine Light Infantry, sometimes known as the 'Red Marines' because of their uniform, were merged with the Royal Marine Artillery, sometimes known as the 'Blue Marines' for the same reason. The Admiralty established a committee, the Madden Committee, which recommended in 1923 that in addition to the traditional role of the Royal Marines in manning the aft turrets of major warships, providing bandsmen and officers' mess-men, they should be formed into an amphibious warfare force and also a mobile force for defending bases overseas. Nothing was done until after war broke out. After the Royal Marine Division was deployed for the invasion of Madagascar, it was disbanded and its brigades gradually became the forerunners of today's Royal Marine Commandos.

By 1944, the Royal Navy was well on its way to its war-end strength of sixty-one battleships and cruisers; fifty-nine aircraft carriers; 846 destroyers, frigates and corvettes, all of which could be covered by the catch-all term 'escort vessels'; 729 minesweepers; 131 submarines; 1,000 minor naval vessels, including trawlers and drifters adapted for patrols, and 3,700 aircraft. Many of the aircraft carriers were the small auxiliary or escort carriers, most of which were supplied by the United States under Lend-Lease.

The fleet included a number of types of vessel no longer in service today. The large battleships with their 14in, 15in or 16in guns, so useful for bombarding targets ashore, were augmented by the much smaller monitors, again with 15in guns but they were smaller and so had a shallow draft, allowing them to operate closer inshore. Two of these were of wartime construction, HMS *Roberts* and *Abercrombie*, of 8,123 tons displacement and each equipped with two 15in guns, rather than the battleship maximum of eight, eight 4in guns, which could also be used as anti-aircraft weapons, and multi-barrelled anti-aircraft pom-poms, known as 'Chicago pianos' to the men of the fleet. Another two, HMS *Terror* and *Erebus*, dated from 1916, and were slightly smaller but still had two 15in guns and eight 4in guns. *Roberts* and *Abercrombie* were off the British beaches while *Erebus* was off Utah Beach.

The bombardment group consisted of the elderly battleships HMS *Warspite* and *Ramillies*, as well as twelve cruisers and thirty-seven destroyers. In reserve were the battleships *Rodney* and *Nelson*, with their 16in guns, and three cruisers. The heavier calibre guns did not simply fire a heavier shell, their range was also greater. Nevertheless, the last British battleship class introduced before the war was the King George V-class, with just 14in guns. A shell from a 15in gun weighed more than a ton and had a range of more than 20 miles (32km).

The Washington Naval Treaty had stipulated that heavy cruisers should have 8in guns, while light cruisers 6in guns – the total tonnage of the ships was not a factor. Nevertheless, prominent amongst the ships off the Normandy coast was the cruiser HMS *Belfast*, now preserved in the Pool of London, which, with her sister Town-class ships, was classified by the Royal Navy as a 'heavy cruiser' despite having 6in guns. Admittedly, with their sheer tonnage, and the impact of twelve 6in guns fired at once in a broadside, *Belfast* and her sisters could do a great deal of damage, but they did not have the range or 'punch' of an 8in shell.

It had been a bad war for the battleship. The Royal Navy's aerial attack on the Italian fleet in its main forward base of Taranto on the night of 11/12 November 1940 had seen three of Italy's six battleships put out of action, proving that the aircraft carrier was the new capital ship. The Japanese attack on the US Pacific Fleet at Pearl Harbor a little more than a year later reinforced this message, while the major sea battles of the Coral Sea and Midway in 1942 were the first in which the opposing fleets did not see each other. The Japanese tried to make use of their battleships at Leyte Gulf, but once again air power was the dominant force. By the time of the Normandy landings, the role of the battleship was to provide heavy bombardment of fortifications and other targets ashore, and anti-aircraft fire to protect the aircraft carriers.

THE UNITED STATES NAVY IN 1944

The Washington Naval Treaty of 1922 had decreed that the size of the United States Navy was to be the same as that of the Royal Navy, which had been the world's largest before the First World War, albeit thinly spread. Even before the First World War, the United States Navy had grown beyond a coastal protection force. During the late nineteenth century and the early twentieth the service started a programme of expansion and modernisation, and was able to operate globally, so that by the time the United States entered the First World War in 1917, it was one of the most modern and powerful navies of the day.

On America's entry into the Second World War, the United States Navy was organised into three fleets, of which the most powerful was the US Pacific Fleet, based on San Diego, California and Pearl Harbor in Hawaii. The Asiatic Fleet was based on Cavite in the Philippines, while the Atlantic Fleet was based on Norfolk, Virginia. The Atlantic Fleet was strengthened following the outbreak of war in Europe, and even before the US entered the war, its naval forces started to escort convoys as far as a mid-Atlantic dividing line, ostensibly to protect neutral shipping.

Much has been written about the Japanese surprise attack on the Pacific Fleet at Pearl Harbor, but the Asiatic Fleet also suffered at the hands of the Japanese, and the resulting decision to create a hastily conceived and poorly equipped ABDA (American, British, Dutch, Australian) Command did little to stop the Japanese advance across the Pacific. Nevertheless, by the Battle of the Coral Sea in May 1942, which consisted of carrier-to-carrier warfare, it was clear that the Japanese could be checked; the Battle of Midway in June, in which the Japanese lost four aircraft carriers in a single day, showed that Japan had no hope of winning the war.

Before the war started, the United States Navy had created a strong air element with aircraft carriers, some of which were very large, operating aircraft that were far superior to those in service with the Royal Navy at the time, and also had a strong submarine arm, albeit plagued at first by problems with torpedoes. Amphibious warfare developed quickly, and by 1944, the USN was driving the Japanese back across the Pacific using airpower and amphibious warfare, while also using its submarines to cut the essential supply lines carrying fuel, rubber and food from the conquered territories to the Japanese home islands.

The strength of the USN had grown from 160,997 personnel in 1940 to more than double by the time of Pearl Harbor. By June 1944, it had 2,981,365 members, to which can be added the 472,380 serving in the United States Marine Corps mainly in the Pacific, and 169,258 members of the United States Coast Guard, who came under USN control in wartime. There were 1,099 ships in 1940, and 46,032 by 1944.

CLEARING THE WAY FOR D-DAY

Most of the minesweepers used to prepare the way for the landing fleet were of the Royal Navy's Bangor-class, with a displacement of 672 tons and a complement of sixty men. They were capable of up to 16 knots. Armament consisted of a 3in gun and one 40mm cannon, as well as four .303 machine guns. Clearly, such ships had little chance of standing up to a German destroyer had they come upon one, but the Allies had never lost naval supremacy in the war against Germany, which had lost many of her all too few destroyers in the two naval battles at Narvik in 1940.

The navies of the day knew how to sweep contact mines, and the Royal Navy had discovered a means – degauzing – of protecting ships from magnetic mines, but acoustic mines, that reacted to the sound of ships' propellers or machinery, were more difficult to deal with. Worst of all were the new pressure mines, known as 'oysters', which responded to the increase in water pressure when a ship passed over them. Acoustic mines could be set not to explode the first time a ship passed, but wait for the second or third ship, all of which made mine clearance more difficult.

Not all of the minesweepers were British, there were many American minesweepers, and on the afternoon before the landings, at 1757, one of these ships, the USS *Osprey*, discovered just how necessary minesweeping was for the landing force. The *War Diary* of Mine Squadron 7, part of Force U covering Utah Beach, tells the tale:

USS *Osprey* (Lt Charles Swimm, captain) was struck by an underwater explosion, under forward engine room; explosion is believed to be from a moored contact mine. Position 50 degrees 12.9N, 01 degrees, 20.4W – about 35 miles south of the Isle of Wight. USS *Chickadee* came alongside *Osprey* to assist. Fire that broke out onboard *Osprey* was under control in 3 to 5 minutes and extinguished in 10 minutes ... In view of the list and irreparable damage and lack of watertight integrity, as a result of the blast, the order to abandon ship was given at 18.15. *Chickadee* took all survivors onboard. (Casualties were six dead, twenty-nine wounded.)[1]

Such a loss in broad daylight and 20 miles north of where the nearest enemy minefield was charted was a sobering warning of what might lie ahead.

Potentially the most serious mine casualty was the Royal Navy's Queen Elizabeth-class battleship HMS *Warspite*, a veteran of the First World War that had seen action at Narvik during the Norwegian campaign in 1940, and later at the Battle of Cape Matapan. This mighty warship, with a full load displacement of 36,450 tons and eight 15in guns, had been repaired in the United States after being damaged at Matapan, and then operated in the Far East before returning to Europe for the Mediterranean landings, but was not fully repaired after being struck by a glider bomb off Salerno. She was given an important part in the Normandy bombardment, hit a mine which damaged her propulsive system to the extent that when needed for further bombardment duties, at Brest, Le Havre and later at Walcheren, she had to suffer the indignity of being towed into position by tug. Even then, her 'X' turret, one of her two aft turrets, was inoperable.

A total of 195,701 seafarers took part, naval personnel and men from the Allied merchant navies, actually outnumbering the men landed ashore.

All in all, the vast armada consisted of 1,213 warships; 4,126 landing ships and landing craft; 736 ancillary ships and 864 merchantmen, many of them the US-built 'Liberty' ships that could be built from prefabricated sections in as little as five days. The Admiralty had originally estimated that 467 warships would be required, but this number was increased as the scale of the invasion became clear.

Overall command of this vast armada was given to a British naval officer, Admiral Sir Bertram Ramsay. His signal to all the ships under his command summed up the situation, and the task, perfectly:

> Our task in conjunction with the Merchant Navies of the United Nations, and supported by the Allied Air Forces, is to carry the Allied Expeditionary Force to the Continent, to establish it there in a secure bridgehead and to build it up and maintain it at a rate which will outmatch that of the enemy. Let no one underestimate the magnitude of this task.
>
> Special Order of the Day, 31 May 1944 by Admiral Sir Bertram Ramsay KCB, KBE, MVO, Allied Naval Commander-in-Chief.

The absence of aircraft carriers did not mean that naval aviation did not play a part. At any one time, a number of the Royal Navy's Fleet Air Arm squadrons would be based ashore, often under the control of RAF Coastal Command, and in 1944 squadrons such as No. 811 NAS, equipped with Fairey Swordfish torpedo bomber biplanes, played a part in protecting the Normandy convoys from German U-boat attack. Amongst the United States Navy squadrons, Cruiser Scouting Squadron Seven, VCS-7, also went ashore and, instead of operating Curtiss SOC Seagulls spotting for the fleet during the naval bombardment phase, 'borrowed' Supermarine Spitfires for the same role, flying out of airfields in the south-west of England.

Several years into the war, the standard of aircraft recognition was still so poor that to prevent British and American aircraft over the Normandy area from being shot at by Allied anti-aircraft gunners, they were painted in 'invasion stripes', that is, the wings and rear fuselage had black and white stripes painted to show clearly that they were Allied aircraft.

HEADING FOR THE SHORE

The convoys bringing the ships from the ports of embarkation, many of them from beyond Land's End, the very tip of Cornwall, had to converge on an area south of the Isle of Wight, naturally enough referred to as 'Piccadilly Circus'. The major naval vessels had come furthest, from the Royal Navy's wartime forward fleet anchorage at Scapa Flow in Orkney, to the north of the mainland of Scotland. These included the elderly battleship HMS *Ramillies*.

No one aboard this vast armada knew whether the Germans were waiting for them or not. The debacle at Dieppe preyed on many minds, while others, just a few, knew what had happened at Slapton Sands. The Germans' reputation for invincibility may have died in the Western Desert, but in an invasion, which is what it was, no matter what Churchill liked to say, the advantage usually lay with the defenders.

German naval power was also an unknown. The two battlecruisers *Scharnhorst* and *Gneisenau* and the heavy cruiser *Prinz Eugen* had been withdrawn from France, but the U-boats remained, as did the E-boats. Attack from below the sea or from small, fast, difficult to hit E-boats was feared more than a naval battle between capital ships and cruisers.

These concerns were valid, but Admiral Ramsay had ensured that these were addressed and, as mentioned earlier in Chapter Ten, the RAF had joined the Royal Navy in extensive anti-submarine patrols. *Grossadmiral* (Admiral of the Fleet or Fleet Admiral) Karl Doenitz, the former head of the *Kriegsmarine*'s U-boats, who was now in command of the service, and who had argued the case for more U-boats before the war, was to be shamed by the fact that not one U-boat penetrated the defences to reach the invasion force.

It was important that the landing ships and landing craft should reach the part of the Normandy coast where they were to land. Matters of command and control were simplified by the establishment of British and American sectors: the British took the eastern sector and the beaches designated Gold, Juno and Sword; the Americans took the western sector and Omaha and Utah beaches. The British sector also included a substantial Canadian force destined for Juno Beach. The disposition of the British and American sectors was dictated by the locations of their troops' bases in England. Some argue that the Americans would have been better equipped to take the eastern sector and the British the western, but that would have complicated an already difficult and demanding convoy system for the landings. Swapping the troops around before embarkation would have avoided this, but created problems of a different kind, stretching transport and logistics resources at a time when everyone was preparing for the cross-Channel assault, and even creating enough of a commotion to have put security at risk.

SHOWING THE WAY

Not everyone could wait until the night of 5/6 June to cross the Channel. Getting the mass of landing ships and landing craft to the right beach was no easy task. Once clear of the rendezvous, the ships headed for the five invasion beaches but, as mentioned in the preface, guidance was necessary, and this came from the crews of midget submarines, the 'X' boats. These craft usually had a crew of four, two officers and two ratings, and when used offensively, they would all be divers capable of fixing mines to the hulls of enemy warships. For Neptune, the officers were drawn from amongst the best of the Royal Navy's navigators.

The men aboard these small craft left what was then the Royal Navy's main submarine base at Gosport, HMS *Dolphin*, just across the harbour from the major naval base of Portsmouth, late on Friday 2 June. They cleared the Isle of Wight, towed most of the way by converted trawlers, and crossed the 80 miles to the coast of Normandy, and once in position submerged and spent the daylight hours sitting on the seabed, just off shore. On Sunday night, the midget submarines surfaced and dropped anchor once in their marking position. Those aboard *X-23* watched as a lorry dropped a crowd of German soldiers who then played a game of volleyball on the shore, unaware that they were being watched, or of what the future held for them.

The midget submarines were part of Force S under Rear-Admiral A. G. Talbot, RN, the assault force for Sword Beach. In wartime, the normal navigational aids were not available, and nor were the ships' pilots, experienced seafarers who would bring ships safely into, and out of, a major port, or take them through a difficult channel, augmenting the ship's own officers. Elsewhere, including operations off North Africa, the Royal Navy had positioned submarines with a shaded light pointed seawards to guide war-ships safely towards their designated positions. For the Normandy landings, midget submarines were used, the famous 'X-Craft', as in the Alten Fjord the previous September against the German battleship *Tirpitz*.

It was necessary to use the small and vulnerable midget submarines as larger submarines would have been spotted easily once on the surface, and, in an area with many natural and manmade obstacles, would have been at risk of grounding or collision.

Two midget submarines, *X-20* and the aforementioned *X-23*, were deployed in the British sector to ensure that the landing craft and landing ships headed for the right position and did not land troops and vehicles in the wrong place. They had to fix their positions accurately by daylight and then submerge, lying on the seabed until the invasion fleet approached, when they were to surface and show shaded lights to seaward. Submarines had never been used to provide guidance for the attackers in such shallow water and so close to an enemy-held shoreline, which was also the most heavily defended anywhere. The task was not without its privations. Even today submarines are neither spacious nor comfortable, but midget sub-marines went beyond spartan. Once submerged, the only air inside was that taken down within the submarine as it dived. Lying low in the water, without a conning tower or fin, even in reasonable sea conditions midget submarines tended to ship water easily, but in bad weather, the small crew of just four men were soaked. There could be so much water aboard that it had to be pumped out, by hand. Added to which, all of the officers aboard both submarines had been swept overboard in the stormy conditions and returned aboard with considerable difficulty, soaked.

These airless and damp conditions had to be endured for nineteen hours a day so that the submarine would not be spotted on the surface during the long daylight hours of summer. Both submarines had two officers aboard, the commanding officer and a specialist navigator, so important was accuracy. *X-23* was the senior vessel, commanded by Lt J. B. Honour, RNVR, with navigational specialist Lt L. J. Lyne, RN. Had the invasion gone ahead as planned on 5 June, there would have been just a few hours to wait, but the day was spent on the seabed. These small craft also had to remain in position after the initial landings until more permanent naviga-tion aids could be positioned.

Lt Honour recorded:

We hoisted our radio mast and got a signal that the invasion had been postponed, so then we had to retreat to the bottom again and wait until Monday night. That night we surfaced and received a message that the invasion was on. So we went back to sit on the bottom and at about 04.30 on Tuesday, 6th June, we surfaced again, put up all our navigational aids: 18-foot telescopic mast with a light shining seaward, a radio beacon and an echo sounder tapping out a message below the surface. This was for the navigational MLs [mine-layers used to guide the fleet] to pick up as they brought the invasion in.

Our particular operation for D-Day was called 'Gambit'. When we looked it up in the dictionary, much to our horror it said the pawn you throw away before the big move in chess, which didn't encourage us too much.[2]

Once their duty was over, the two X-Craft went alongside the headquarters ship *Largs*, where the crews were described as 'all in' and treated for exposure and exhaustion before their craft were towed back to England. Their role had been vital to the success of Overlord and once completed there was no need for ships to be guided in what had become, in maritime terms at least, a well-worn path to the invasion beaches.

'So ended an exploit of fine courage and no ordinary hazard and endurance,' reported Rear-Admiral Talbot, who was well placed to appreciate the value of the submariners and their hardships. 'The weather was such that all officers were washed off the casing [deck] at one time or another and much water was shipped, which necessitated continued pumping. Sixty-four out of seventy-six hours were spent submerged in this small craft.'[3]

The variety of the naval vessels assembled for Overlord was unprecedented. The Allies had realised that using converted merchant or naval vessels was not adequate for an opposed landing, and so a wide variety of landing ships had been developed. At the bottom end was the LCI, which could run onto the beaches enabling infantrymen to splash ashore; at the upper end was the LST, which could launch tanks into the shallow waters close to the coast; in between these two extremes were other craft carrying vehicles and artillery. Some of the landing craft were taken over and modified to fire artillery rockets offshore against the German defences, augmenting the heavy naval gunnery of the battleships and cruisers, and that of the coastal monitors, small ships with a shallow draft and heavier armament designed to provide covering fire.

Minesweepers were necessary not just for the passage across from the south of England, ensuring that a swept channel was provided, but also before the invasion off the shores of Normandy. Midget submarines were to act in the place of the normal navigational buoys, removed in wartime, and guide the invasion force towards the shore. Other naval vessels were deployed on the flanks of the invasion force to stop any attack by German coastal forces, such as the dreaded E-boats, fast motor gunboats or torpedo boats, or even submarines.

Each of the five beaches had its own fleet, a wide cross-section of warships and ships used for invasion, carrying troops in landing ships down to landing craft.

Further preparations were necessary before landing on the beaches at H-hour. The troops arriving aboard the landing craft would need to be shown the way off the beach to reduce their time exposed to German fire on the beach. The Royal Navy Commandos were given the task of landing to set up signs and indicators for the main assault force. One of their landing craft was hit before it reached the beach, its ramp blown down so that it dropped below the bows, forcing those aboard to disembark by the stern, dropping to the rough seas. They were none too pleased as they had spent weeks training for the landing on windswept beaches in Scotland.

On coming ashore, they were met by the discouraging sight of bodies being swept in and out with the waves, and hastened to seek shelter in the sand dunes.

Reaching the beaches was an ordeal in itself. The Germans had placed obstacles along the coast, tetrahedral steel posts with shells and mines attached. A number of landing craft had been modified with twenty-four 60lb spigot bombs so that they could blow up the beach obstacles at half-tide. Immediately behind them came the LCTs carrying tanks with flails, which would clear the beaches of any mines to allow infantry to follow them ashore. The landing craft heading for the beach obstacles sailed in under a heavy destroyer bombardment, but at H-hour minus one minute, the bombardment lifted and the landing craft let go their spigot bombs. Within seconds the air was rent with massive explosions.

It seems that not all of the beach obstacles could be cleared in time for the landing force. For the beach master, a naval officer responsible for operations ashore and ensuring that the beaches were cleared quickly, the priority was to dismantle the Rommel's asparaguses, each of which had an unhealthy 88mm shell on the end. Able Seaman Ken Oakley, a Royal Navy Commando, later wrote:

> All around the sea was one mass of craft, landing craft of all kinds, shapes and sizes. A lot in our immediate area were LCAs because we were going for the initial assault. There was a good feeling as we went forward, except that most of the army was seasick. I wasn't very happy myself. However, when we got within sight of the shore we were getting splattered with light gunfire, nothing very heavy at this moment. Finally, we got within sight of the stakes, the dreaded stakes, with the shells and mines on, which protected the beaches. Our coxswain did a marvellous job. We were headed straight for this stake and I could see the 56-lb shell lashed to it. In just the last second, he missed it. He got it just right. He steered us in between the stakes and got ashore without touching one of those shells. At the order 'Down ramp', we were all surging ashore. We were in a few inches of water. All around were craft beaching and chaos and more gunfire was pouring down on us. We ran, under fire, up to the top of the beach where we went to ground, about a hundred yards from high water. People were going down and screaming and crying all around us. As we hit the sand at the top of the beach we took stock of our bearings and realised that we had landed almost exactly in our correct positions. We landed on Queen Red One, Sword Sector, Colleville sur Orne.[4]

The LCIs sailed towards the shore in tight circles, and when they closed on the beach, they peeled off one by one and rammed their bows onto it next to each other. Some of the landing craft had been hit by German artillery fire, and were ablaze, often with many casualties aboard. After the rough seas, many must have been longing to reach the shore.

It was probably better to be on deck in the open. As for those in the troopships, the poor ventilation below decks added to their misery. Many had to endure both discomforts, even torture. The LCTs sailed all the way from the ports on the south coast of England to the Normandy beaches, but the infantry spent time aboard troopships before scrambling down into LCIs.

'Morale was getting pretty low,' recalled Sergeant-Major William Brown of D Company, 8th Battalion, Durham Light Infantry, aboard a troopship:

People were getting sick and spewing. The smell when you went downstairs, where the men were trying to lie in the bunks with their equipment on – the smell was vile. Chewing gum was supposed to stop you from feeling sick – but in fact it made you worse. The handiest things were the spew bags, because you could take them and throw them over the side.[5]

The problem was no better for the officers. In fact, it was worse for during the passage they had to ensure that their subordinates knew what had to be done as briefing before the operation had been limited to senior officers for security reasons. In any case, it would have taken time to spread the word amongst the 75,215 British and Canadian troops and the 57,500 American troops landed on D-Day alone. There were also 23,400 British and American paratroops.

Major Ian Hammerton was struggling to get maps to his men in the Royal Armoured Corps' 2nd County of London Yeomanry as their LCT left harbour:

As we crossed the bar, I said, 'I suppose I better open my bag' – my sandbag with the maps in it. And while I was going down to the cabin to get it, I passed the exhaust from the motors of the engines of the ship – and I began to feel queasy. Up to that point, I'd enjoyed the smell of diesel smoke – but from that point onwards in my life, I didn't. I got them opened – I got the relevant maps to the other tank crews on the ship, and that was it – I was sick. As the landing craft headed into the rollers, there was a thud, it slipped sideways and upwards and downwards and all ways. Water splashed onto the deck and began sloshing from one end of the ship to the other, carrying with it sandwiches, oil and vomit. This went on all night as we were going pretty slowly.[6]

In theory, disembarking should have been easy, the infantrymen running down the ramp as soon as it was lowered and on to the beach. That was the theory. Nevertheless, the weather was still not good and the huge waves of the previous day had still to settle. Lieutenant William Jalland, a platoon commander in the 8th Battalion Durham Light Infantry, had an unnerving experience:

I stepped off the ramp into the water. The water rushed over my head and I went straight to the bottom on my hands and knees. The prow was smashing into the shingle next to me and I watched it smashing against my legs and arms whenever it came near me. My waders were full of water and I couldn't get to the surface. I threw away the folding bicycle that I was carrying. Then I started to tear at the waders and I managed to get them off. I unfastened my webbing and slipped that off and eventually I landed on Hitler's Fortress Europe on my hands and knees, wet through, very frightened and completely unarmed.[7]

Some of those present at the time might have said that Jalland was lucky. Earlier in the war, a German naval officer who had narrowly missed being killed when a torpedo hit his ship described his similar experience as 'good fortune in misfortune'. Someone else recalled that there were bodies lying all along the beach, and that many of the dead had been overridden by their own landing craft as they stepped off. The problem was that the landing craft became lighter as they emptied, and were swept forward by the waves, going over anyone ahead of them and either crushing or drowning them.

Others also landed in France with far less military aplomb than anticipated. One of these was Philip Crosfield, a young officer in the Royal Artillery. As he went ashore in a truck towing the leading artillery piece ashore, his vehicle hit a crater and he was catapulted out, arriving in France headfirst. 'This did the general morale a lot of good,' he observed later.[8]

During the crossing Crosfield had been ordered by his commanding officer to keep his troop entertained, so he had organised a boxing match, in which he took part, only to be knocked senseless by his opponent. In fact, he could count himself lucky to have been present at the landings at all as he had been threatened with court-martial during officer training for defying an order to yell 'I hate the Germans' during bayonet drill. His explanation was that he 'hated Hitler and everything his gang were doing and would gladly do my bit in defeating them, but hatred wasn't my line'.

He survived and left the army as a captain before becoming an Anglican priest.

Yet these scenes existed alongside others more sombre and typical of the approach of many fighting men on the eve of battle. Many had discussed whether they would survive the landings. Lieutenant Gardner Botsford of the US 1st Infantry Division recalled that 'even though huddled together and cramped, one felt very private'.

'My thoughts turned to home and family,' recalled another American soldier. 'I wondered how they would take the news of my death. I consoled myself with the fact that I was insured for the maximum amount of the GI insurance plan, and that my parents would at least have ten thousand dollars to compensate them for my death'.[9]

Aboard the USS *Bayfield*, a young officer noted that he felt he was 'approaching a great abyss – not knowing whether we are sailing into one of the world's great military traps or whether we have caught the enemy completely off guard.'[10]

The *Bayfield* was an attack transport, one of many ships specifically designed for operations such as the Normandy landings, with a crew of almost 600 personnel and an admiral's staff of around 150; she could carry over 1,200 troops and use seventeen landing craft to put them ashore. Not surprisingly, her light displacement of 8,100 tons rose to more than 16,000 tons when fully loaded.

BOMBARDMENT!

Other ships, including converted merchant vessels as well as landing craft, were fitted with artillery rockets to clear the beaches and to put the defences under pressure. All this, of course, was in addition to gunnery. Destroyers at the time were generally fitted with a main armament of 4in guns, although a few of the more modern ships had 4.5in. Cruisers had 6in guns with 4in as a secondary armament. One of these was HMS *Danae*, and on her bridge was Captain J. H. B. Hughes, a Royal Marine:

> Just before dawn, those of us on the bridge of HMS *Danae* had a tot of the most superb 1812 brandy from a bottle laid down by my great-grandfather in 1821; sent to me by my father with the comment, 'You may find this of some use in the near future.' We then commenced the operations for which we had been trained, namely engaging and knocking out three enemy batteries. At about 10.00 we closed the beaches to knock out the opposition to the landing forces in the Ouistreham area. Our open 6-inch and twin 4-inch guns went into independent fire, the guns being laid, trained and fired by the crews stripped to the waist. This was real 'Nelson stuff'. We knocked up a fantastic rate of fire. X and Y* guns were firing at least 19 rounds per minute on occasion. We all joined in, jumping in to relieve the exhausted crew members where we could. It was exhilarat-

ing beyond description and even my thirteen-year-old boy bugler fired Y gun with the lanyard while the captain of the gun, a corporal, leapt to get more charges into the breech.

Then it all came to a halt and we sailed to Portsmouth for re-ammunition.[11]

HMS *Danae* had been in Greenock when the plans for the landings had been finalised. Her commanding officer assembled her ship's company in their respective divisions on the quarterdeck in freezing cold weather to tell them of her role. He commented that they had 'the honour to be expendable', to which someone in the ranks of the stokers' division promptly commented: 'Fuck that for a lark!'[12]

Another rating aboard one of the ships in the bombardment force remarked: 'Cor! I'm sorry for those poor bastards on the other side.' The Germans might not have seen the invasion fleet coming, but they certainly heard it when it arrived. The bombardment started before the landing craft went in, and crept ahead of the troops once they were ashore. There seem to have been no reports of 'friendly fire' casualties once on the beaches.

The naval bombardment started at 0530 and the landings commenced at 0630, by which time the bombardment had moved away from coastal targets and headed inland.

There was a sense of improvisation even in this, the largest amphibious assault in history, and with first call upon the British resources; while the Americans had much to do in the Pacific, there was no doubt that this was their biggest effort in the Atlantic. The naval commander in the eastern sector was Admiral Philip Vian, whose flagship was the light cruiser HMS *Scylla*. Aboard the ship, the volume of messages to be decoded and encoded meant that extra officers were required, but there was no space to accommodate them. The result was that they were sent every other day from Portsmouth aboard MTBs and stayed aboard working for forty-eight hours before being returned to Portsmouth.

Despite the minesweepers' best efforts, by the time Operation Neptune officially ceased on 30 June, fifty-nine ships had been sunk and another 110 damaged, many by pressure mines. Nevertheless, despite a storm that wrecked one of the two Mulberry harbours, that at Saint-Laurent serving the US forces on Utah and Omaha beaches, ensured that 850,279 men, 148,803 vehicles of all kinds and 570,505 tons of supplies were landed.

Once the initial landings had been made, the major warships went back to bombarding enemy-held territory. Ships were routinely rotated out of the Normandy coastal waters and back to Portsmouth or even Plymouth to re-ammunition and refuel. Their fire could be so devastating that at one point Rommel authorised the movement of a *Panzer* division away from the coast to a much safer location further inland. Even the armour of a tank was not proof against a 15in shell.

Throughout June 1944, more than 70,000 shells were fired by the Royal Navy at German shore targets. Naval shellfire is more constant and wearing than that of land-based guns as the mechanised handling equipment means that a warship gun can fire six times as many shells in a given period than a land-based artillery piece, and often the shells are much heavier.

The German Commander-in-Chief, Army, West, Gerd von Rundstedt, reported later:

> The enemy had deployed very strong naval forces off the shores of the bridgehead. These can be used as quickly mobile, constantly available artillery, at points where they are necessary as defence against our attacks or as support for enemy attacks. During the day their fire is skilfully directed by ... plane observers, and by advanced ground fire spotters. Because of the high rapid-fire capacity of naval guns they play an important part in the battle within their range. The movement of tanks by day, in open country, within the range of these naval guns is hardly possible.[13]

Another German report discovered later noted that:

> Even more disastrous than the material effect was the morale effect of the rapidly and precisely firing naval guns. Even when not reinforced by simultaneous air bombing, the drum fire inspired in the defenders a feeling of utter helplessness, which in inexperienced recruits caused fainting or indeed complete paralysis. The supporting fire of warships was extremely accurate and made the movement of strategic reserves impossible within the 20 mile range of their guns.[14]

So that was it. The constant hammering of exploding shells all around them kept many Germans imprisoned within their shelters and concrete gun emplacements.

The Germans were not the only ones to suffer though. Those aboard the ships got no rest until they withdrew to refuel and re-ammunition. The firing and recoil of a heavy gun aboard a warship sends sound and shock waves right through the ship. The battleship *Nelson* had nine 16in guns spread over three turrets, the heaviest calibre in the Royal Navy at the time, and these fired a round once every minute on the night of 12/13 June, bombarding Caen. Those aboard the bombarding ships showed great endurance. They also had to be ready for action at a moment's notice, day or night. Some of the officers did not change their clothes for several days, some reports suggest as long as seventeen days. It was tiring, but it says much about the poor state of the defenders and the weakness of the *Kriegsmarine* that the Germans never tried to take advantage of their weariness. Hitler had, of course, brought home his battlecruisers *Scharnhorst* and *Gneisenau* and the heavy cruiser *Prinz Eugen* earlier in the celebrated 'Channel Dash' of February 1942. Based at Brest, they had been subjected to heavy bombing by the RAF, and with great daring had taken the direct route through the Straits of Dover rather than going around the west of Ireland. Because of excessive secrecy, the British reaction was too little, too late, the one aerial attack mounted against the ships having little impact despite great courage and loss of life.*

The Allied navies continued to shell for as long as was needed and there were enemy targets within range. On 30 June, US troops seized the port and city of Cherbourg, one of the great Channel ports. Elsewhere, the Allied armies took Caen on 9 July, followed by Saint-Lô on 18 July, and Avranches on 25 July, which finally allowed the bombardment fleet to leave the Normandy coast, their work done.

FRIENDLY FIRE

While Neptune ended on 30 June, the Royal Navy's involvement did not, and the service continued to patrol the waters off the coast of Normandy looking for mines, and remained alert to the threat of E-boats and U-boats. The campaign had seen relatively few naval casualties, a tribute to the use of overwhelming force and a reflection of the weak state of the German *Kriegsmarine* and *Luftwaffe*. The Germans were, after all, by this time on the defensive in Italy and the south of France as well as in Normandy and on the Eastern Front.

What happened next was all the more distressing because it did not come as a result of an engagement with the enemy but was a clear case of 'blue on blue', or 'friendly fire'. On 27 August, two of the Royal Navy's minesweepers were sunk and a third lost its stern in an attack by rocket-firing Hawker Typhoon fighter-bombers from the Royal Air Force's 263 and 266 squadrons.

The Royal Navy's First Minesweeping Flotilla was operating off the French coast in the region of Cape d'Antifer when it was decided to move into a new area, and details of the change were sent by signal to all interested parties. Later that day, another naval officer came on duty and decided to send the flotilla back to its original area of operations, and again a signal was sent, but somehow the area naval headquarters was not included in the recipients and therefore could not notify the Royal Air Force. As a result, when Allied radar spotted five ships sweeping in line abreast at noon on 27 August, it was immediately assumed to be a German formation. Not having received the signal detailing the change, the Flag Officer, British Assault Area, FOBAA, agreed that any ships must be German. Two of the ships, HMS *Hussar* and *Britomart*, were larger than most minesweepers and had served as sloops on convoy escort duties. From the air they seemed large enough to be small German destroyers. A Polish airman flew over the ships in a Spitfire and reported that they seemed to be Allied vessels, but gave the wrong position. FOBAA then attempted to contact the officers controlling minesweeping, but could not get through as the lines were down. FOBAA then called for an anti-shipping strike, and sixteen Typhoons of the RAF's 263 and 266 squadrons were ordered into the air. As he approached the flotilla, the strike leader thought that he could see Allied ships, so he radioed questioning his orders, only to be told to attack. He subsequently queried his orders twice.

At 1330, the attack began. Sweeping out of the sun towards the first ship, *Britomart*, the Typhoons started strafing and firing anti-tank rockets, deadly against the thin-plated hulls of minor warships. In less than two minutes, the ship had lost its bridge and was listing heavily, while another, *Hussar*, was on fire. Those aboard the ships immediately assumed that the aircraft must belong to the *Luftwaffe* and *Jason* signalled that she was under attack by enemy aircraft, but as the aircraft raced away, the distinctive D-Day black and white 'invasion stripes' could be seen and another ship, *Salamander*, fired recognition flares, forcing the hapless leader of the strike to query his orders yet again, for the fourth time. Yet again, he was ordered back into the attack, and at 1335 dived down again towards the warships, hitting *Britomart* once again and strafing *Jason* while rockets went into both *Salamander* and *Colsay*. Despite a large white ensign and a Union flag being draped over the stern of *Jason* as she fired further recognition flares, a third attack followed at 1340, hitting *Hussar*, which exploded, and *Salamander*, whose stern was blown off by rocket strikes. As the crippled *Salamander* drifted shoreward, a no doubt bemused German artillery battery with 9.2in coastal guns opened fire, forcing *Jason* to launch her small boats to tow *Salamander* out of danger.

This was the Royal Navy's worst friendly fire incident of the Second World War, with 117 officers and ratings killed and another 153 wounded. The whole incident was covered up and those involved sworn to secrecy on threat of prosecution and it only came to light in 1994, when the then Public Record Office, now the National Archives, released the papers.

The three officers who were responsible for this appalling and unnecessary loss of life and valuable ships were court-martialled, but two were acquitted and the third severely reprimanded. No doubt the strike leader would have been dealt with far more severely had he disobeyed his orders.

NOTES

1. US National Archives.
2. Imperial War Museum Sound Archive.
3. Imperial War Museum Sound Archive.
4. Imperial War Museum Sound Archive.
5. Imperial War Museum Sound Archive.
6. Imperial War Museum Sound Archive.
7. Imperial War Museum Sound Archive.
8. Obituary, *The Scotsman*, 27 March 2013.
9. US National Archives.
10. US National Archives.
11. Imperial War Museum Sound Archive.
12. Imperial War Museum Sound Archive.
13. Imperial War Museum Sound Archive.
14. Rundstedt, Gerd von *German Commander-in-Chief West, Field Marshal Karl R. Gerd von Rundstedt's Report on the Allied Invasion of Normandy*. U.S. Department of the Navy – Naval Historical Center.
15. Foreign Military Studies, United States Army Military History Institute.

* X and Y turrets, the two turrets closest to the stern, were manned by Royal Marines rather than naval gunners on British warships.

* Lieutenant-Commander Eugene Esmonde was awarded the Victoria Cross posthumously for leading a detachment of six Fairey Swordfish biplanes to face the three ships. While most of the planned fighter cover of Supermarine Spitfires failed to materialise, the Swordfish were caught between the Luftwaffe's strong fighter patrols and the heavy anti-aircraft fire of the German ships. All six aircraft were shot down and all but five of the eighteen naval airmen killed.

13

THE ASSAULT – THE BRITISH SECTOR

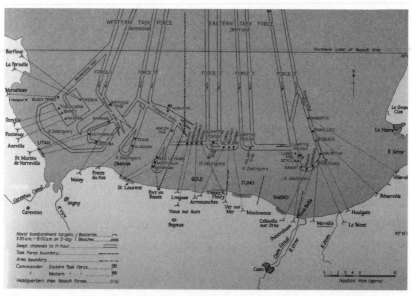

The Normandy beaches, the British having Sword and Gold, and the Canadians predominating at Juno, combining to make the British sector, and the American sector at Omaha and Utah. The east-west split between British and Canadian troops on the one hand and those of the US on the other was dictated by the location of their bases in England. (from an original in the Imperial War Museum archive)

Clearly, the whole object of the exercise was to get the required number of men and vehicles ashore as quickly as possible. For the British and Canadians, this meant landing on three beaches code-named, from east to west, Sword, Juno and Gold.

Gold Beach lay between Port-en-Bessin and the River Provence in the Baie de la Seine, and included Arromanches, the site of one of the two Mulberry harbours. The British 50th Infantry Division landed here. Between the River Provence and Saint-Aubin-sur-Mer in the Baie de la Seine lay Juno Beach, used by the 3rd Canadian Division. Also in the Baie de la Seine was Sword Beach, between Saint-Aubin-sur-Mer and the mouth of the River Orne. This is where the 3rd British Infantry Division landed.

The convoy of landing craft and ships, warships and merchant vessels heading for the British sector was known as the Eastern Task Force for, as noted earlier, the basing of British and Canadian troops ashore in England dictated that the British sector was to the east and the American sector to the west.

While we are primarily concerned with the naval aspects of Operation Overlord, itself code-named Operation Neptune, the amphibious assault was matched by air-landed troops, many of them paratroops but others used gliders. Both the British and the American sectors benefited from this two-pronged approach. Much had been done to improve air landings, lessons having been learnt from the problems that had affected Operation Husky, the landings in Sicily, which had also suffered from bad weather.

Being flown over the coastal defences to land, as it were, behind the lines, brought problems of its own. The bad weather had meant some flooding, but the Germans had also conducted some defensive flooding of their own to make the arrival of paratroops or glider-borne troops as difficult as possible.

The British 9th Parachute Battalion was landing inland from Sword Beach. Its commanding officer, Lieutenant-Colonel Terence Otway, hit the wall of a house, having been blown out of his aircraft, a Short Stirling bomber, when it was hit by an anti-aircraft shell. Out of a reinforced battalion of 750 men, he suffered 40 per cent casualties. Many of the 300 lost were captured by German units based in the area, but these were the lucky ones for many others were drowned, either in the rivers and flooded areas, or in the mud, sucked down by their packs before they could find their feet.

'We saw several men who had been caught in the floods,' Otway recalled later, 'and were weighed down with their packs, just sinking. We tried to pull them out, but there was nothing we could do except watch them be sucked down by the mud. It was very unpleasant.'[1]

Bombing raids before the landings had left many gun batteries unscathed, but had also left the ground pock-marked with large bomb craters, some of which had filled with water, though others did at least provide some cover as the paratroops advanced to attempt to destroy the batteries before the amphibious landings on Sword Beach.

Fierce fighting followed, with a hole blown in a barbed wire fence by Bangalore torpedoes (a long pipe filled with explosive), before four guns in the coastal artillery battery were spiked and of the 130 defenders, all but twelve were killed or incapacitated. Later that day, they captured the village of Amfreville, followed by the Château St Come, securing the ridge that protected the eastern flank of the bridgehead spring out from Sword Beach.

SWORD BEACH

The need for an effective artillery barrage before committing ground forces to an advance, or even a landing, had been proven in both world wars. At Sword Beach, the battleships HMS *Warspite* and *Ramillies*, and the monitor *Roberts*, were offshore, supported by four cruisers, one of which was the Polish *Dragon*, as well as an escort of thirteen destroyers, although these too played a part, bombarding targets with their 4in guns. This was a far heavier naval support than originally proposed, but the planners had taken into account the number of German coastal batteries in the area.

The barrage of naval gunfire started at 0530, as the first landing craft were lowered into the water, circling while the gunfire continued and their occupants were suffering from seasickness having briefly swallowed breakfast, with a tot of rum, before boarding the landing craft.

Their plight and discomfort was as nothing compared to that of the men of the 13th/18th Hussars, who were equipped with the amphibious DD tanks. It was small comfort when the order to release the tanks was given, 'Floater 5,000!', that originally they had been expected to launch 8,000 offshore rather than 5,000, as the waves were still running at up to 5ft.

The landing craft and tanks were supposed to reach the shore at 0630. At 0650, the division's self-propelled guns, also placed aboard landing craft, opened fire, adding the sound of their guns to the thunder of the battleship, monitor and cruiser guns. To everyone's surprise, as the first infantrymen from the 1st Battalion the South Lancashire Regiment and the 2nd East Yorkshires streamed ashore, the first DD tanks were already ashore and firing at the German positions. Out of forty tanks, just six had been sunk, two of them after being rammed by landing craft, which, being flat-bottomed, were extremely difficult to control in stormy seas. One of the first successes came when a Bren-gun platoon, coming ashore in their tracked carriers, raced across the beach to a German position whose occupants immediately surrendered. The first prisoners were already being taken, and one German officer complained when he found himself and his men having to crouch by a sea wall to escape the effects of their own side's artillery fire. Nevertheless, casualties were already beginning to mount, the South Lancashires losing their CO 10ft from the top of the beach, the battalion's medical officer falling wounded beside him.

Amidst the sound and the fury, and the chaos, the 2nd Battalion of the Middlesex Regiment were welcomed by the mayor of Colville, wearing a brass fireman's helmet, and accompanied by the first of many young women who, in the midst of a raging battle, started to bandage wounded soldiers.

'Hobart's Funnies' were also ashore, the flail tanks clearing paths through the minefields. The exits from Sword Beach were opened more quickly than at any other of the D-Day landing sites. More conventional mine disposal was also being carried out by the Royal Engineers.

Enemy armour did not appear while the battle raged. This was partly because of the indecision at the top of the German chain of command, with Rommel in Germany on leave and the *Panzer* units waiting to be unleashed, but only if ordered by Hitler, who was still in bed since his staff officers refused to wake him, not even for the long-awaited invasion.

Amidst the chaos, there were surreal moments. The arrival of the mayor to welcome the troops ashore was one. Lord Lovat's 1st Special Service Brigade had also landed in the area, and as they swept ashore his men abandoned their helmets and proudly wore their green berets instead. Lovat led the way off the landing craft, which pleased many as, being 6ft tall, he would show them how deep the water was. Lovat had his personal piper, Bill Millin, whose old regiment was the Cameron Highlanders, with him, wearing his kilt, which spread around him as he entered the cold water. Nevertheless, as he strode ashore he started to play 'Highland Laddie', the regimental march of the Scots Guards, Lovat's old regiment. Lovat then asked Millin to march up and down the beach while the rest of the men disembarked playing 'The Road to the Isles'. Some of those coming ashore were buoyed up by the sound, but some others were angry at Millin being presented as a target for a sniper.

Once ashore, Lovat led his men on a forced march towards Bénouville, where two bridges had been seized by Major John Howard's glider troops. Once again, Millin was asked to play, Lovat explaining that the glider troops would know relief was coming once they heard the pipes. As it happened, the men of a parachute battalion had beaten him to it, and even some of his own men reached the bridges before their distinguished commanding officer.

Meanwhile, the warships had come in as close to the shore as possible, reasoning that even if a ship was sunk in shallow water, her guns could continue firing, and once the fighting stopped, salvage would be easier. By the following day, minesweepers had cleared a substantial pear-shaped area between the eastern limit of Sword Beach and the major port of Le Havre, so that the bombarding ships had more room in which to operate. Another day and a mine-free channel had been swept between this area and the swept area just off Sword Beach.

On one occasion, some British warships charged through an area still known to be an unswept minefield, fortunately without losses, on reports that German warships were leaving Le Havre.

Given the overwhelming success of the landing on Sword Beach, life aboard the warships after the initial euphoria soon seemed tedious and uneventful, a situation made worse not just by the need to keep awake, but the sheer impossibility of getting any rest while the bombardment continued, with the sound of heavy guns firing and the recoil running through the ships. Nevertheless, as the troops ashore moved inland the targets switched from the German coastal batteries to providing supporting fire for the troops. This required specially trained naval officers, forward officers, bombardment, FOBs, and bombardment liaison officers, BLOs, alongside the troops, radioing orders back to the ships. The battleships and cruisers had their own spotting aircraft, which were launched and helped with the artillery spotting and targeting. The battleships could give support at ranges of more than 20 miles, while the cruisers could do so at ranges of between 10 and 12 miles. As mentioned earlier, German *Panzer* commanders found their units being blown apart by this gunfire and attempts to organise a counterattack were foiled. The impact on German morale can be imagined.

This was all achieved at some cost. Under intensive use, artillery gun barrels wear out quickly, and even before Caen was taken, the battleships *Warspite* and *Ramillies*, and the cruiser *Orion* had to have new barrels fitted. The ships of the fleet were moved around so that even when a ship was away re-ammunitioning or even having new gun barrels fitted, the rate and intensity of fire continued unabated. While firing at such an intense rate, the heat and the stench of the gases used in the propellant was unimaginable, and many gunners were to suffer deafness later.

JUNO BEACH

At Juno Beach, the bulk of the 21,400 men coming ashore on the morning of 6 June were members of the 3rd Canadian Division, many of whom wanted to avenge the Dieppe raid. The beach was in the middle of the British sector and lay between the River Provence and Saint-Aubin-sur-Mer, again in the Baie de la Seine.

As elsewhere, the waters offshore were packed with mined obstacles placed between the high and low water marks, and a few actually below the low water mark. Landing craft obstacle clearance units, or LCOCUs, were deployed, but to succeed the initial assault had to have momentum and the landing craft and landing ships carrying infantry and vehicles had no option but to drive through such obstacles. The smaller landing craft attempted to thread their way through such obstacles, but the larger and heavier landing ships trusted to their size. Armoured bulldozers landed with the first wave also attempted to clear as many obstacles as possible, but there was not enough time to clear everything if the landing fleet was not to be left waiting offshore and within range of the German defences.

One Canadian account recalls how difficult the situation was at Juno Beach. HMCS *Prince David* landed her first body of Canadian troops exactly on schedule on the beach at Bernieres-sur-Mer:

> The soldiers, members of a French-Canadian regiment recruited from the lower St Lawrence, were ferried from the parent ship by the landing craft flotillas, commanded by Lieutenant R.G. Buckingham. It was not until the assault infantry and tank landing craft were practically on the beach that they ran into trouble in the form of mines. The small assault boats were

the heaviest sufferers. The boats rode in with a stiff wind that sent the surf crashing on the beach. Their way lay through a section of crossed scantlings which gave the piece of water the appearance of a field filled with stumps. These were the mine supports. First Lieutenant J. McBeath's boat was mined; then Lieutenant Buckingham, Lieutenant Beveridge and Leading Seaman Laverne had their craft smashed by mines. It was a wild scramble for shore, but everyone made it but for two French-Canadians in Lieutenant McBeath's boat. They were killed outright by the mine which their boat hit. While our boats were emptying their men, others were taking punishment from mines farther up the beach. Chunks of debris rose a hundred feet in the air and troops, now hugging the shelter of a breakwater, were peppered with pieces of wood. The bigger landing craft did not escape, but they could take it.[2]

This was a far more difficult landing than along the coast at Sword Beach, but it was, as we will see in the next chapter, far from being the worst.

The Canadians, led by Major-General Rod Keller, wore British uniforms, but not surprisingly, felt more of a rapport with the Americans. They shared the Americans' air of superiority and were doubtful about the British, and especially the piles of paperwork that seemed to come from the headquarters of the British Second Army. Some wits referred to Operation Overlord as 'Operation Overboard'.

Supporting the Canadians as they swarmed ashore was Task Force J, led by the heavy cruiser HMS *Belfast** with the light cruiser HMS *Diadem*, five British fleet destroyers, three Norwegian destroyers, a Free French destroyer and the two Canadian destroyers HMCS *Algonquin* and *Sioux*. The French destroyer, *La Combattante*, would later make her mark in history by bringing General de Gaulle to France a week after the landings.

At Juno, the bombardment commenced at 0527, while rocket ships, usually converted landing craft, also sent salvoes over the heads of the troops heading aboard their landing craft through the shallows. As Canadian troops and six LCIs carrying members of No. 48 Royal Marine Commando approached the shore, everyone was surprised that there was no fire, and even after the bombardment ceased for the landings, there was an eerie silence. The Germans were not asleep, not still hiding in their deep shelters, but waiting. As soon as the landing craft ramps went down at 0730, field guns and machine guns opened up. When the Canadians arrived at

0749, the same reception awaited them. Despite being ordered to abandon those who had been hit and press on with the attack, many of the Canadian troops helped their wounded comrades to safety. All in all, 961 Canadian casualties were incurred on Juno Beach.

The Royal Marines had actually crossed the entire Channel in their small LCIs, and in addition to the packs and heavy equipment, there were also bicycles and motor cycles and a number of handcarts.

Heavier support for the attack came from the DD tanks of the Fort Garry Horse and the 1st Hussars.

At Courseulles-sur-Mer, the 7th Canadian Brigade's Royal Winnipeg Rifles secured the west bank of the River Sculles before joining the Canadian Scottish in advancing towards Vaux and Graye-sur-Mer. On the other side of the river, clearing the east bank proved more difficult for the Regina Rifles, who had suffered particularly heavy casualties during the landings. It took several hours before the town could be secured.

Meanwhile, back on the beaches, the 8th Canadian Brigade also ran into fierce resistance at Saint-Aubin-sur-Mer, and the North Shore Regiment took heavy losses. The Fort Garry Horse squadron of DD tanks arrived late, and in the confusion they ran over many corpses and Canadian wounded on the beach.

The advance went more smoothly at Bernières-sur-Mer, where the use of artillery and more DD tanks of the Fort Garry Horse had the Germans retreating by 0900, when civilians emerged from their cellars and a bar was opened for drinks. Despite warnings from their officers that food or drink offered by the French might be poisoned, many accepted the hospitality. Elsewhere, other French civilians were delighted when French Canadian troops arrived, speaking French, and were viewed as the next best thing to being liberated by the Free French.

Kellar, the Canadian commander, arrived in the midst of the chaos with war correspondents and photographers, having made a show of sending a highly optimistic radio report to Lieutenant-General Harry Crerar, the senior Canadian officer for the Normandy landings.

Things improved somewhat after the destroyer *Algonquin* knocked out a battery of guns near Bény-sur-Mer. Nevertheless, the advance to the Canadians' prime objective, the airfield at Carpiquet, was slow, and it was sheer luck that the *Luftwaffe* failed to destroy the airfield, its fuel and its installations properly before it finally fell to the Allies.

GOLD BEACH

The most westerly of the British landing beaches, lying between Port-en-Bessin and the River Provence east of Mont Fleury in the Baie de la Seine, Gold Beach was the landing place for the British 50th Infantry Division and 24,970 troops landed on D-Day. The beach lay near Arromanches and was the site of the Mulberry harbour that survived the bad weather.

Jim Tuckwell, a private in the 1st Battalion of the Dorsetshire Regiment, or '1st Dorsets', saw the ramp of the landing craft go down, and then turned and asked one of his comrades why he was hitting him. His friend was not hitting him – he had been struck by bullets fired from a German machine gun. He staggered ashore and lay on the beach nursing his wounds for the next three hours, hoping that he would not be run over by a British tank coming ashore. He accidentally exposed himself to a German sniper and was shot in the chest. Delirium and then unconsciousness followed before he was found by a medical team and evacuated.

Gold was the British beach closest to the American sector and the British troops took some of the pressure off the Americans bogged down on Omaha Beach, who had landed at 0630, an hour before the British 50th Northumbrian Division arrived. Gold and Omaha seem to have had the worst of the weather, or at least been the most exposed, so much so that the two armoured regiments with DD tanks pressed ahead until they were within 1,000yd of the beach before launching the two squadrons of Sherwood Rangers Yeomanry tanks, but even so, eight were lost. The 4th/7th Dragoon Guards launched even closer to the shore, to the right of the Sherwoods, and lost fewer tanks.

The decision of when to launch lay with the commanding officers of the landing craft, and it took some heated discussion between the Dragoons and their landing craft commanders before the launch was delayed.

The difficulties faced by the armoured units in the rough seas meant that the most westerly brigade, which included the 1st Battalion of the Royal Hampshires and the 1st Dorsets, faced strong resistance when they arrived east of Le Hamel and Arromanches-les-Bains. The naval bombardment came from the two light cruisers HMS *Ajax* and *Argonaut*, aimed mainly at a German heavy coastal battery at Longues, which had been expected to be destroyed by heavy bombing. Evening was drawing in before German resistance was overcome.

To the left, far better luck lay with the Green Howards as they advanced on Mont Fleury, having been told by their second-in-command that if they stopped on the beach, 'you are never going to get up again'. When the Germans began to surrender, they were ordered back to the beach and went obediently without an escort. Yet, further left still, at the most easterly point on Gold Beach, at La Rivière, where the coastal defences had not been destroyed by bombs or naval bombardment, the 5th Battalion, East Yorkshire Regiment, faced strong resistance. It was not until an AVRE tank (or assault vehicle, Royal Engineers) appeared and fired a 40lb petard bomb that the anti-tank gun emplacement there was destroyed, but it still took several more hours to clear La Rivière, even with the assistance of flame-throwing Crocodile tanks.

NOTES

1. *Daily Telegraph*, 5 June 2004.
2. Canadian War Memorial.

* According to the Washington Naval Treaty, with her 6in guns, she was really a light cruiser, despite her tonnage and the fact that there were twelve guns in four turrets. The RN decided that Belfast and the other Town-class cruisers were heavy cruisers.

14

THE ASSAULT – THE AMERICAN SECTOR

As with the British sector, the priority was to get the American forces ashore as quickly as possible. The basing of the American troops in England meant that the simplest arrangement was for the Americans to take the western sector and so, naturally, the convoy of landing craft and ships, warships and merchant vessels was known as the Western Task Force.

The Americans had two beaches, Omaha and, further west, Utah. Both were far broader than the British beaches. Omaha Beach lay between Port-en-Bessin and the mouth of the River Vire in the Baie de la Seine. It was to be the location for one of the two Mulberry harbours, which was installed at Saint-Laurent, but two weeks after the landings, on 20 June, was destroyed in a storm, along with some 700 small craft, cutting Allied supplies by 80 per cent initially. On D-Day, 34,250 troops landed on Omaha, but they faced the fiercest resistance of the entire Normandy landings, taking 2,000 casualties, and at times it seemed as if the Americans might not gain a foothold.

The situation was less fraught at Utah Beach, the westernmost of all the invasion beaches, which lay alongside the eastern coast of the Cherbourg Peninsula, and ran northwards from the mouth of the River Vire, the actual landing spot being south of Les Dunes de Varreville. On D-Day, 23,250 troops of the 4th US Division went ashore at Utah Beach.

OMAHA BEACH

Probably the most experienced of all the forces landed on D-Day, the 1st US Infantry Division was the oldest active division in the US Army and as well as carrying the nickname of the 'Big Red One', it was also known as the 'First Team', again a reference to the '1' badges worn on the uniforms. What mattered more than its age was the fact that it had already seen action during the Second World War in the landings in North Africa and then the following year in Sicily. Nevertheless, there was still a substantial element amongst the troops on their first major operation, coming under fire for the first time.

As in the British sector, the Americans had their own mine and obstacle clearance teams, the equivalent of the Royal Naval Commandos being the Naval Combat Demolition Units. This was hard and dangerous work at the best of times, but saw men crawling on their stomachs under heavy fire, dragging the explosives with which they were to blow gaps in the obstacles for landing craft situation between the low water and high water levels.

'The Jerries started pouring lead at us right off the bat,' recalled J. L. Jeffries, a member of one of the teams:

> They used everything they could muster, 88-mm guns, mortars and machine guns, and the snipers were busy too. But we managed to wire our charges to the obstacles, which were pyramids of railway iron with mines attached, and blow the gaps. We worked on those things all day and for the next two days with the Jerries working on us all the time with their 88-mms. As soon as we heard them go off we'd try to make it to foxholes, but often we didn't have time, so we'd just hit the deck and hope.[1]

It was not always enough. In one US Naval Demolition Unit there was just one survivor, but it managed to complete its assigned task despite being pinned down by fire for fifteen hours by the dreaded 88mm guns. These were amongst the most effective anti-aircraft guns deployed by any side during the war, but they proved just as effective when turned against armoured formations, and the American seamen struggling to clear the beaches had no armour to protect them. The result was that only five of the planned sixteen lanes through the beach obstacles could be opened, and most of the tanks coming off the landing craft were knocked out by 88mm fire before they had a chance to fire themselves. Some of the landing craft coming from the attack transport USS *Samuel Chase* were hit and on fire even before they reached the beach. All of the first wave of landing craft from the *Samuel Chase* all foundered.

What had happened at Omaha was that the German 352nd Field Division was in the area, having moved there just two or three days previously to conduct anti-invasion training and manoeuvres. This was the one instance of Allied intelligence failing to detect a major German formation in the preparations for Operation Overlord. The presence of the division was entirely down to luck – good luck for the Germans, but very bad luck for the Allies. The 352nd Field Division was well trained, prepared to a degree that no other German unit managed on D-Day, and was also overwhelmingly stronger than the 1st US Infantry Division. This particular German division had not had its strength and cohesion diluted by foreign conscripts, elderly or wounded soldiers. The Germans had also managed to prepare a strong defensive position, which one senior American naval officer reported as being 'highly organised, strongly built, and skilfully designed'.[2]

Perhaps most tragic of all, this also happened to be the one beach where the initial pre-H-hour aerial attack had not materialised. In short, the German defenders had the advantage and had not even had to suffer a pre-landing softening up.

The tank landing craft delayed launching the DD tanks until around 5,000yd off the shore, but even so the rough seas and offshore obstacles meant that only two reached the tank landing site code-named 'Fox Green', another three failed to launch due to a damaged ramp, and the remaining twenty-seven sank, although somehow most of the crews survived.

At around 0830 a beachmaster from the 7th Naval Beach Battalion signalled that the landing of vehicles should be suspended, and shortly afterwards aboard the cruiser USS *Augusta*, Lieutenant-General Omar Bradley wondered whether he should save his troops and evacuate Omaha Beach.

This had to change. The actual assault was under the command of Rear-Admiral J. L. Hall (Jr), USN, who quickly realised what was happening and signalled the commander of the Western Task Force, Rear-Admiral Alan Kirk, USN, for support. Even before Kirk could order the warships offshore to commence a heavy bombardment of the German coastal defences, many commanding officers had taken the initiative and heavy shelling had begun, despite the fact that most of the Navy's Shore Fire Control Parties did not make it ashore, or if they did, did not survive long enough to direct naval gunfire. Air cover was also on its way, and before long the Germans were also suffering bombs and rockets.

'The initial check on the beach was overcome because of the initiative displayed by gunfire support ships, the assistance of the air force and the intrepidity of the infantry on the shore line,' recalled Kirk. 'The performance of battleships, cruisers and destroyers in support of the operation was magnificent.'[3]

The biggest impact on the German defenders was made when the battleship USS *Texas* began firing shortly after midday. The 14in and 5in shells from this World War I veteran's guns soon brought the Germans out of their shelters and fortifications to surrender.

Not all of those involved with Omaha Beach were American. Many of the landing craft had been manned by the Royal Navy. Aboard the former Grimsby trawler *Olvina*, which was converted into a convoy escort, the crew had been expecting leave when they arrived at Plymouth on 3 June.

'We'd dropped anchor at Plymouth after a convoy and thought we were in for some leave,' explained Harry Marrington, who was a naval rating, aged just 19 at the time. 'But then we were ordered to store up. I thought we were going out with another convoy.'[4]

Instead, *Olvina* joined the rest of Operation Neptune, sailing to Fowey in Cornwall before following the rest of the ships to 'Piccadilly Circus', south of the Isle of Wight, ready for the final stage of the passage to Normandy. Marrington noted that the vast armada gave the impression that one could have 'walked across the Channel without getting wet'.[5]

Omaha was already the scene of heavy fighting by the time the old trawler arrived, shepherding landing craft towards the beaches. Some of the landing craft had been sunk and men were struggling in the water, but *Olvina* dared not stop for fear of becoming an easy target for the German gunners.

'You were an instant target if you stopped,' recalls Marrington. 'It was indescribable. We were pushing bodies aside as we went through the water.'[6]

A landing craft drew alongside and informed *Olvina*'s commanding officer that the Royal Navy beachmaster, whose role it was to keep the vehicles and troops landing on the beach moving, was short of men. Five men were requested, and the commanding officer, a lieutenant-commander, agreed to provide them. Within minutes, Marrington was on his way ashore, without a rifle and without any training. For the next two or three hours he was fighting for his life:

All hell let loose and everyone tried to find shelter. I thought, 'Oh my God. What am I doing here? I got behind one of the steel hedgehogs the Germans had put there to wreck landing craft. The bullets were pinging off it every now and then and I dived under the water to escape the firing.

You were on your own. My only thought was to survive. There were terrible sights – a man with no arms and all that. I could hear people screaming and calling out for their mothers. But if you started worrying about them, you'd soon be joining them. I thought: how mad is it that people can do this to each other.[7]

Eventually he reached the beach and sheltered in the sand before joining his comrades. For the next three days he helped clear damaged vehicles, sleeping in the open, but he, and indeed all five of the men from the *Olvina*, survived.

Nevertheless, the battle for Omaha Beach did not end for six hours, until after 1300, and it was not until the beach had been secured that the armoured bulldozers could start to demolish the obstructions on the beach itself and at the exits into the area beyond. One of the major achievements of the battle was the scaling of the cliff face of the Pointe du Hoc by the US 2nd Rangers in order to dispose of a German gun emplacement, supported by gunfire from the destroyers USS *Satterlee* and HMS *Talybont*. On reaching the emplacement, the Rangers discovered that the guns had been moved elsewhere. They were eventually discovered and destroyed.

The worst casualties on D-Day were on Omaha Beach: 2,000 men were killed or seriously wounded.

UTAH BEACH

The most westerly beach, Utah, lay alongside the eastern shores of the Cherbourg Peninsula, running north from the River Vire in the Baie de la Seine. It was the landing area for the 4th US Division, which landed south of Les Dunes de Varreville, 23,250 troops coming ashore on D-Day. Of all five beaches, Utah was the easiest, and least bloody.

As the troops landed, there was no enemy machine gun fire or shelling, and mine clearance units were able to clear the small number of mines and booby traps found on the beaches. It was not until the second wave of US troops landed that German resistance started, by which time the first wave were off the beaches and had even started establishing supply depots inland.

The first landings on the Cotentin Peninsula, often known as the Cherbourg Peninsula because of the important port at its head, were made by US paratroops of the 82nd Airborne Division. Though their landings were unopposed, they were scattered and the high hedgerows of the fields made orientation and communication with other clusters of troops more than a little difficult. It was not until daylight that units began to form and attack their objectives, but they still had no radio contact with headquarters and it was fortunate that the Germans were in an even worse state after telephone wires had been cut by the French Resistance and the various groups of saboteurs dropped by the Allies in the weeks before the invasion. The Germans had no idea where the Americans were, and with one of their generals, *Generalleutnant* Falley, dead from an ambush and another, *Generalleutnant* Karl-Wilhelm Graf von Schlieben, absent, in a hotel near Rennes preparing for a planned Seventh Army exercise. He was telephoned at 0630 and told that he was requested to return to his unit immediately. He realised that the Allies must have invaded, and this was confirmed as his staff car approached the coast and he could hear heavy gunfire.

In fact, a number of US paratroopers had been taken prisoner by the Germans after landing too close to the 91st *Luftlande* Division. Heavy fighting was soon to follow.

Meanwhile, back at Utah Beach, German attempts to organise a defence had been seriously hindered by a heavy bombardment, once again commanded by Rear-Admiral Alan Kirk aboard the heavy cruiser USS *Augusta*. The *Augusta* was accompanied by a mixed Anglo-American bombardment force that included the battleship USS *Nevada* and the heavy cruisers *Quincy* and *Tuscaloosa*, as well as the monitor HMS *Erebus* and the light cruisers HMS *Black Prince* and *Enterprise*, and twelve destroyers. There were also rocket ships, usually converted landing craft, which seemed to be surprisingly inaccurate. While the bombardment failed to destroy many of the German positions, it did play a part in clearing many of the minefields. The US Ninth Air Force bombed the German positions close to the landing area, although without doing much damage. Despite all of this, the landings went smoothly.

Major-General J. 'Storming Joe' Lawton Collins' VII Corps came ashore after their landing craft had been pushed by the current towards the Vire

Estuary, to a point where the German defences were negligible. The only DD tanks lost were the four aboard a landing craft that struck a mine, but those that reached the shore were, initially, short of targets to attack. When the first senior officer reached the shore, Brigadier-General Teddy Roosevelt Jnr, son of the former president, he wisely saw that there would be no point in redeploying to the assigned landing positions, and famously announced that, 'We'll start the war from here!'

It took less than an hour of what some officers described as being 'more like guerrilla fighting' to clear the beach. Even the Allied aircraft roaring overhead found no *Luftwaffe* aircraft to engage, and Thunderbolt squadrons racing inland to destroy German armoured reinforcements heading for the landing sites were similarly disappointed as there were none.

The 4th Infantry Division suffered just 200 casualties on D-Day.

NOTES

1. US National Archives.
2. US National Archives.
3. US National Archives.
4. *Daily Telegraph*, 5 June 2004.

15

THE BATTLE FOR
THE CHANNEL PORTS

Normandy was only the beginning, a beachhead. There was some debate over whether the land war should be fought on a narrow front, directed first towards Paris and then on into Germany, or on a broad front. The latter held the prospect of liberating Belgium and the Netherlands, but at the risk of the Soviet armies reaching Berlin first and even cutting across northern Germany towards Denmark.

Finally, on 12 June, HMS *Kelvin*, a Royal Navy destroyer, brought British Prime Minister Winston Churchill to Normandy. Two days later, *La Combattante*, a former Royal Navy Hunt-class destroyer now manned by the Free French, brought General Charles de Gaulle back to his home country. Then, on 16 June, the landing beaches were visited by His Majesty King George VI aboard the cruiser HMS *Arethusa*, accompanied by the First Sea Lord, Admiral of the Fleet Sir Andrew 'ABC' Cunningham.

Now it was time for nature to take a hand.

A fierce gale began to blow in the early hours of 19 June and soon developed into the worst June gale that had been experienced in Normandy for forty years. It sprang up suddenly at 0330. Commodore G. N. Oliver, RN, in charge of the Juno area, was aboard his headquarters ship, HMS *Hilary*, and while she rode out the gale, it took two anchors to hold the ship, but only for so long as the following day, shortly after noon, the ship began to drag her anchors. Other ships had already been swept off-station, taking the line of least resistance until the weather moderated and they could return.

Unable to move, of course, were the two Mulberry harbours. The one in the British sector off Arromanches was nearly completed and enjoyed a relatively sheltered position, and was able to provide shelter for the many small craft caught offshore in the bad weather. The situation at the American sector's Mulberry harbour near Saint-Laurent was far worse, and the commanding officer of one of the small craft seeking shelter described the scene in graphic terms:

> The scene inside the Mulberry was one of unutterable chaos. Literally hundreds of landing craft from LCV (landing craft, vehicle) to LST (landing ship, tank) were ashore piled one upon another. The 'whales' (caissons on which the pier roadways floated) had vanished. The bombardons were chasing one another madly around the bay. The 'phoenixes' (the big concrete breakwater caissons) had cracked. Even the blockships were breaking up, and what little sea room remained was packed with wreckage, DUKWs and more and more landing craft, coasters and barges, dragging their anchors steadily towards the beach.[1]

The British Mulberry harbour, being almost complete, was better able to stand the battering of the gale. It was also sheltered by the Calvados Rocks. It did not escape damage completely, as the outer floating bombardon breakwater broke away and then broke up. The two harbours were still far from complete, and every one of the sections on tow towards Normandy that day was lost. Nevertheless, both provided shelter for small craft, even the ill-fated harbour at Saint-Laurent, and many of the 155 small ships and landing craft that took shelter in the Mulberry harbours would no doubt have been lost otherwise. Gooseberry shelters had created some additional safe harbours and these also played a part in saving many small craft and ships.

Even so, more than 800 ships and craft of all sizes were stranded. Out of 650 LCTs employed in the initial assault and then retained for the steady build-up of reinforcements, no less than 320 were put out of action.

One observer noted that the gale did more damage to the invasion than the Germans had managed in fourteen days, with the weather accounting for some 700 ships and small craft against 261 by the enemy. The American sector Mulberry harbour at Saint-Laurent was damaged beyond repair and even though the British sector Mulberry harbour at Arromanches survived, it too was damaged and needed repair. Ships had to be salvaged at both sites. The number of ships arriving with supplies and reinforcements fell after the gale and was less than during the week after D-Day when, of course, no such harbours existed.

This is why the loss of LCTs and LCVs was felt very acutely, as these had enabled the Allies to function without a harbour. After the gale, they had many fewer LCTs and LCVs, one harbour damaged and in need of repair, and another so badly damaged it had to be abandoned.

Improvisation was the order of the day. The Royal Navy and the United States Navy both had repair ships in the area. The British ships were HMS *Adventure*, a former minelaying cruiser, and HMS *Albatross*, which had been a seaplane carrier and had been transferred to the Royal Australian Navy before being brought back to European waters. The *Albatross* alone was credited with saving seventy-nine landing craft and restored 132 vessels of all kinds to fighting service, despite coming under heavy fire from German artillery, including mobile guns. Her stay was cut short when a serious underwater explosion, believed to have been caused by a German torpedo striking the ship, forced her to withdraw for dockyard attention.

The German mobile artillery was far more troublesome than the fixed coastal artillery, largely because no sooner were the artillery batteries located than they moved to a fresh firing position. They were also manned by better trained and fitter troops. German mine laying was also another hazard as the enemy started to fight back more effectively.

Nevertheless, once completed and with the weather damage repaired, the solitary Mulberry harbour near Arromanches was able to handle an average of 7,000 tons of supplies and equipment daily. It had originally been planned to have a working life of ninety days, but in the end was kept on throughout most of the winter of 1944–45. The supply situation for the Allies also improved as two small harbours at Courseulles and Port-en-Bessin fell into their hands.

As ever, there was disagreement between the navies and the armies about how best to maintain the flow of supplies and equipment. The armies believed in a policy of 'selective unloading' so that ships were called into port not in turn but as those ashore needed their cargo. The armies believed that this stopped the creation of large and vulnerable dumps ashore. The navies, on the other hand, saw the ships offshore as being vulnerable to enemy attack, and almost as bad, not fulfilling their proper use as transport whilst lying waiting to be unloaded. In short, the nautical view was that the ships were vulnerable as supply dumps offshore.

The life of the temporary port came to an inevitable end as other ports were seized and cleared by the Allies, and each of these successive ports were far closer to the fighting as the armies approached Germany itself. The Arromanches Mulberry also began to silt up, and the tides swept sand from one part of the harbour to another, making one part too shallow and the other so deep that the caissons began to settle and even topple into the deeper parts. The roads around Arromanches had also started to deteriorate, not being meant for such heavy volumes of traffic, or for the heavy and destructive tracks of armoured vehicles.

CHERBOURG

Despite the Mulberry harbours, the Allies knew that it was vital that a good deep water port be seized as soon as possible so that supplies, equipment and reinforcements could sail directly from the United States without having to be unloaded into smaller ships or landing craft at a British port. In any event, landing ships and landing craft able to use beaches to unload their contents were far from the most efficient means of shipping, while anything being moved in this way not only had to be unloaded in a British port, but then water-proofed before onward movement.

With American troops landed on the Cotentin Peninsula, the port of Cherbourg at its head was the most obvious port to take. It was the largest and most easily accessible port from the landing sites. At one stage during the planning of the landings, it was decided not to land troops on the peninsula as they would be separated from the British and Canadian forces by the valley of the River Douve, which was flooded by the Germans to prevent airborne landings. This decision was reversed by the British ground commander, General Montgomery, when appointed in January 1944, partly to prevent landings on too narrow a front, which could have made the initial landings vulnerable to a strong German counter-attack, but also because of the importance of taking Cherbourg.

The first troops to land on the Cotentin Peninsula were those of the US 82nd and 101st Airborne Divisions, who landed at the base of the peninsula before dawn on D-Day and, despite being widely scattered, managed to secure most of the routes needed by the US 4th Infantry Division as they advanced inland from Utah Beach. In contrast to the bloodshed at Omaha, the landings at Utah shortly after dawn incurred few casualties. Nevertheless, after the landings the overriding priority was to establish a broad front and that meant connecting the US and British sectors. Despite the flooding, on 9 June, the US 101st Airborne Division crossed the Douve to capture the town of Carentan the following day after prolonged house-to-house fighting. This move united the Allied front, and held it, despite a powerful armoured German counter-attack on 13 June.

Uniting the fronts freed the US VII Corps, of which the 82nd, 101st and 4th were part, to move west, cutting off German forces on the Cotentin Peninsula. The corps commander, Major-General Lawton Collins, did not spare his men, sacking officers if progress was not fast enough for his liking, and even withdrawing units that failed to meet his demanding expectation. Progress was helped by the fact that the German defenders had not only suffered heavy casualties from Allied aerial attack and naval bombardment, as well as from the landings and battles with the American airborne troops, but their *Panzer* units were detained to the east because of the Allied threat to the key town of Caen. Even infantry units found movement to join the defences difficult as the flooding of the Douve now worked against the Germans, protecting the Allied southern flank.

Faced with an increasingly desperate situation, the German commander in the field, *Generalfeldmarschall* Erwin Rommel, wished to pull his troops back into the fortifications of Cherbourg, part of the Atlantic Wall, to defend the port, knowing that they could withstand a lengthy siege. Hitler ignored their advice and experience and ordered that they did not withdraw, even though this meant them fighting in the open and under constant Allied attack. It was not until late on 17 June that Hitler relented and allowed a limited withdrawal, but this was to a new defensive line that spanned the entire peninsula to the south of Cherbourg. Again Rommel protested that the new line was unsustainable.

The following day, the US 9th Infantry Division crossed the peninsula, cutting off the German defenders. By 20 June, the 4th, 9th and 79th Infantry Divisions had established a broad front forcing their way north towards Cherbourg. The defences around Montebourg collapsed. At Brix, the Americans discovered V-1 flying bombs and a V-2 rocket firing ground.

On 22 June, the US units were close to Cherbourg, whose defensive forces no longer had the option of crack troops withdrawn safely into the port; instead many of the 21,000 personnel defending the city and port were naval personnel hastily transferred, or from labour units. By this time, food, fuel and ammunition were in short supply, and the few German troops who had escaped the clutches of the advancing Americans were exhausted and organisation was lacking. The situation was not helped in any practical sense when the *Luftwaffe* managed to drop some supplies, but these included supposedly morale-boosting items such as Iron Cross decorations. Even so, the German commander rejected an Allied invitation to surrender, even though defeat was inevitable, and ordered his engineers to start to demolish key port installations so that it would be some time before it could be used by the Allies.

As the Americans advanced, Allied warships began a concentrated bombardment of the city's fortifications, and after several days of heavy fighting, cleared the Germans from bunkers and concrete pillboxes, the 79th Division's capture of Fort du Roule on 26 June ended any organised defence. Even so, the port and the arsenal did not fall until 29 June, and even then some isolated German troops cut off outside the city continued to fight until 1 July.

As a result of the German demolitions, the port was not in immediate use, and despite the odd cargo ship entering it at the end of July, use was still limited by the middle of August.

BREST

By the time Cherbourg was capable of limited use in mid-August, the Allies were already attempting to take the port of Brest, both further south and west than Cherbourg. At the north-western tip of the Brittany Peninsula, Brest had been an important French naval base and after the fall of France became the most important of the German U-boat bases. The attack started on 7 August, after the Americans had cut off German forces in Brittany in 'Operation Cobra'.

Because of its role as a naval base, Brest was even more important to the Germans than Cherbourg, and was defended by around 40,000 troops, led by *General der Fallschirmtruppe* Hermann-Bernhard Ramcke, a German paratroop general and a veteran of the *Afrika Korps*. German propaganda made much of the fortified status of the port, which was known as *Festung Brest*, 'Fortress Brest'. Spearheading the thrust towards the city was General George Patton's Third United States Army; the US VIII Corps was also diverted to Brittany to help secure Patton's breakthrough.

As they advanced through Brittany, earlier, on 17 August, the old port and fortified city of St Malo was captured from the Germans by 83rd Infantry Division, but at the time this was a much smaller port than Cherbourg or Brest, and in any case its harbour installations had been badly damaged by the retreating Germans. Despite the withdrawal from the port, the German garrison at Cézembre Island only surrendered after several days of aerial attack, including one of the earliest uses of napalm bombs, and heavy naval bombardment from the Allies.

Brest was surrounded and on 7 August the US VIII Corps began their attack. On this occasion, the defenders were well-trained and battle-hardened, many of them being paratroops, or *Fallschirmjäger*, who stood their ground despite heavy aerial attack and intensive naval bombardment. The outlying defences surrendered more easily. The attackers made slow progress and suffered heavy losses, despite the extensive use of artillery to reduce the level of hand-to-hand fighting. Another difference at Brest was that by the time of the American assault, the defenders were still well armed. In an attempt to flush the defenders out of their bunkers and pillboxes, the British 79th Armoured Division was called upon to send in flame-throwing Crocodile tanks, a variant of the Churchill, supported with US infantry, to take the heavily fortified Fort Montbarey. The result was that by the time the battle ended with surrender on 19 September, the city had been razed to the ground, but again the Germans had managed to sabotage the port installations.

The cost of the attack and the damage done to the desperately-needed port installations forced the Allies to decide against surrounding and seizing other ports, unless these could be easily taken during the advance, or, in military terms, 'on the march'. The sole exception to this rule was the Normandy port of Le Havre, but many of the remaining Breton ports were not taken before German surrender. As it was, Brest was not operational until after the fall of Paris.

LE HAVRE

One of the best-known and largest French ports, Le Havre had not only been a cross-Channel ferry port before the war, but was a major port for transatlantic liners, and indeed was the main French port for such ships. For the advancing Allies, Le Havre was a prize not just because of its capacity to handle large ships, but because it was far closer to Paris and the frontline than the other ports such as Cherbourg and, even further away, Brest.

The move to take Le Havre was code-named 'Operation Astonia' and, because of its location, the operation was given to British and Canadian troops. The actual battle lasted from 10–12 September 1944.

Heavily fortified by the Germans to make it one of the strongest parts of the Atlantic Wall, Le Havre also had good natural defences with access from the south, east and west prevented by bodies of water. As a result, the Germans concentrated their man-made defences to the north, with an anti-tank ditch 10ft (3m) wide which was 20–23ft (6–7m) deep, covered by anti-tank weapons in pillboxes and an estimated 1,500 mines laid on the approaches. The Allies believed that there were up to 8,700 troops defending the city and port, of which 4,000 were artillery and 1,300 naval personnel, and that there was also a battalion from the 36th Grenadier Regiment, while the remainder consisted of infantry.

To soften up the defences, the Royal Air Force bombed the area over three days between 5 and 7 September with no less than 1,900 bomber sorties dropping 8,200 tons of bombs. There was also bombardment from the sea, with the battleship HMS *Warspite*, crippled off the Normandy beaches, towed into position and accompanied by the monitor HMS *Erebus*.

The assault began at 1745 on 10 September, with the two warships attacking the coastal batteries and the RAF dropping a further 5,000 tons of bombs over a period of ninety minutes before the ground attack began. The ground attack by British I Corps and Canadian II Corps was led by the Canadians. It was supported by a number of specialised units, with 'Kangaroo' and 'Crab' tanks, which quickly cleared gaps through the minefield and breached the anti-tank ditch, at great cost – the 79th Armoured Division lost no less than thirty-four Crab anti-mine flail tanks, two command tanks and six AVRE tanks. First through the defences was the 49th (West Riding) Infantry Division, while the 51st (Highland) Infantry Division broke through to their right. The battle continued until 1400 on 11 September with German troops surrendering when flame-throwing Churchill Crocodile tanks appeared. It was not until 1145 on 12 September that the garrison commander finally surrendered and the Allies found that the garrison was far larger than expected and 12,000 German personnel were taken prisoner.

As always, the Allies were hoping that the port would be intact and that it would be handling ships soon after its liberation, but the damage was so extensive that the port was not opened to Allied shipping until October. The damage was not entirely due to German engineers sabotaging the facilities, but was also the result of the naval bombardment and bombing. While the assault had cost the British and Canadians few casualties, no less than 350 ships had been destroyed as well as more than 10 miles (16km) of quayside. No less than 15,000 buildings had been razed to the ground.

DIEPPE

Meanwhile, on 1 September the Canadians had taken Dieppe, the port over which so many lives had been lost in 1942. In 'Operation Fusillade', the 2nd Canadian Infantry Division advanced on the port and city expecting to have to face determined German resistance, but the 8th Reconnaissance Regiment (14th Hussars) approached from inland in the direction of Rouen and reported that the Germans had abandoned the city on 31 August. A planned raid by RAF Bomber Command was called off when the leading formation was just twenty minutes from the city.

In contrast to the debacle of August 1942, the welcome was warm as the entire population lined the streets to greet the liberators, with the two motorcyclists sent in advance being surrounded so that they could move no further. On 3 September, the Canadians paraded through Dieppe.

For the locals there was another pleasant surprise in store when they discovered that many of the Canadians spoke French!

BOULOGNE

Boulogne and Calais, in the Pas-de-Calais, long considered by many German senior officers to be the most likely invasion points, were at one stage in danger of being bypassed. Eisenhower and his colleagues in SHAEF favoured advancing on a broad front, but others, including Montgomery, favoured a single thrust. The advocates of the single thrust believed that victory lay in getting Allied forces into Germany as soon as possible. Those who advocated a broad front knew the dangers of a spearhead or single thrust being cut, leaving forward troops isolated, and there was also the pressing question of obtaining ports through which supplies could be landed. As the armies advanced, their supply lines became ever longer, and yet they needed 27,000 tons of supplies and fuel daily. The ports in Normandy were to have limited usefulness, and in any case, after capture, Le Havre, and Rouen, further upstream on the Seine, were allocated to the Americans.

There were a number of unusual features about the moves to liberate Boulogne. The first of these was that the 3rd Canadian Infantry Division to which the operation, code-named 'Wellhit', was assigned, agreed with the Germans that many of the town's civilians should be evacuated before the assault, and 8,000 were moved out before the operation began on 17 September. The second was that there was no naval gunfire support, but instead two 14in and two 15in guns located in Dover fired across the English Channel, mainly firing at German 16in coastal gun positions around Calais and Cap Gris Nez, preventing them being used against the Canadians. There were, however, heavy air raids with 800 sorties and 3,200 tons of high explosive bombs dropped.

It took until 22 September for the German garrison to surrender, with around 9,500 German personnel becoming prisoners-of-war. Once again, the town and the port were badly damaged, but in addition the presence of the German guns at Calais and Cap Gris Nez also meant that Allied ships had to avoid the area. The Canadians knew that they had to silence these guns and capture the port of Calais. No doubt the presence of these weapons had also influenced the decision not to deploy a battleship or monitors to bombard Boulogne as the Royal Navy insisted that the guns in the Calais area would have to be silenced before Boulogne could be brought back into use as a port. This was disappointing news for the commander of Canadian troops, Lieutenant-General Henry Crerar, who had simply hoped to surround Calais and wait for the isolated German garrison to surrender.

CALAIS

One of the busiest ports for cross-Channel traffic, Calais was also the port closest to the English mainland. It was not just the importance of such a well-positioned port that spurred the Allies to seize it and liberate the town; it was also the pressing need to silence the German coastal batteries with their powerful 16in guns. These were menacing Boulogne once liberated, and during the war they had had a similar effect on the English port of Dover, where shellfire rather than bombing raids had been the problem.

Calais was well defended and the attack had to wait for the armour and artillery used at Boulogne to become available. This was to be expected as Boulogne lay along the route from Dieppe to Calais anyway.

So important were the guns at Calais that there had in fact been an attempt to tackle them before the move on Boulogne. The Canadian 7th Reconnaissance Regiment (17th Duke of York's Royal Canadian Hussars) had started screening Calais on 5 September, and they were joined on 10 September by the Toronto Scottish Regiment, part of the Canadian 2nd Division. Later, the 3rd Division's 7th Infantry Brigade and the Royal Winnipeg Rifles followed and on the night of 16/17 September these forces attacked the four gun batteries on Cap Gris Nez, which had a total of seventeen guns between them. The batteries were in concrete pillboxes and bunkers, and protected by minefields, electrified fences, and anti-tank ditches and tank traps as well as anti-tank guns. For the cost of six Canadian tanks, three Hussars dead and another wounded, the assault made no impression on the German defenders.

Boulogne was secured on 22 September and the following day the Canadian 3rd Division redeployed, its 8th Brigade going to Calais and the 9th Brigade to Cap Gris Nez, ready for the start of 'Operation Undergo', the liberation of Calais. Aerial reconnaissance had spotted no less than forty-two heavy artillery batteries in the 20 miles (32km) around Calais. The Canadians had already moved two batteries of 7.2in howitzers and two regiments of heavy anti-aircraft guns into position on 21 September, but after 23 September, this grew to eight medium regiments. Heavy bombing had started on 20 September, with more than 600 sorties dropping 3,000 tons of bombs, but aerial operations were then suspended until 24 September due to bad weather.

In addition to the German defences, Calais was also surrounded by marshland and the surrounding countryside had also been flooded by the

Germans, doubtless recalling how the British had held them at bay in this same countryside in 1940. The centre of the city was fortified and a network of canals was augmented by a moat surrounding the central citadel. Despite this, the German commandant, a mere lieutenant-colonel, regarded most of his 7,500 troops as 'mere rubbish'.[2]

On 25 September the battle began at 1000 as soon as a heavy bombing raid that had started at 0815 ended. One of the Canadian brigades was assigned to the fortifications at Cap Gris Nez, while the other two, with British and Canadian armour support, were to take the city. A smoke screen was laid to prevent the attack on the city being seen by the guns at Cap Gris Nez, and a heavy artillery bombardment was laid before the assault began.

The first day saw Cap Blanc Nez, halfway between Cap Gris Nez and Calais, taken along with 200 German prisoners, but the Germans were not giving in without a fight, and elsewhere ceded ground only to lure the Canadians into an exposed position. Nevertheless, the use of flame-throwing Crocodile tanks helped the Canadians make progress, and eventually further ground was taken, with another 300 prisoners.

The assault on the city was much more difficult. Nevertheless, the Germans were not without difficulties of their own, including 20,000 French civilians who had steadfastly refused to be evacuated, and German troops were beginning to desert. Eventually, early on 29 September, a truce was agreed, which took effect at noon. Neither side was allowed to regroup, while the French civilian population was eventually persuaded to leave, and the Germans were given twenty-four hours in which to organise the evacuation, the Canadian forces providing relief for the population once clear of the city.

The truce ended at noon on 29 September. What happened next features in the regimental history of the Regina Rifles:

On September 30 a terrific artillery and fighter-bomber attack began which was to be a prelude to the main effort. This show of force was too much, by 13.15 hours we received reports that they were surrendering in masses to the Queen's Own Rifles and the Cameron Highlanders of Ottawa who had been containing the city on the north. We were ordered to attack at once and Colonel Matheson with the intelligence officer started out to tactical headquarters in an amphibious jeep. The jeep sank.

Objectives were rapidly occupied and by early evening the prisoners totalled were three hundred and seventy-two including nine officers.

It was all over but the shouting. Company areas in the city were searched and occupied. The battalion's vehicles had to travel ten miles around the water in order to find a route into the city.

During the truce at Calais, RAF Bomber Command made another heavy attack on the fortifications at Cap Gris Nez, followed by a Canadian assault. The assault was hampered by minefields and after further attempts it was not until 29 September, after a heavy artillery bombardment, that Cap Gris Nez was in Allied hands and the guns were silenced.

With the fall of Calais and the occupation of Cap Gris Nez, the Canadians took more than 9,000 prisoners, of which some 1,600 were from Cap Gris Nez. Nevertheless, once again it was something of a Pyrrhic victory, since the port facilities had been badly damaged both by German sabotage and by the bombing and shelling of the Allies.

DUNKIRK

While Boulogne and Calais were still to be liberated, the Canadian 2nd Division had moved to Dunkirk, starting with initial probing attacks on 15 September. This vital port was under the command of a German naval officer, Admiral Friedrich Frisius. The Allies surrounded the port, but after pushing into Belgium and seizing Antwerp, the one major port captured with its facilities more or less intact, General Montgomery decided to bypass Dunkirk and simply keep the Germans besieged. It was not until after Frisius surrendered unconditionally to the commander of the Czechoslovak Brigade, Brigade General Alois Liska, on 9 May 1945, that the heavily fortified port and town was taken by the Allies.

As at Calais, a truce was arranged for French civilians to be evacuated, but on this occasion it was arranged by the International Red Cross and did not take place until 4 October, when thirty-six hours were allowed for 18,000 French civilians to leave, and for the evacuation of wounded German personnel.

Meanwhile, far more important, and pressing, was the taking of the island of Walcheren and the clearing of the Scheldt Estuary so that the port of Antwerp could re-open. Antwerp was at the time Europe's largest port, and was also far closer to the frontline as it advanced through the Netherlands towards Germany.

OSTEND

The Belgian port of Ostend was liberated by Canadian troops on 8 September 1944, five days after Brussels was liberated and four days after the liberation of Antwerp. As Antwerp had still to be opened and the Scheldt was impassable due to the German presence on Walcheren, Ostend assumed a greater importance to the Allies than would have been justified otherwise. It was the nearest port to the fierce fighting that continued in the Netherlands and on the border between Belgium and Germany.

Access from the sea was to be the main problem at Ostend as the Germans had managed to sink no fewer than fourteen ships, all close together, and in three lines across the harbour entrance. Salvaging so many ships would have taken time, so drastic measures were called for, as Commodore T. Mackenzie, RNVR, the Allied Naval Commander-in-Chief's Principal Salvage Officer explained:

> The removal of these three lines of wrecks by ordinary salvage practice would have taken three to six months. The use of the port was vital to the army. I decided therefore to disperse the wrecks by mass demolition. Our wreck disposal vessels were called forward, and a few days after they commenced operations our salvage vessels entered the port astern of the minesweepers and commenced clearing the berths of wrecks. Two days later troops carrying thousands of tons of vital war material for the army entered the port and commenced discharging. The volume of traffic increased as the channel at the blockships was deepened by our wreck disposal vessels and more berths were cleared by the salvage vessels.[3]

This makes it sound deceptively easy. It was a quick method of re-opening the port, but it was far from easy. Divers had to position explosive charges on the blockships, with the ever-present danger of a mine nearby being detonated. Placing the explosive charges was far from easy, and there was always the risk of their air lines being entangled in the rigging, masts or superstructure of the sunken ships. The explosive charges were sufficiently large and heavy that they had to be dropped to the divers, who then had to move these dangerous loads carefully into the position where they would do the most damage. There was always the risk that explosive charges could be moved by tides or currents, or the passage of other ships. Lines had to be taken from the explosives to the detonators, either ashore or onboard the ships supporting the divers.

Nevertheless, Ostend was open and it was no longer necessary to convey thousands of tons of fuel, supplies and ammunition from Normandy.

But tragedy awaited the Allied navies at Ostend.

Even by spring of the following year, most of the Netherlands was under German control, including the major naval bases of Ijmuiden and Den Helder, acting as bases for E-boats. The E-boats posed a major threat to the steady stream of shipping crossing the southern North Sea, and as always, the best defence against E-boat attacks on the northern flank of the Allied convoys was to provide motor gunboats or motor torpedo boats as escorts or on patrol to ward off E-boat attacks before they could get within reach of a convoy. Two MTB flotillas were based at Ostend, the Royal Navy's 55th and the Canadian-manned 29th, with a mobile base unit to service the motor torpedo boats. These two units had been fighting alongside each other since June 1944. The 29th had eleven 72ft 6in MTBs while the 55th had the larger Fairmile 'D' boats, more usually known as 'Dog Boats'. Most British MTBs and MGBs had petrol engines rather than the safer diesel engines, which meant that accidents involving fuel vapour-induced explosions and fires were relatively common.

On 14 February 1945, there were no less than thirty-one MTBs of all kinds as well as other small craft gathered in the harbour at Ostend, many of the MTBs moored alongside one another. Many of the crew members had been granted shore leave, but others were busy preparing for that night's patrols.

Amongst these latter were four of the Canadian boats of the 29th MTB Flotilla. Of these, *MTB464* was carrying out an armament check at sea when one of its engines cut out due to water in the fuel system. This was a common problem as one of the tankers supporting the MTBs had pumped water contaminated fuel ashore. The base maintenance staff were too busy to provide assistance, and simply suggested that the MTB's crew pumped water from their fuel tanks into buckets and then disposed of it over the side. Before long, a strong smell of petrol spread throughout the harbour. Many noticed this, but no one reported it or took any action.

What actually ignited the major fire that ensued remains unknown. One witness was Ken Forrester, serving aboard one of the Royal Navy's MTBs, *MTB771*, in the 55th Flotilla:

It was a rest day, and half the crew had been taken on a sightseeing trip to Brugge for the afternoon. It was around 3 o'clock in the afternoon. I had volunteered to make the tea and went up on deck to go to the potato locker which was just below the bridge. Before I got there I saw flames and smoke rising from the middle of a group of Tony Laws' 72' 6" [British] Power Boats that were berthed in a large lock entrance some 30 yards away. Our boat was tied up to the wall with two others of our flotilla tied alongside us. The tide was low which meant that our torpedoes were below the level of the seawall. There was a raised gangway over the torpedoes bypassing the 0.5 turret. This gangway was level with the top of the wall. On seeing the fire I ran to the forward hatch – the crew's quarters – and yelled out *Fire!* Ran to the stern of the boat, took hold of a fire hose that was permanently rigged and ran unreeling it as I went. I was just passing over the gangway that was level with the wall when the boat that was on fire blew up with a huge *Woomph* noise. There was a rush of seething hot air which blew me over. The next thing I remember was picking myself up on the dockside with burning debris everywhere covering the quayside and all of our boats. Our own boat had been protected somewhat with being shielded by the dockside. I was still dazed, realised I'd lost my shoes and beard mostly singed off. I had blood running down my face by that time. Someone was running past me, so I ran while pandemonium was going on. Ammunition was exploding, torpedoes going off, pieces of flaming boats everywhere.[4]

It seemed as if the entire harbour was ablaze, with torpedoes and other ammunition exploding, and fuel tanks rupturing and exploding, adding their contents to the fire.

Thirty-six members of the Royal Navy were killed, with the loss of seven boats, while the Royal Canadian Navy lost twenty-six personnel and five boats.

NOTES

1. Imperial War Museum Sound Archive.
2. Stacey, C. P., *Official History of the Canadian Army in the Second World War: Volume III: The Victory Campaign: The Operations in North-West Europe 1944–45* (Ottawa, ON: Queen's Printer, 1960).
3. Imperial War Museum Sound Archive.
4. Forrester, Ken, *If Only I had Known*, believed privately published, 2013.

16

WALCHEREN

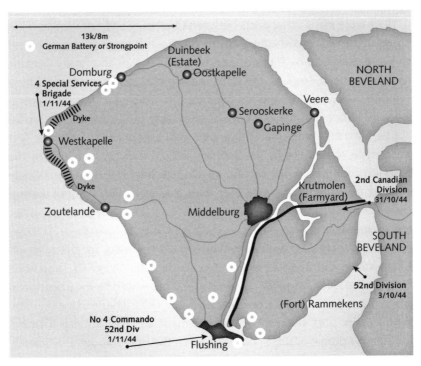

Often described as being like a saucer, with dykes around the edges and a centre below sea level, the Dutch island of Walcheren was heavily defended by the Germans as it commanded the estuary of the River Scheldt, and hence the approaches to the Belgian port of Antwerp, at that time Europe's largest. (Library & Archive of Canada)

It took far longer to break out of Normandy than the Allies had planned. The *bocage*, the small fields with high hedges and deep lanes were natural obstacles that looked so innocent, and even attractive, but were a blessing to the defenders and a source of frustration and loss to the attackers. This was not tank country.

A big gain had come on 30 June with the capture of the port of Cherbourg, followed by the fall of the key city of Caen on 9 July and then Saint-Lô on 18 July. The fall of Avranches left the Allied armies too far inland for the bombardment fleet to continue shelling useful targets.

Even after the Allies' break out of Normandy, which started on 13 August 1944, fresh problems arose, not least with the supply lines, which were extending daily. The Germans resisted Allied attempts to take the French channel ports, appreciating their significance to the enemy, which left the Allies dependent on the surviving Mulberry harbour, and the port of Cherbourg, which was actually further away from the advancing frontline.

There were many other ports between Cherbourg and Antwerp, as mentioned in the previous chapter. Moving eastwards through France there was Le Havre, followed by Dieppe, then Boulogne, Calais and finally Dunkirk, before moving to Belgium with Ostend and then Zeebrugge. Most of these involved heavy fighting, and the combination of Allied attack and German sabotage meant that the vital port facilities were badly damaged and could not be used for some time. There were two exceptions to this. The first was Dieppe, abandoned by the Germans and so taken 'on the march' by the Canadian 2nd Division. The second was Dunkirk, heavily fortified, but simply 'masked' by the Allies or, in civilian terms, besieged, and left until the war ended when the port was surrendered. Antwerp was the prize the Allies really wanted.

Antwerp was taken by General Bernard Montgomery for the Allies on 4 September. This was a far greater success than the Allies had dared hope for, with the Germans taken by surprise and prevented by local resistance groups from destroying the port's extensive dock facilities and lock system. With a major port intact, the Allies had made a significant leap forward, but for one problem, ships could not reach the port through the Scheldt Estuary, as Antwerp is more than 37 miles, 60km, from the open sea.

Antwerp was the largest port in Europe and strategically well placed for the Allied advance, but without being able to use the port, the Allies could not contemplate invading Germany, as the Germans well understood.

With so much in the balance, the attempt to clear the Scheldt Estuary involved some of the fiercest fighting on the Western Front.

Another reason for the importance of the operation was that it followed the failure in September of Operation Market Garden, the attempt to take the Rhine bridges at Arnhem. This was seen by Montgomery, and then by Eisenhower, as a means of bringing the war in Europe to an early end. Despite dropping 16,500 paratroops and another 3,500 glider-borne troops with astonishing accuracy, the operation failed, partly because two German SS *Panzer* divisions were unexpectedly refitting in the area, and by coincidence had just completed an exercise in repelling an Allied airborne landing. The units intended to relieve the airborne troops were delayed, while, unknown to the Allies, an American officer was captured with a copy of the operational order.

Had Market Garden succeeded, the Allies had the prospect of capturing the ports of Rotterdam or Amsterdam, which would have been excellent alternatives to Antwerp as supply ports, provided that they were captured intact and with little damage, and the approaches were free of blockships and mines. Without either of these ports, Antwerp was vital and the only hope of providing adequate supplies for the growing Allied armies as they prepared to push into Germany.

The Allies started by clearing the land on either side of the Scheldt, Dutch territory, a process that was finished by the end of October, but this still left Walcheren Island. The low-lying island with dykes and sand dunes around its coastline has been compared to a saucer. The island's dykes bristled with coastal batteries that commanded the approaches to Antwerp. In an attempt to destroy the batteries and force the Germans to withdraw from Walcheren, RAF Bomber Command made repeated attacks on the dykes. The first of these was on 3 October, when the dykes at Westkapelle were breached, but with considerable loss of civilian lives. A further attempt was made on 7 October, striking at two points to the east and west of Vlissingen. The third attempt on 11 October was at Veere, and this saw the central part of the island completely flooded, the Germans forced to retreat onto high ground and around the outside of the island as well as into the towns.

To the east of Walcheren Island was South Beveland, taken by the 2nd Canadian Infantry Division. South Beveland was linked to Walcheren Island by a causeway just over 130ft (40m) wide, and 1,200yd (1,100m) long. In anticipation of an amphibious crossing of the River Seine after the Normandy landings, the Calgary Highlanders had been trained to use small boats, but this tactic was not needed in Normandy, and although a few boats were launched, for the most part it was not possible at Walcheren because the ground along the river banks was too soft and swampy for boats to be launched.

As British and Canadian troops prepared to take the island of Walcheren, the strong air support needed was not available, despite clear skies over the target area, because Allied aircraft were stuck on their fogbound airfields. The attack was conducted on two sides, with the Canadians, supported by troops from the British Army's 52nd (Lowland) Division, attacking from landward at South Beveland, across the Scheldt, while the British 4th Special Service Brigade comprising Royal Marine and Army Commandos attacked from seaward. The Royal Navy provided a heavy bombardment of the island and its defences.

As with some of the defensive positions at Normandy, many of the troops defending Walcheren were men unfit for normal combat duties. Reports indicate that many of them suffered from stomach problems, but even so, they were well supplied with food and munitions. No doubt someone had foreseen that resupply might become difficult, and by the time the Allies were ready to seize the island this was indeed the case as the island was cut off from the remaining German forces.

On the late afternoon and evening of 31 October, 'C' Company of the Royal Regiment of Canada, attempted to make a surprise attack to seize the causeway. The causeway was straight and did not offer any cover for attacking troops. Their efforts were rewarded by heavy casualties, and stopped while halfway along the causeway, where they found that the Germans had blown a deep crater to act as an anti-tank obstacle. 'B' Company of the Calgary Highlanders were then ordered to advance along the causeway just before midnight, but also brought to a halt. Despite these two costly setbacks, 'D' Company was ordered forward and, in the face of facing intensive gunfire from the defenders, managed to secure the causeway by dawn on 1 November, aided by the British 52nd (Lowland) Division, who had found a way across the Sloe channel to the island.

The Germans then began a series of strong counter-attacks, using all of the weaponry available to them, including flame-throwers. Considerable bravery was shown by the Canadians, whose Company Sergeant-Major 'Blackie' Laloge of the Calgary Highlanders received the Distinguished Conduct Medal, DCM, after throwing back hand grenades before they could explode.

The following day, two platoons of *Le Regiment de Maisonneuve* took over the bridgehead on the island, before being forced back onto the causeway, and the situation did not change when a battalion of the Glasgow Highlanders were ordered into the battle.

Meanwhile at 0554, the three Royal Marine Commandos of the British 4th Special Service Brigade attacked from seaward at Westkapelle, in Operation Infatuate I, accompanied by troops of the No. 4 (Belgian) and No. 5 (Norwegian) Commandos from Brigadier Peter Laycock's No. 10 (IA) Commando. No. 4 Commando with French troops in support then crossed from Breskens to attack Flushing with support from No. 155 Infantry Brigade in Operation Infatuate II, aided by a heavy naval bombardment from the crippled battleship HMS *Warspite*, two monitors, including HMS *Roberts*, and other naval vessels, despite many of their landing craft being sunk by heavy fire from German coastal batteries. The crossing was made mainly in Buffalos, which one Royal Marine present described as being like tanks with no tops.

The run ashore was not easy, as Captain J. Linzel of No. 10 Commando recalled:

> This operation had more impact on me. The objective was to clear the seaway to Antwerp. We went to Belgium, where the No. 4 Troops Brigade and the No. 10 Commando were billeted. We were an attached unit of 14 men. We entered our LCT's Buffalo's amphibious vehicles to go to Walcheren where we experienced heavy German artillery. Our vehicle got hit direct by a grenade, setting our flamethrowers and ammunition on fire. This was a chaos. Our burning Buffalo was pushed into the sea and I can remember that together with 10 other men I ended-up in another Buffalo and landed at Westkapelle. We experienced some serious fighting there and a lot of the Brigade were killed. It took us 3 days to capture the German dyke at Vlissingen, there were about 300 casements.[1]

Frederick Weston was a sergeant in No. 41 Royal Marine Commando:

> We were in the open, unlike D-Day, so we saw everything as we went in. It was very heavily defended, we manned gunboats to take these on and we also had rocket ships that shot off scores of shots at a time. We'd also been told that there could be fixed flame-throwers on this part of the beach, so that was something to look forward to. We managed to get on

all right and got into the village there, and saw their strongpoint at the base of a lighthouse. We got cover in an old house and found the old hands in there getting a brew of tea going. As we were pretty wet and miserable at the time, we had a quick cup of tea.

Unfortunately our troop commander was killed when we reached their strongpoint. It was a very sad occasion for us, it seemed like they were giving themselves up and then one man decided not to, and that was the end of our troop commander. It made us all very angry.[2]

This was the one thing that most fighting men could not accept: enemy troops surrendering and when approached to be taken prisoner, shooting their exposed would-be captors. It says much for the discipline of the Royal Marines that they did not shoot the Germans, or at least the man who betrayed their trust.

Two days of street fighting followed before the regional capital Middleburg could be seized and the Germans surrendered there on 5 November. Nevertheless, some resistance continued in the north of Walcheren and it was not until 8 November that this ended.

The arrival of the Commandos unfortunately showed that the sacrifices made by the Canadians and the Scots to secure the causeway and establish a bridgehead on the island were unnecessary – a waste of brave lives.

Between 1 and 26 November, the Royal Navy's minesweepers set about clearing the Scheldt from the North Sea to the port of Antwerp. The delay in making use of Antwerp had given the Germans breathing space and without it, they would probably not have been able to mount the Ardennes offensive, or the 'Battle of the Bulge', in December.

Of course, Walcheren had not been subdued on 1 November, so the first attempts at minesweeping were made under heavy fire from German coastal artillery. This is an indication of the importance of the work. Starting in earnest on 3 November, no less than 150 minesweepers conducted a careful sweep of the Scheldt, sweeping and detonating 267 mines by the time their work was completed on 26 November.

On 28 November, local dignitaries and the leaders of the Allied armies, including Admiral Ramsay, gathered at a formal celebration to declare Antwerp open for shipping, the first ship to arrive being the Canadian-built but British-manned *Fort Cataraqui*, and within days more than 10,000 tons of supplies had been landed. A military band played both the Belgian and the British national anthems.

Antwerp was open only just in time. When the Germans launched the Ardennes offensive, catching the Allies by surprise, their advance saw many large Allied supply bases fall to the enemy. Had Antwerp not been operational, and the Allies still dependent on Cherbourg and the sole surviving Mulberry harbour, the setback would have been disastrous. It is doubtful that the Allies could have been pushed back into the sea, but they could have been pushed back into France.

As it was, regaining Antwerp had been one of the objectives of the Ardennes offensive, and E-boats were sent to harass Allied shipping entering and leaving the port. The war was far from over for the citizens of the liberated port as Hitler then turned his V-1 and V-2 missiles on Antwerp, which received far more of these 'revenge' weapons than did London.

NOTES

1. Imperial War Museum Sound Archive.
2. Imperial War Museum Sound Archive.

17

WHAT COULD HAVE HAPPENED

When looking for a new general, Napoleon Bonaparte is supposed to have asked whether a candidate was lucky. There can be little doubt that, as in so much else, luck plays an important part in warfare. Others have declared that within minutes of a military operation being launched, the plans and any timetable go out of the window.

So, the first question has to be whether or not the Allies were lucky, or simply reaping the benefits of their growing experience in amphibious assault, and of their meticulous planning?

'Simply' is hardly the right word. There was nothing simple about Overlord and nothing simple about Neptune either. It was the largest and most complex amphibious assault in history, and remains so today. It was also the largest and most complex airborne assault, and again, that holds true to this day.

THE GERMAN RESPONSE

The first big question really concerns the German response, which was uneven and varied wildly, being at its best at Omaha, which became a bloody and hard won victory for the Americans.

The German ability to respond was initially hampered by Hitler's decision to withdraw the battlecruisers *Scharnhorst* and *Gneisenau* from Brest. Had these ships been present, the Allies would have had to fight their way to Normandy. In fact, there would have had to be a major naval battle to remove them before the landings could even be contemplated.

This begs the question whether they would have survived at Brest in the first place. They were ordered back to Germany in February 1942 because they had been bombed frequently by the Royal Air Force. The bombing had done relatively little damage because bombs bounce off armour plating or break up, but by 1944 things were changing. It was not just that bombs were getting heavier and armour penetration was better, but even before the invasion RAF Bomber Command was already using the 14,000lb 'Tallboy' earthquake bomb and knew that most damage was done if the bomb was aimed at a point next to the target, instead of directly onto a solid target such as concrete submarine pens or a heavily armoured warship. The concept of the earthquake bomb was that it started to spin as it dropped and then buried itself deeply before exploding. Heavy concrete structures crumbled as they were undermined and warships capsized.

The advent of bombs such as 'Tallboy' and the even heavier and more effective 22,000lb 'Grand Slam', the largest and heaviest bomb of the Second World War, meant that ships in sheltered positions once again became targets, and even a Norwegian *fjord* was no protection for the remaining German battleship, *Tirpitz*. Before such weapons became available, torpedo attack was the most certain means of sinking a major warship for, as one American admiral once commented, 'it is easier to sink a warship if the water comes in through the bottom'. Torpedo attack was not easy, as dropping a torpedo too soon gave time for evasive action, while dropping it later gave the target time to shoot at the torpedo-bomber as it slowly held its course to aim at the target. There was also the danger of a torpedo being dropped from too high, in which case it broke up on hitting the sea.

For once in his dismal record of second-guessing his senior military and naval officers, Hitler was right to bring the ships back to Germany. He was not to know about the earthquake bombs at the time he made the decision, but even so, the ships were safer away from Brest.

The German U-boats were conspicuous by their absence from the scene. The reasons for this were simple. First, their codes had been broken and the Allies knew where to find them. The Battle of the Atlantic was by this time won by the Allies. Second, their bases in France were soon lost to the Allies and, with the 'Tallboy' bomb, vulnerable even before they were lost. This meant that any U-boats had to run the risk of escaping from

Germany, travelling around the north of Scotland and the west of Ireland, then moving up the heavily patrolled Western Approaches and into the English Channel, before attacking. Their chance of closing in on the landing beaches or of tackling convoys running in to Normandy was slight. The passage from Germany was long and hazardous. They would also have to make it back, saving enough fuel for the homeward journey.

The Germans were kept guessing about where the Allies would land until it was too late. The fact that even after the landings they still expected landings in the Pas-de-Calais is astonishing as the scale of the landings was unprecedented and they surely could not have believed that the Allies could manage the same again? True, the landings in the south of France followed in August, but these were not on the same scale.

The Germans would have done much better to have withdrawn the bulk of their army from Norway, leaving the *Kriegsmarine* to ward off any Allied landings. The ideas that the Allies would return to Europe via Norway was one of Hitler's fancies, and no doubt, as usual, he paid little regard to the difficulties of moving overland in such a mountainous country with a heavily indented coastline.

Some German officers would have liked to abandon Italy and concentrated their forces in France. There is some logic to this, but had the fighting ended in Italy, the Allies would also have been able to bring greater air, land and sea power to bear on France.

Troops were also kept in the Channel Islands, which Hitler believed could be used by the Allies as a stepping stone for a return to France. The fact that these small islands, with their very narrow country lanes and small harbours, would have made poor bases escaped him.

It is true, however, that the Germans had overreached themselves, and were possibly already overstretched by the time they invaded the Soviet Union, but even that debacle was made worse by Hitler changing the objectives. By 1944, they were under increasing pressure on the Eastern Front, while still tied down in Greece and Yugoslavia and had also lost substantial forces in the invasion of Crete, an island that proved of little use to them once occupied.

The relative weakness of much of the Atlantic Wall and the poor quality of many of the defending troops was another sign of German weakness, lacking sufficient fit and trained manpower and also the industrial resources and raw materials necessary to provide a strong defence. As mentioned earlier, the Germans were basically in the position of choosing between completing the Atlantic Wall or building U-boat pens, but could not have both, after the invasion of France. Then, later in the war, they could either repair the damage done by Allied bombing or concentrate on completing the Atlantic Wall, but again, could not do both. The famous raid on the Ruhr dams needed 7,000 labourers to repair, who could not be transferred to the Atlantic Wall until the chronic shortage of water for the steel industry had been rectified by repairing the dams.

The fortifications such as gun emplacements and look-out posts built at great cost on the Channel Islands might be tourist features today, but at the time this was just more wasteful use of slave labour and materials.

Defeating any landings on the beaches sounded fine in theory, but in practice it depended on the quality and depth of the initial defences, and also overlooked the fact that the Allies might divide their forces and air-land troops behind the defences. This is what happened. The Germans, who had done much the same thing in the Netherlands, should have realised this. They had also attempted a combined air and sea assault on Crete, but the assault by sea was crippled by the Royal Navy's command of the seas and that from the air was costly.

In fact, the German failure lay in their inability to prepare a fast, flexible mobile defence. This would have been difficult enough, but failure was guaranteed by holding troops in reserve for landings in the Pas-de-Calais.

Insisting that army commanders should not withdraw forces as they thought necessary meant that losses mounted and the numbers taken prisoner increased. Cynics always say that a 'strategic withdrawal' is simply a euphemism for retreat, and while this is often true, there are times that a strategic withdrawal is necessary if the battle is to continue.

The fact that so many of the port facilities were sabotaged shows that many German commanders were realists, but Hitler's insistence on using the Channel ports as strongpoints to be defended to the last man again shows his poor grasp of strategy.

Churchill and Stalin also never hesitated to interfere in military planning and decision making, but Stalin, after his initial refusal to accept the reality of a German invasion, had a good grasp of strategy, even impressing the British General Sir Alan Brooke, who never suffered fools gladly. Churchill was more often right than wrong, and as the leader of a democracy had the benefit of senior officers who could stand up to him without the fear of imprisonment. Hitler was in this respect slightly kinder than Stalin, who did not hesitate to use the *gulag* system of prison camps and even sent the families of his immediate circle to them to guarantee their loyalty. Even so, one cannot imagine the case of Rommel's alleged disgrace and forced suicide being repeated in either the United Kingdom or the United States.

ALLIES

That the British and the Americans were close allies made the planning and execution of the assault easier, but it did not make it easy. Churchill hit the nail on the head when he said, as quoted in Chapter Three, that: 'There is only one thing worse than fighting with allies, and that is fighting without them.'

Churchill's comment makes sense. The British and the Americans were not, and never have been, two sides of the same coin. They never will be. Both sides had to swallow their pride and their prejudices, and their own military theories, and find a solution to the problems presented by the landings in Normandy. The differences were almost as wide as the Atlantic itself. It was not made any easier that these two nations and their armed forces were not the sole participants. Out of necessity, the substantial Canadian contribution was essential to make up the numbers, both of men and equipment, including warships. Out of expediency, the 'free navies' of countries overrun by the Germans had to be involved. Their contribution, at the time even for the French, was relatively small, but it meant that they were sharing in the liberation of Europe and committed to the Allied cause.

The French were by far the most difficult ally for both the British and the Americans to handle. Much of this was due to the personality and vanity of one man, the leader of the Free French, General Charles de Gaulle. As mentioned earlier, Churchill had to remind him on at least one occasion that without the Americans, there could be no liberation of occupied Europe. Almost without exception, de Gaulle could not see or hear of an Allied plan without wishing to change it. Perhaps de Gaulle was embarrassed by French defeat, even though few with experience of the Battle of France doubted that many French troops fought bravely and that many sacrificed their freedom to allow the British and many of their compatriots to escape at Dunkirk and, less well known, Cherbourg. Many French people blamed the British for abandoning them, but there was little more that could be done.

The British contribution to the Battle of France was not strong enough and, more importantly, not well enough equipped. It was also clear that the British Expeditionary Force, BEF, and the attendant Advanced Air Striking Force, AASF, was neither large enough nor well trained enough for expeditionary warfare.

Of course, this brings us to a major strength of the Anglo-American alliance. Whatever the frictions, both countries worked together most of the time. The French and British knew that they would have to fight alongside each other, but did not exercise together. The French would not allow offensive bombing by the RAF's AASF in case it brought retribution on French cities, even though this was the only way of bringing home to the Germans the truth that they were at last facing an opponent that would fight back, and even breaking up German formations and lines of communication before the assault in the west, *Falle Gelbe*.

If anything, the situation with the Belgians was even worse. Most Belgians knew that they would need British and French support if their country was not to be overrun by the Germans, as it was almost entirely (but not quite) in the First World War. Again, little tangible cooperation or collaboration existed between Belgium and her much needed allies. As for the Dutch, neutrality had saved their country in the First World War, and perhaps they can be excused for believing that the same would happen again. After all, everyone else thought that the Second World War in Europe would be a re-run of the earlier conflict. Dutch military planning was inhibited by the presence of a strong pacifist movement between the two world wars, but pacifism leaves a country without a fall-back situation, without a 'Plan B' in modern terms.

The same applied to Denmark and Norway, although the latter fought valiantly against the German invaders. Perhaps if Norway had cast its lot with the British and French before the German invasion, the outcome could have been different.

It is easy to criticise the early conduct of the war by the British and French and the other nations involved in the campaigns of early 1940, but Anglo-French appeasement had generated a belief amongst many Germans that the two countries did not mean to draw a line over Poland. Hitler believed that war would not break out for another three or even four years and had given this impression to many of his senior officers, including, crucially, the head of the *Kriegsmarine*, Raeder and his submarine commander, and eventual successor, Doenitz.

After all, Germany had gained first a portion of Czechoslovakia, then Austria, and then the remainder of Czechoslovakia. Italy meanwhile had escaped war over Ethiopia, and then acquired Albania.

ANGLO-AMERICAN RELATIONS, AND ATTITUDES

It has been said that the British and the Americans are two nations divided by a common language, but the divisions run far deeper than that. The dislike of many Americans for a heredity monarchy and a class system is only another fairly superficial difference. Far more serious was the dislike of many Americans, especially politicians, for the British Empire and the concept of colonialism. This in fact was somewhat hypocritical, as the Americans were running the Philippines virtually as a colony during the late 1930s, and while the state of Panama was nominally independent, it excluded the Panama Canal Zone, which at the time was administered by the United States.

Also more serious was the so-called 'Munro Doctrine', which lacked any constitutional basis and had no force of law behind it, but which decreed that the Americas were an area of United States interest and rejected the right of any outside state to interfere. It was somewhat inconvenient that Canada shared the North American continent, but also very irritating that Britain had so many Caribbean territories, even more than the Netherlands or France.

As the United States started to fight back against Japan, many Americans were none too keen to have the Royal Navy supporting them in the war in the Pacific because they suspected that the British involvement was motivated by desire to recover their lost colonies. They did not want to assist this venture. It was also true that the Americans knew that they could handle the Japanese on their own, and some were even contemptuous of the way in which the British had failed to hold the Japanese, but the Americans had also failed miserably in the Philippines. Even so, the Royal Navy made a massive contribution as the Allies closed upon Japan, deploying the most balanced fleet in its history and stopping the Japanese attempts to reinforce and resupply their air combat squadrons.

Many Americans had in fact wanted to give priority to the war against Japan. Possibly, if Hitler had not declared war on the United States after Pearl Harbor, they might have won the argument. Nevertheless, others wanted to accord priority to the war in Europe. There were good strategic reasons for this. Using airfields in England, the United States Army Air Force could strike at Germany and occupied Europe, while it was to be some time before it could play a major part in the war against Japan, which had to be left to naval air power and the submarine force at first. There had in any case, even before the United States entered the war, been clashes between U-boats and US warships escorting convoys to the mid-Ocean handover point. In escorting convoys, providing aircraft, warships and other equipment under 'Lend-Lease', using British Caribbean bases, and providing vital support in training British naval airmen, the United States was already at war with Germany in all but name: a situation not dissimilar in many ways to the 'Cold War by proxy' conflicts of South-East Asia in later years.

Yet, in a sense, these were political considerations. What mattered almost as much, and possibly even more, were the differences in approach at command level, and below, in the military.

The American attitude was much more 'gung-ho' than the more considered British approach. The Americans viewed the British as over-cautious and less than ambitious, but the British regarded the Americans as reckless and inexperienced. There was much truth in this as many of the American senior officers in the Second World War had not enjoyed, or perhaps 'suffered' would be a better word, frontline combat experience in the First World War. There can be little doubt that American entry into the First World War hastened its end, but the tide had already turned in favour of the Entente Powers by the time the first American troops arrived in Europe.

Certainly at first many Americans did not understand why landings in Europe could not take place in 1943. Given the difficulties faced on Omaha Beach, no doubt many soon understood why.

The British preferred a gradual approach. They had lost many men, both killed or as prisoners of war, in Europe prior to and at Dunkirk, in North Africa, and in Hong Kong, Malaya and Singapore. Manpower was a problem. In any case, they were a maritime power, and although throughout most of the preceding nine centuries they had become involved in continental wars and joined the Crusades, victory at sea and control of the seas was the essential preliminary to landings and land battles. There was no history of large standing armies, and no history of a small professional cadre supported by conscription as in most European nations.

The United States was different. As mentioned earlier, manpower was not a problem and what the American military historian Edward Luttwak has described as an infantry mass of 'disposable sons' encouraged a more forceful attitude. The Americans were fully familiar with the importance of sea power and even before the start of the twentieth century had concentrated on creating a strong ocean-going navy, or in terms of maritime strategy, a 'blue water' navy. Nevertheless, US attitudes were still those of a continental power.

On the ground, this attitude translated into the adoption of 'marching fire', a tactic pioneered by the US Army officer General G. S. Patton Jnr, with all riflemen and light machine gunners advancing in a single thin skirmish line, firing as they marched at anything that hid or contained enemy troops. This tactic meant that heavy casualties from marching troops in an exposed position were accepted, while the infantry fire was less accurate, and if co-ordinated action was not an impossibility, there was at least a delay in organising it. The alternative favoured elsewhere was 'fire and movement', which divided infantry into teams that alternatively fired and moved, the former providing covering fire for the latter.

The demands on US servicemen, and especially the infantry, were enormous. There was no circulation of units between the front and rearward areas for rest, recovering, training and absorption of new arrivals. US units were kept in the front line as long as they were viable, that is, not so diminished by casualties that they were no longer cohesive units. New arrivals, rookies straight from the training depots, were posted to the front line and suffered heavy casualties as a result.

Oddly, the greatest convergence of approach between the British and the Americans was in the air. The Royal Air Force, formed at the height of the First World War on 1 April 1918, and the United States Army Air Force, which did not become the autonomous United States Air Force until after the war, in 1947, both saw themselves as strategic air arms. This was in contrast to the German *Luftwaffe* and the Russian air forces, which were strongly biased towards tactical warfare. Though the British believed that the German term *Blitzkrieg*, or 'lightning war', referred to the 'Blitz', the German bombing of British cities in 1940–41, in reality it applied to co-ordinated advances spearheaded by armour units and heavy aerial assault. One reason why the German 'Blitz' was less effective than the Anglo-American bombing campaign was the lack of a heavy bomber in the

Luftwaffe until 1943, when the four-engined Heinkel He 177 heavy bomber entered service, but in numbers that were too small to make a difference, especially as the RAF's night fighter capabilities had improved enormously over the preceding two years.

The big difference in the air was that the Americans favoured heavy defensive armament on their bombers and defensive formations were flown, so in order to keep losses to an acceptable level the RAF's Bomber Command mainly operated at night while the USAAF operated mainly daylight missions. The latter were still costly, with heavy losses, but by the time the bomber campaign was in full swing, there would not have been enough airspace over southern and eastern England for the bombers of both air forces to operate safely. There was also much logic in maintaining round-the-clock attacks on a target so that the defenders did not have time to recover from the RAF by night and the USAAF by day.

Inevitably, both air forces had much to learn about air-ground co-ordination, and this really became effective in North Africa, with the Western Desert Air Force and the Eighth Army bringing co-ordination to a fine art. This was continued during the Italian campaign and reached its peak with the formation of the US 1st Tactical Air Force and the British 2nd Tactical Air Force, which joined the ground forces in France shortly after the landings, and followed them into Germany, even with bases in Germany itself as the war in Europe ended.

At sea, the British desire to play a role in the Pacific meant that much co-ordination was necessary. The signals by carrier batsmen for pilots attempting on aircraft carriers had to be co-ordinated, and the Royal Navy's Fleet Air Arm had to adopt the US signals – essential as before this some signals had meant the opposite! The British learnt that the American abeam method of refuelling while ships were under way at sea was superior, indeed vastly superior, to their bow and stern method, not just in the rate that fuel could be transferred but also in the range of weather conditions in which refuelling could take place.

It does seem, though, that this learning was one-way. When British naval pilots warned their American counterparts of the dangers of flying straight and level near German anti-aircraft fire, and especially at certain altitudes where such fire was at its most accurate, their advice was ignored, and off the south of France a formation of four USN aircraft was shot down before the pilots could manoeuvre.

In the Pacific the Royal Navy was under no illusion that it was there under sufferance and was told that it had to find its own bases and its own resources, although fortunately at a lower level many USN officers ignored this advice from above and did all they could to help.

Despite the collaboration and the desire to operate together, there were always going to be problems of communication, co-ordination and control, as well as different tactics and much different equipment, which also had an impact on supplies and support. These reasons lay behind the division of forces for the Normandy landings. The location of British and Canadian bases in England and those of the Americans also decided which country had which beaches. There was no way that the forces could be completely integrated. This was probably fine as far as the British and Americans were concerned, but possibly galling for some Canadians, who often found it easier to communicate with their American counterparts. On the other hand, many Americans treated the Canadians as poor cousins, something the British never did, although some British senior officers had doubts about the quality of the Canadian senior officers, but they had the same doubts about many in the Territorial Army, Britain's army reserve.

What becomes clear, when considering the way in which the Allies fought the war, is that very senior officers were thrown together by politicians for political and diplomatic ends. There were Canadian troops, so Montgomery had to have Crerar, their commander-in-chief, on his team, when he really wanted to sack him. This was just one example. No one could risk an ally dropping out because their senior officers were overlooked. The quality of senior officers mattered, but the need to have a senior representative of an important ally in the right place mattered even more. One of the few examples of a senior officer being dismissed was that of McNaughton, Crerar's predecessor as Canadian commander, but this was largely because of his opposition to dividing his forces, and because he not only upset the other senior Allied officers, but also came into conflict with the Canadian defence minister.

By contrast, the Germans commanded many joint forces, but, as Japan was too far away to be involved in such groupings, with the exception of the Italians, the Germans dominated the forces contributed by countries such as Hungary and Romania. In North Africa, after an uncertain start, Rommel was left in no doubt that he was expected to take the decisions and bear responsibility. The other contrast was, of course, that relatively few of the non-German units performed with any great distinction, while those of the Allies often made great sacrifices. As has been shown earlier, in the chapters on the landings, many of the defending troops were Axis officers, but from across occupied Europe, with some, such as the Russians, having 'volunteered' simply to escape the prisoner-of-war camps, but were still treated as inferiors by the Germans and lacking in commitment.

Churchill and Hitler had some things in common. Both men stayed up late and rose late. Both interfered in strategy. Both enjoyed painting!

BEFORE AND AFTER OVERLORD: THE SEQUENCE OF EVENTS IN 1944

January 1944

22: Allies begin Operation Shingle, the landing at Anzio, Italy. The US Army 45th Infantry Division stand their ground at Anzio against violent assaults for four months. Time and again aggressive German artillery and troop attacks nearly overwhelm the beachhead.

31: Americans are still struggling to protect the beachhead at Anzio.

February 1944

1: In Italy, the battles at both Monte Cassino and Anzio intensify.

6: The Germans have continuing success in staving off the Allies at Cassino.

7: In Anzio, German artillery attacks continue to threaten the Allies.

8: The plan for the invasion of France, Operation Overlord, is confirmed.

14: SHAEF headquarters are established in Britain by US General Dwight D. Eisenhower.

15: The 'second' Battle of Monte Cassino begins. The monastery on the summit of Monte Cassino is destroyed by Allied bombing. The bombing is controversial since the Germans deny the Allied charge that the grounds were being used as observation posts.

16: The Germans launch a major counter-attack at Anzio, threatening the American beachhead.

18: The Light Cruiser HMS *Penelope* is torpedoed and sunk off the coast of Anzio, with the loss of 415 crew.

March 1944

15: The National Council of the French Resistance approves the Resistance programme. The 'third' Battle of Monte Cassino begins and the small town of Cassino is destroyed.

24: The Fosse Ardeatine massacre in Rome. Three hundred and thirty-five Italians are killed, including seventy-five Jews and over 200 members of various groups in the Italian Resistance; this is a German response to a bomb blast that killed German troops.

April 1944

4: General Charles de Gaulle takes command of all Free French forces.

21: The Badoglio government in Italy falls and he is quickly asked to form another.

27: The Slapton Sands tragedy: American soldiers are killed in a training exercise in preparation for D-Day at Slapton in Devon.

30: Vast preparations for D-Day are going on all over southern England.

May 1944

6: Heavy Allied bombings of the Continent in preparation for D-Day.

8: D-Day for Operation Overlord set for 6 June.
   The Battle at the 'Gustav line' near Monte Cassino continues without resolution.

11: The British cross the River Rapido. A 'fourth' battle of Monte Cassino begins, concurrent with the opening of an offensive campaign towards Rome.

18: Battle of Monte Cassino ends with an Allied victory; Polish troops hoist their red and white flag on the ruins of Monte Cassino. The Germans cede it and depart.

21: Increased Allied bombing of targets in France in preparation for D-Day.

23: Allies advance towards Rome, after a linkup of American II and III corps.

25: Germans are now in retreat in the Anzio area. American forces break out of the beachhead and link up with the Fifth Army; both then begin their advance on Rome.

June 1944

2: The provisional French government is established.

3: There are daily bombings of the Cherbourg Peninsula and the Normandy area.

4: Operation Overlord is postponed twenty-four hours due to high winds and heavy seas. American, British and French troops enter Rome.

5: Rome falls to the Allies, becoming the first capital of an Axis nation to do so. Operation Overlord commences when more than 1,000 British bombers drop 5,000 tons of bombs on German gun batteries on the Normandy coast in preparation for D-Day. The first Allied troops land in Normandy; paratroopers are scattered from Caen southward.

6: D-Day begins with the landing of Allied troops on the beaches of Normandy. The Allied soldiers quickly break through the Atlantic Wall and push inland in the largest amphibious military operation in history.

7: Bayeux is liberated by British troops.

10: At Oradour-sur-Glane (a town near Limoges), 642 men, women, and children are killed in a German response to local Resistance activities.

13: Germany launches a V-1 flying bomb attack on England, in Hitler's view a kind of revenge for the invasion. He believes Germany's victory will be secured with this 'secret weapon'. The V-1 attacks will continue through June.

17: Free French troops land on Elba.

18: Elba liberated.
The Allies capture Assisi.

19: A severe Channel storm destroys one of the Allies' Mulberry harbours in Normandy.

22: V-1s continue to hit England, especially London, sometimes with horrifying losses.

26: Cherbourg is liberated by American troops.

July 1944

2: V-1s continue to have devastating effects in terms of material destruction and loss of life.

3: The Allies find themselves in the 'battle of the hedgerows', as they are stymied by the agricultural hedges in western France, which intelligence had not properly evaluated.

9: After heavy resistance, Caen is liberated by the British troops on the left flank of the Allied advance.

11: President Roosevelt announces that he will run for an unprecedented fourth term.

17: Field Marshal Rommel is badly wounded when his car is strafed from the air in France.

18: Saint-Lô is taken, and the Allied breakout from hedgerow country in Normandy begins.

19: American forces take Leghorn (Livorno) far up the Italian boot.

20: The 20 July plot is carried out by Col. Claus von Stauffenberg, failing to assassinate Hitler, who was visiting headquarters at Rastenburg, East Prussia. Reprisals follow against the plotters and their families, who even include Rommel.

24: US bombers mistakenly bomb American troops near Saint-Lô.

24: Operation Cobra is now in full swing: the breakout comes at Saint-Lô in Normandy with American troops taking Coutances.

August 1944

4: Florence is liberated by the Allies, particularly British and South African troops; before exiting, however, the Germans under General Kesselring destroy some historic bridges and historically valuable buildings.
The trials of the bomb conspirators against Hitler are underway in a court presided over by notorious Judge Roland Freisler.
Rennes is liberated by American forces.

8: The conspirators in the bomb plot against Hitler are hanged, their bodies hung on meat hooks; reprisals against their families continue.

14: The Allies' failure to close the Falaise gap in France proves advantageous to the Germans fleeing to the east, who escape their pincer movement.
A clash between Italian POWs and American servicemen ends in the Fort Lawton Riot.

15: The Allies reach the 'Gothic Line', the last German strategic position in north Italy.
Operation Dragoon begins, marked by amphibious Allied landings in southern France.

19: The French Resistance begins the uprising in Paris, partly inspired by the Allied approach to the River Seine.

25: Paris is liberated; de Gaulle and Free French parade triumphantly down the Champs-Élysées. The German military disobeys Hitler's orders to burn the city. Meanwhile, the southern Allied forces move up from the French Riviera and take Grenoble and Avignon.

28: The Germans surrender at Toulon and Marseilles, in southern France. Patton's tanks cross the Marne.

30: The Allies enter Rouen, in north-western France.

31: American forces hand the government of France to Free French troops.

September 1944

1: Canadian troops capture Dieppe, scene of their humiliation in August 1942.

2: Allied troops enter Belgium.

3: Brussels liberated by the British Second Army while Lyon is liberated by French and American troops.

5: Antwerp is liberated by the British 11th Armoured Division.

:   United States III Corps arrives in the European theatre.

6: In the UK, the 'blackout' is diminished to a 'dim-out') as the threat of invasion and further bombing seems unlikely.

Ghent and Liège are liberated by British troops.

8: Ostend liberated by Canadian troops.

9: The first V-2 rocket lands on London.

De Gaulle forms a provisional government in France; Bulgaria makes peace with the USSR, then declares war on Germany.

10: Luxembourg liberated by the US First Army.

Two Allied forces meet at Dijon, cutting France in half.

The first Allied troops enter Germany, entering Aachen, a city on the border.

Dutch railway workers go on strike. The German response results in the Dutch famine of 1944.

11: The United States XXI Corps arrives in the European theatre.

13: American troops reach the Siegfried Line, the west wall of Germany's defence system.

17: Operation Market Garden, the attempted liberation of Arnhem and the turning of the German flank begins.

Assorted British and commonwealth forces enter neutral San Marino and engage German forces in a small-scale conflict known as the Battle of San Marino.

18: The important Channel port of Brest falls to the Allies.

19: Nancy is liberated by the US First Army.

20: The United States XVI Corps arrives in the European theatre.
   The Battle of San Marino ends.

21: British forces take Rimini.
   San Marino declares war on the Axis.
   The Germans surrender at Boulogne.

25: Operation Market Garden fails and British troops pull out of Arnhem. Over 6,000 paratroopers are captured. Hopes of an early end to the war are abandoned. The United States IX Corps arrives in the Pacific theatre.

30: The German garrison in Calais surrenders to Canadian troops. At one time, Hitler had thought it would be the focus of the cross-Channel invasion.

October 1944

2: American troops are now engaged in a full-scale attack on the German 'West Wall'.

5: Canadian troops cross the border into the Netherlands.

12: The United States XXIII Corps arrives in the European theatre.

14: Field Marshal Rommel, under suspicion of being one of the 'bomb plotters', voluntarily commits suicide to save his family. He is later buried with full military honours.

15: The Allied bombardment of Aachen continues, the first major battle on German soil.

18: Hitler orders a call-up of all men from 16 to 60 for Home Guard duties.

21: Aachen is occupied by the US First Army; it is the first major German city to be captured.

23: The Allies recognise General de Gaulle as the head of a provisional government of France.

27: The Battle of Hürtgen Forest is developing, and will continue through October and November and have its last spasms in December.

November 1944

1: Operation Infatuate: An Allied attempt to free the approaches to Antwerp; notably there are amphibious landings on Walcheren Island.

2: Canadian troops take Zeebrugge; Belgium is now entirely liberated.

6: Franklin Delano Roosevelt wins a fourth term.

9: General Patton's troops and tanks cross the River Moselle and threaten the city of Metz.

10: V-2 rockets continue to hit Britain, at the rate of around eight a day.

20: Hitler leaves his wartime headquarters at Rastenberg, East Prussia, never to return; he goes to Berlin, where he will soon establish himself in the bunker.

23: Metz is taken, and Strasbourg, in eastern France, is liberated by French troops.

26: The war in Italy is at a stalemate, partly because of heavy rain.

28: Antwerp is now a major supply port for the onward moving Allies.

30: The United States XXII Corps arrives in the European theatre.

December 1944

3: The British Home Guard is stood down.

5: The Allies are now in control of Ravenna.

16: The Ardennes offensive or 'Battle of the Bulge' begins as German forces attempt a breakthrough in the Ardennes region. The main object of Hitler's plan is the taking of Antwerp.

17: The Malmedy massacre: SS troops execute eighty-six American prisoners in the Ardennes offensive. The SS troops are led by SS commander Jochen Peiper.

18: Bastogne, an important crossroads, is surrounded.

22: The battle for Bastogne is at its height, but the Americans are running low on ammunition.

23: The skies clear over the Ardennes, permitting Allied aircraft to begin their attacks on the German offensive, the one factor that Hitler feared in his planning.

24: The American counter-attack at the 'Bulge' begins.
Manchester is attacked with V-2 flying bombs.

26: The siege of Bastogne is broken, and with it the Ardennes offensive fails.

APPENDIX II

BRITISH, CANADIAN AND 'FREE' WARSHIPS IN OPERATION NEPTUNE

The vast majority of the warships engaged in Operation Neptune were British, but the Royal Canadian Navy provided a significant number of ships, and there were also ships from the 'free' navies of France, Greece, the Netherlands, Norway and Poland. Many of these were transferred from the Royal Navy and these are noted, along with significant events in the life of the ship.

BATTLESHIPS

HMS *Nelson*: 1925, Nelson-class, 38,000 tons, main armament: 9 x 16in guns in three turrets. Held in reserve until 10 June.

HMS *Ramillies*: 1915, Revenge-class, 33,500 tons, main armament: 8 x 15in guns in four turrets.

HMS *Rodney*: 1925, Nelson-class, 38,000 tons, main armament: 9 x 16in guns in three turrets.

HMS *Warspite*: 1913, Queen Elizabeth-class, 35,000 tons, main armament: 8 x 15in guns in four turrets.

HEAVY CRUISERS

HMS *Frobisher*: 4 x 7.5in guns in single turrets.
HMS *Hawkins*: Original 8in guns reduced to 6in.

LIGHT CRUISERS

Usually 6in or 5.25in guns (French).
* Officially classified by the Royal Navy as a heavy cruiser.
HMS *Argonaut*; *Ajax*; *Arethusa*; *Belfast** (Flagship of Rear-Admiral Frederick Dalrymple-Hamilton); HMS *Bellona*; *Black Prince*; *Capetown*; *Ceres* (Flagship of US Service Force); *Danae*; *Diadem*; *Emerald*; *Enterprise*; *Glasgow*;* *Mauritius* (Flagship of Rear-Admiral Patterson); *Orion*; *Scylla* (Admiral Vian's flagship, mined and seriously damaged; out of action until after the war); *Sirius*. In reserve until 10 June.
Free French: *Georges Leygues*; *Montcalm* (Flagship of Rear-Admiral Jaujard).

ESCORT VESSELS (INCLUDING DESTROYERS, FRIGATES AND CORVETTES)

HMS *Bleasdale*; *Boadicea* (torpedoed and sunk 13 June); *Cattistock*; *Cottesmore*; *Eglinton*; *Faulknor*; *Fury* (mined 21 June and not repaired); *Grenville*; *Jervis*; *Kelvin*; *Kempenfelt*; *Melbreak*; *Middleton*; *Pytchley*; *Saumarez*; *Scorpion*; *Scourge*; *Serapis*; *Stevenstone*; *Swift* (mined and sunk 24 June 1944 off Normandy); *Talybont*; *Tanatside*; *Ulster*; *Ulysses*; *Venus*; *Verulam*; *Vigilant*; *Virago*; *Wanderer*; *Whimbrel*; *Wrestler* (damaged by a mine and not repaired).
Canadian: HMCS *Algonquin*; *Cape Breton*; *Chaudière*; *Kitchener*; *Sioux*. French: *La Combattante* (former HMS *Haldon*). Greek: RHN *Kriezis* (formerly HMS *Coreopsis*); *Tobazis* (formerly HMS *Tamarisk*). Norwegian: HNoMS *Glaisdale*; *Stord*; *Svenner* (hit by German torpedo and sunk off Normandy at dawn, 6 June). Polish: ORP *Krakowiak* (former HMS *Silverton*); *Slazak*.

SUBMARINES

HMS *Undaunted*; *Undine*; *Urania*; *Urchin*; *Ursula*.

OTHER WARSHIPS

508 ships (352 British, 154 US and two other Allied vessels):
HMS *Bulolo* (HQ ship for Gold Beach carrying tri-service commanders and staff); *Centurion* (an old battleship sunk as a blockship in Gooseberry breakwater); *Dacres* (Captain-class frigate converted to act as a headquarters ship); *Durban* (a light cruiser used as a blockship in Gooseberry breakwater); *Erebus* (a First World War monitor with two 15in guns); *Hilary* (HQ ship for Juno Beach carrying tri-service commanders and staff); *Kingsmill* (Captain-class frigate converted to act as a headquarters ship); *Largs* (HQ ship for Sword Beach carrying tri-service commanders and staff); *Lawford* (Captain-class frigate converted to act as a headquarters ship; bombed and sunk); *Roberts* (monitor with two 15in guns).
The British 9th and 159th minesweeping flotillas provided minesweeping protection. A distant anti-submarine screen to the operation was provided by HMS *Onslow*, *Offa*, *Onslaught*, *Oribi*, *Melbreak* and *Brissenden*. Additional protection from E-boats was provided by various motor gun boat flotillas.
Canadian: HMCS *Cowichan*, minesweeper. French: *Courbet* (an old battleship sunk as a blockship in Gooseberry breakwater).
Netherlands: HNLMS *Flores* (gunboat); *Soemba* (gunboat); *Sumatra* (decommissioned due to crew shortages and losing her guns to HNLMS *Flores* and *Soemba*, used as a blockship in Gooseberry breakwater).
Norwegian: HNoMS *Nordkapp* (patrol boat).

APPENDIX III

AMERICAN WARSHIPS IN OPERATION NEPTUNE

BATTLESHIPS

USS *Arkansas*: Wyoming-class, 26,100 tons, main armament: 12 x 12in guns. Eastern Omaha Beach primarily in support of the US 29th Infantry Division.
USS *Nevada*: Nevada-class, 29,000 tons, main armament: 10 x 14in guns. Utah Beach (damaged and beached to avoid sinking at Pearl Harbor).
USS *Texas*: New York-class, 27,000 tons, main armament: 10 x 14in guns. Western Omaha Beach primarily in support of the US 1st Infantry Division; flagship of Rear-Admiral C. F. Bryant.

HEAVY CRUISERS

All with 8in main armament.
USS *Augusta*: Flagship of Rear-Admiral Alan Kirk, with Lt General Omar Bradley embarked.
USS *Quincy*; *Tuscaloosa*.

LIGHT CRUISERS

All light cruisers were provided by the Royal Navy, the Free French and the Free Polish Navy. See Appendix I above.

ESCORT VESSELS (INCLUDING DESTROYERS, FRIGATES AND CORVETTES)

USS *Amesbury*; *Baldwin*; *Barton*; *Carmick*; *Corry* (sunk during the invasion); *Doyle*; *Frankford*; *Glennon* (hit by mine 8 June, sunk by German artillery 10 June); *Harding*; *Hobson*; *Laffey*; *McCook*; *Murphy*; *O'Brien*; *Rich* (sunk by mines 10 June); *Satterlee*; *Thompson*.

OTHER WARSHIPS

USS *Bayfield*; *Charles Carroll*, attack transports. The US 7th Minesweeping Squadron provided minesweeping protection.

APPENDIX IV

ALLIED ORDER OF BATTLE

The Allies landed on beaches code-named Sword, Gold and Juno, running from east to west, while the Americans landed on Omaha and Utah beaches, the latter being the most westerly. Further inland, paratroops and glider-landed troops were dropped to secure import objectives, such as bridges, or to protect the flanks of those troops arriving ashore.

American units were part of the US First Army, while the British and Canadian units were part of the British Second Army. Throughout the war, armies were created and abandoned for administrative and command reasons and no particular significance can be attributed to these designations, even though for those who served in them, there was a sense of belonging and well-justified pride amongst veterans at having been part of particular armies.

Although we are concerned with the naval aspects of the Normandy landings, the part played by airborne troops was an integral part of the whole exercise and so they are included here to provide a complete picture.

US FIRST ARMY

The eastern of the US landing sites was Omaha Beach, lying between Port-en-Bessin and the mouth of the River Vire in the Baie de la Seine. The V Corps, comprising the 1st Infantry Division and 29th Infantry Division, a total of 34,250 men, landed between Sainte-Honorine-des-Pertes and

Vierville-sur-Mer, accompanied by the 2nd and 5th Ranger Battalions at Pointe du Hoc, the Rangers being diverted to Omaha.

Utah Beach was further west and lay along the eastern coast of the Cherbourg Peninsula, running north from the mouth of the River Vire in the Baie de la Seine, and the US 4th Infantry Division landed south of Les Dunes de Varreville. A total of 23,250 men landed around Pouppeville and La Madeleine, all part of the US Army's VII Corps, augmented by men from the 90th Infantry Division.

The landings on Utah Beach were supported by the 101st Airborne Division landed by parachute around Vierville, while the US 82nd Airborne Division also landed by parachute around Sainte-Mère-Église, protecting the right flank. The 82nd had originally been tasked with dropping further west, in the middle of the Cotentin, which would have given the amphibious forces easier access across the peninsula, and prevented the Germans from reinforcing the north part of the peninsula. At the last minute, the German 91st Air Landing Division was believed to be in the area and the plans were changed to bring the 82nd much closer to the beachhead.

Altogether, the First Army consisted of some 73,000 men, of whom 15,600 were members of the airborne.

BRITISH SECOND ARMY

The British Second Army landed three divisions on D-Day, two from I Corps and one from XXX Corps, on Sword, Gold and Juno beaches. Support was provided by the 79th Armoured Division, which operated specialist armour ('Hobart's Funnies') for mine-clearance, recovery and assault tasks, with the unit's armour spread around the Anglo-Canadian beaches.

British and Canadian forces, plus some French troops, landed to the east of the US forces. The most easterly of the beaches was Sword, in the Baie de la Seine between Saint-Aubin-sur-Mer and the mouth of the River Orne, where the 1st Special Service Brigade comprising Nos. 3, 4, 6 and No. 45 (RM) Commandos landed at Ouistreham; No. 4 Commando was augmented by the French 1 and 8 Troop of No. 10 (Inter Allied) Commando. These forces were augmented by I Corps, 3rd Infantry Division and the 27th Armoured Brigade which landed between Ouistreham and Lion-sur-Mer, while No. 41 (RM) Commando (part of 4th Special Service Brigade) landed on the far west of Sword Beach. Once again the flanks were protected by airborne troops, the left flank of Sword Beach protected by 6th Airborne Division commanded by Major-General R. N. Gale, which landed by parachute and glider to the east of the River Orne. The division contained 7,900 men, including one Canadian battalion.

Between the River Provence and Saint-Aubin-sur-Mer in the Baie de la Seine lay Juno Beach in the middle of the British amphibious landing zone, where I Corps, 3rd Canadian Infantry Division, 2nd Canadian Armoured Brigade and No. 48 (RM) Commando came ashore from Saint-Aubin-sur-Mer to Courseulles-sur-Mer. It was intended that No. 46 (RM) Commando (part of 4th Special Service Brigade) should also land on Juno to scale the cliffs on the left side of the Orne Estuary and destroy an artillery battery, but when this produced little artillery fire, No. 46 were kept offshore as a floating reserve and were not landed until the following day, D+1.

The most westerly of the British beaches was Gold, lying between Port-en-Bessin and the River Provence in the Baie de la Seine, and included Arromanches, the site of one of the two Mulberry harbours, on which 25,000 men of XXX Corps, 50th (Northumbrian) Infantry Division and 8th Armoured Brigade landed between Courseulles and Arromanches, while No. 47 (RM) Commando (part of 4th Special Service Brigade) landed on the west flank of Gold Beach.

Of the 83,115 troops in the Second Army contingent, 61,715 were British. Most of the rest were Canadian, but eight Australian officers were attached to the British forces as eyewitnesses. The nominally British air and naval support units included a large number of personnel from Allied nations, including several RAF squadrons manned almost exclusively by overseas aircrew. For instance, the Australian contribution to the operation included a regular Royal Australian Air Force (RAAF) squadron, nine RAAF reserve squadrons and hundreds of personnel posted to RAF units and RN warships.

APPENDIX V

GERMAN ORDER OF BATTLE

Germany's military manpower, if not its military might, reached a peak during 1944, although her resources were widely spread and no doubt the quality of troops had diminished when conscription was extended to include both younger and older men, hitherto regarded as unfit for active service. Apart from casualties, many experienced and highly-trained men had been taken prisoner-of-war by the increasingly strong Soviet advance, and others captured in North Africa and Italy. By D-Day, 157 German divisions were stationed in the Soviet Union, six in Finland, twelve in Norway, six in Denmark, nine in Germany, twenty-one in the Balkans, twenty-six in Italy and fifty-nine in France, Belgium and the Netherlands. Worse, the strengths given for the units in the east were no better than nominal as the severe weather and the heavy casualties meant that many units were at no more than half strength.

ATLANTIC WALL

The Germans saw the English Channel as their first line of defence, despite the fact that at its narrowest it was little more than 20 miles across. This was augmented by the so-called 'Atlantic Wall', designed to provide a strong defensive position and supposed to run from Norway to the Pyrénées, but in fact only really strong in the Pas-de-Calais and Normandy. Even so, when assigned to the area, Rommel augmented the fortifications with pillboxes, artillery, machine gun positions and extensive barbed wire as well as laying hundreds of thousands of mines to deter landing craft.

In theory, the Atlantic Wall fortifications had large bunkers, sometimes intricate concrete constructions containing machine guns and large-calibre weapons and were integrated into the cliffs and hills overlooking the beaches, but this was only when at their best. Rommel discovered much that needed to be completed, but demand for concrete, steel and other materials was such that he did not get everything that he wanted. On the plus side, the German defences used an interlocking firing style, so they could protect areas that were receiving heavy fire.

The Allies were fortunate in their choice not to attack at Calais but at the more distant beaches of Normandy in that this was the sector boundary between the 7th and 15th German armies, and on the extreme eastern flank of the former, which allowed them to make the most of divided German commands, hampering the German reaction. The landing sector was occupied by four German divisions.

THE GERMAN DIVISIONS

Facing the British and Canadian beaches was the 716th Infantry Division (Static) defending the eastern end of the landing zones, and which largely consisted of Germans who were not considered fit for active duty on the Eastern Front, either because of serious wounds or poor physical fitness. They were augmented by soldiers drawn from occupied territories, including former Soviet prisoners-of-war who had chosen to fight for the Germans to escape the prison camps, and formed into 'Ost-Bataillone', or East Battalions, of doubtful loyalty, and in any case were regarded with disdain by their German officers.

By contrast, at Omaha Beach the 352nd Infantry Division was a well-trained and equipped formation defending the area between approximately Bayeux and Carentan. Many of its men were veterans of the Eastern Front, as the division had been formed in November 1943 with the help of cadres from the disbanded 321st Division, which had been destroyed in the Soviet Union that same year.

Nearby was the 91st *Luftlande*, or Air Landing Division under *Generalmajor* (Major-General) Wilhelm Falley, consisting of the 1057th

Infantry Regiment and 1058th Infantry Regiment. This was an infantry division, trained and equipped to be transported by air, but with few heavy weapons and located in the interior of the Cotentin Peninsula, including the drop zones of the American parachute landings. It had been augmented by the 6th Parachute Regiment, which had been rebuilt as a part of the 2nd Parachute Division stationed in Brittany.

On the Cotentin Peninsula, including Utah Beach, was the 709th Infantry Division (Static), consisting of the 729th Infantry Regiment, 739th Infantry Regiment and the 919th Infantry Regiment, but the first two included a number of Ost troops. This coastal defence division protected the important port of Cherbourg as well as the rest of the northern coast and also the eastern coast of the Cotentin Peninsula.

There were other divisions occupying the areas around the landing zones, mainly static, such as the 243rd Infantry Division (Static), protecting the western coast of the Cotentin Peninsula, consisting of the 920th Infantry Regiment (two battalions), the 921st Infantry Regiment and the 922nd Infantry Regiment. There was also the 711th Infantry Division (Static), comprising the 731st Infantry Regiment, and the 744th Infantry Regiment, defending the western part of the Pays de Caux. The 30th Mobile Brigade included three bicycle battalions.

ARMOUR

No German general was more adroit at exploiting the use of large armoured formations, and of maintaining a flexible and highly mobile defence, yet Rommel's defensive measures were frustrated by a dispute over strategy. The Commander-in-Chief West, *Generalfeldmarschall* Gerd von Rundstedt, had two army groups plus the headquarters of *Panzergruppe West* under General Leo Geyr von Schweppenburg (usually referred to as von Geyr). This formation was nominally an administrative HQ for von Rundstedt's armoured and mobile formations, but it was later to be renamed the Fifth Panzer Army and brought into the line in Normandy. Von Geyr and Rommel disagreed over the deployment and use of the vital *Panzer* divisions.

Rommel recognised that the Allies would possess air superiority and be able to harass his movements from the air and proposed that the armoured formations be deployed close to the invasion beaches. He believed that it was better to have one *Panzer* division facing the invaders on the first day than three *Panzer* divisions three days later, when the Allies would already have established a firm beachhead. Von Geyr argued for the standard doctrine that the *Panzer* formations should be concentrated in a central position around Paris and Rouen, and deployed *en masse* against the main Allied beachhead when this had been identified.

The argument was eventually brought before Hitler, who decided on an unworkable compromise. Just three *Panzer* divisions were given to Rommel, too few to cover all the threatened sectors. The remainder, nominally under Von Geyr's control, were actually designated as being in 'OKW Reserve', but only three were deployed close enough to intervene immediately against any invasion of Northern France; the other four were dispersed in southern France and the Netherlands. Hitler reserved for himself the authority to move the divisions in OKW Reserve, or commit them to action. On 6 June, many *Panzer* division commanders were unable to move because Hitler had not given the necessary authorisation, and his staff refused to wake him upon news of the invasion, doubtless because news of any military reverses always led to fury, and although there is no record of Hitler ever having shot the messenger, no doubt no one wanted to take that chance. The Fuhrer had in fact retired to bed at 0300, after spending much of the night chatting with Eva Braun and Goebbels. When later that morning he heard the news, to everyone's surprise he reacted with glee, predicting that his V-1 flying bombs would destroy London!

While the 21st *Panzer* Division was deployed near Caen as a mobile striking force as part of the reserves for Army Group B, Rommel placed it so close to the coastal defences that, under standing orders in case of invasion, several of its infantry and anti-aircraft units would come under the orders of the fortress divisions on the coast, reducing its effective strength. As the other mechanised divisions capable of intervening in Normandy were retained under the direct control of the German Armed Forces HQ (OKW), these were also denied to Rommel at a time when he could have made good use of them.

BIBLIOGRAPHY

Alanbrooke, Field Marshal Lord, *War Diaries 1939–1945* (London: Weidenfeld & Nicolson, 2001).

Ambrose, Stephen, *Parameters* (New York, 1990).

Badsey, Stephen & Bean, Tim, *OMAHA BEACH* (Stroud: Sutton Publishing, 2004).

Balkoski, Joseph, *Utah Beach – The Amphibious Landing and Airborne Operations on D-Day* (Mechanicsburg: Stackpole Books, 2005).

Beevor, Antony, *D-Day, The Battle for Normandy* (London: Viking, 2009).

Churchill, Winston, *The Second World War* 6 vols (London: Cassell, 1948–54).

Edwards, Commander Kenneth, RN, *Operation Neptune* (London: Collins, 1946).

Falconer, Jonathan, *The D-Day Manual* (Yeovil: Haynes, 2013).

Forrester, Ken, *If Only I had Known*, believed privately published, 2013.

Gelbe, Norman, *Desperate Venture* (London: Hodder & Stoughton, 1992).

Hall, Anthony, *D-Day: Day-by-Day* (Hoo: Grange, 2003).

Johnson, Group Captain 'Johnnie', *Wing Leader* (London: Chatto & Windus, 1956).

Kennedy, Paul, *Engineers of Victory: The Problem Solvers Who Turned the Tide in the Second World War* (London: Allen Lane, 2013).

Laffin, John, *Damn the Dardanelles! The Story of Gallipoli* (London: Osprey, 1980).

Montgomery, *Memoirs of Field Marshal the Viscount Montgomery of Alamein* (London: Collins, 1958).

Norman, Albert, *Operation Overlord: Design and Reality, the Allied Invasion of Europe* (Westport, CT: Greenhill Press, 1970).

Nye, R., *Parameters* (New York, 1991).

Stacey, C. P., *Official History of the Canadian Army in the Second World War: Volume III: The Victory Campaign: The Operations in North-West Europe 1944–45* (Ottawa, ON: Queen's Printer, 1960).

Stagg, J. M., *Forecast for Overlord* (London: Ian Allan, 1971).

INDEX